LIFE ON THE ROCKS

Robin Hazell

with kind regards
Robin

LIFE ON THE ROCKS
Copyright © 2012 Robin Hazell.
All rights reserved.

First paperback edition printed 2012 in the United Kingdom.

A catalogue record for this book is available from the British Library.

ISBN 978-1-907308-99-4

No part of this book shall be reproduced or transmitted in any form or by any means, electronic or mechanical, including photocopying, recording, or by any information retrieval system without written permission of the publisher.

Published by Compass Publishing

For more copies of this book, please email: robin.hazell@gmail.com

Designed and Set by Robin Hazell and Palace Printers
Illustrations by MATT
Printed in Great Britain by Palace Printers Lostwithiel Cornwall

Although every precaution has been taken in the preparation of this book, the publisher and author assume no responsibility for errors or omissions. Neither is any liability assumed for damages resulting from the use of this information contained herein.

This book is dedicated to Sam, who will understand.

CONTENTS

Introduction

As a profoundly non-academic geologist, much of my life was occupied by travel to remote corners of the world, generally helping to find water supplies for the less developed parts. Temperamentally unsuited to armchair geology and not by nature competitive, I inevitably worked where there were few geologists and a great many rocks. By day the work was hard and physical but evenings in camps, clubs and rest houses were relaxed, with discussion of a strongly non-intellectual nature aided by cold lager. The most congenial, jovially vocal non-conformists are to be found in wild and distant corners, far from central authority,

These friendly folk, when utterly relaxed, often urged me to write my memoirs; though I suspect some shared my inner view that elegant prose is not my strong suit. On the borders of Rwanda a benevolent British disc jockey, working up a programme about refugees, offered to lend me a tape recorder to capture anecdotes but I could see this ending in tears and declined.

Over the last 20 years some notes have evolved, though with difficulty. It is easy enough to write about the good times but often painful to resurrect memories from the darker ages. Buried and left to lie, they simply will not go away. So I put them in.

This collection of notes would have become lodged in an obscure directory, overgrown and forgotten, but the gentle drift of my declining years was rocked by a sudden and unexpected heart attack. Lying in an unyielding hospital bed, feeling far from jovial, there opened a very mixed vista. There was ample time for meditation, though the collected human wrecks around me were not always entertaining. One shared his bleak view of his future with a captive audience; another had an excruciating cough that peaked almost triumphantly at three in the morning. There were moments of hilarity. A well-built Welshman who, as the senior resident, felt able to conduct his business by phone was curtained off one day while preparations were made for his angiogram. This entertaining little procedure is routine, consisting of sliding a slender probe into a blood vessel – under a local anaesthetic - and steering it up to the heart, where it takes tasteful photos. The nurse who prepared the site, known as shaving the 'groin area', with a Remington razor may have had an unsteady hand, for from behind the curtains came a scream of agony. Even the gloomiest patient joined in the burst of hilarity and contributed to the fusillade of bawdy advice.

Calling to mind the dying words of Lytton Strachey: ('if this is dying I don't think much of it') I resolved there and then to stay alive and tidy up the traces of a rather untidy life.

So here is a collection of snapshots. Though dedicated to Sam, my grandson, fragments have leaked over the years to others. But when I am taken off to hammer the celestial outcrops it will be comforting to carry with me the thought that Sam will have a notion of how some of his ancestors conducted their lives. Warning! Some of the tales are not attuned to ears polite nor to the susceptibilities of the politically correct.

Author as a young man

Who wishes the kernel must first crack the nut

James Temple Hazell, the great genealogist

Chapter 1. Nigeria Airways

'How fortunate that we were not in the air.'

At its peak of mismanagement in the Seventies there brooded over every Nigeria Airways flight an exciting aura of uncertainty. Mercifully, private airlines came into being and the national carrier inevitably, deservedly and mercifully died. The period of mourning was short indeed but it deserves a candid obituary. A few snapshots from personal experience may help the obituarist in this task.

Though only a water geologist, unversed in aeronautical parlance, even I knew there was something odd about the announcement during a noisy Nigeria Airways domestic flight: 'Your excellency, lady and gentlemen: on this short leg from Ikeja to Ibadan we have reached our cruising height of 2,500 feet below the sea level.'

On domestic flights a sense of humour was a pre-requisite. I needed to travel from Yola to Kano and, with inner reservations, bought a ticket. The airstrip bordered a swamp beside the Benue river. The aircraft, an F27, had a full passenger complement and a cargo space stuffed with sacks of rice. Heavily overladen, we lumbered along the metal strip to the highest end of the runway, the passengers strapped in and white knuckled. The first wild charge down the runway towards the river was prudently abandoned with a noisome, rubbery stench clouding around us. The second attempt, even more alarming than the first, ended abruptly when the nose wheel exploded and bits of smoking rubber flew everywhere. We grated to a halt uncomfortably close to the swamp. After a lengthy dead silence the cockpit door opened and a beaming face announced: 'Your Excellency, lady and gentlemen, we have had a puncture. Please leave the aircraft through every available exit.'

As there was but one door, the scramble could have ended with fatalities with heavily built alhajis frantically scrambling through the door. Mercifully the leading and largest alhaji fell flat so that the descent of the others was squashily cushioned. I happily sat quietly and descended decorously just before the fire tender arrived. This was worth watching as the crew assumed a heroic pose, pointing a heavy looking hose nozzle at the stone-cold aircraft. I longed, but did not dare, to take a photo appropriate to a Victorian magazine. At the end of a one-mile trudge with a heavy suitcase to the control tower I was in time to hear a message being radioed to Kano airport requesting a spare nose wheel.

Another flight, from Kano to Ikeja, began uneventfully and ended in drama. As we swung off the runway to the terminal the aircraft stopped abruptly. No one could have foreseen the oration from the pilot as he put on his cap and addressed us thus: 'Your Excellency [there is always an Excellency on the aircraft] lady and gentlemen. We have had complete hydraulic failure.' After a dramatic pause he added peacefully and philosophically: 'How fortunate that we were not in the air.'

Boarding an aircraft was an art form. Domestic flights were insufficient to meet demand and tickets could be bought only immediately before the flight. This led to a flourishing racket, whereby off-duty staff would intercept travellers at the terminal doorway and, as consultants, offer their services. This meant buying a ticket complete with boarding pass at double the proper price.

Nor did a boarding pass guarantee one could board the aircraft, as the number issued usually exceeded the number of seats. It was critically important to guess in advance which of the many aircraft on the apron was the right one. Following an educated guess, the ploy was to stand outside and listen keenly for the loudspeaker to crackle. The main opposition lay in the bevy of stout alhajis having the same objective. Having already adopted an Olympic crouch, they usually got away with a good turn of speed to lead the 100-metre sprint. Being human, they sometimes got it wrong. I recall with great joy the occasion when they targeted the wrong aircraft. They poured up the rear companionway, overpowering the ground staff, before meeting stronger opposition from the pilot. He directed them down the front companionway but the sheer impetus from the rearguard resulted in telescoping and some minor casualties were sustained as they met the ground.

In the wettest part of the wet season and the dustiest part of the dry season reaching one's destination by air was by no means a certainty. When the *harmattan* wind was blowing dust from the Sahara visibility could diminish quickly and, before modern technology caught up, the result was often a return to base. The most vulnerable were the small turbo-prop aircraft that could not climb above the weather. One F27 flight had almost reached its destination in the Chad basin when it met a dusty line squall and in exasperation the pilot tried to plough through. Violently thrown around, we were all terrified. Sitting next to me was an elderly Ibo businessman, grey in the face and shaking with fear long after we turned tail and fled. Between audible prayers he poured out his inmost thoughts in rapid, feverish bursts to keep his mind off what he feared was certain death. The most telling, accurate and revealing statement was - 'Us Nigerians are religious people with high moral standards, except when it comes to money.'

Nigerians have many virtues, common to many black African nations, absent or feeble in European cultures, and by choice I have spent many happy years working with Nigerians. One is courtesy towards strangers, especially in northern regions with an Islamic culture. I consider their enthusiasm for religion to be a virtue.

Another is the extended family system. A family is far wider and more complex than the European model, where even grandparents do not reside in the family home. The main breadwinner of the extended family might be approached by a distant relative with the exhortative greeting: 'You are my father and mother and senior brother' and would be expected to help that relative as far as his means would allow. These family bonds, though weakened by European influences, have persisted through the corroding era of the oil boom. A Nigerian family would be ashamed to consign an elderly relative to a 'care home'.

Related to the extended family system and strong in rural areas is that of community self help. Though dormant in hard times, in their culture is the desire to better their hamlet or village and the communities tax themselves to achieve this.

Two social aspects are derogating from progress. The first is corruption, which paradoxically emerged as a significant force in the days when the Emir or paramount chief held court and exacted tribute. In return he was expected to donate freely from his chest to worthy causes. When the money was recycled in the community this was relatively harmless. In colonial times a newly successful politician would be expected to promote construction of a school or road or whatever, depending on his degree of influence. When, however, the money could be stashed away in overseas accounts and when leaders became excessively aware of their own importance and desires, corruption became systematic and institutionalised; nowadays even with the vast oil income the economy is utterly stifled by it.

The other social problem is improvidence, known in southern Spain as manana. Before the 20th century, a relaxed, improvident view of life was perfectly acceptable, just as it was in Spain. The population was kept low by malaria and the climate benign enough to allow an annual crop to be gathered from the earth. But in the competitive contemporary world many Nigerians cannot accept the need for maintenance of vehicles, machinery, plant, utilities and so on, or for planning for an expanding population; money set aside for this tends to evaporate. Planning and associated pressures are foreign to the Nigerian psyche; the laughter and joking of former times has for those in public office largely disappeared, replaced by hypertension and health failure.

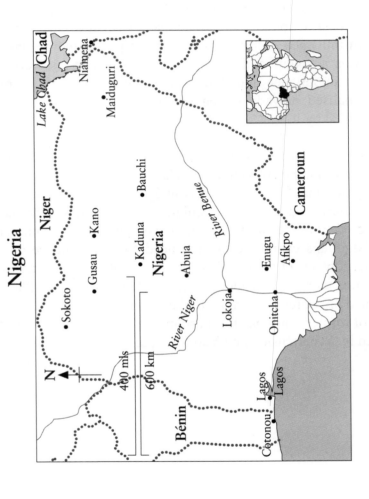

Africa North of the Equator

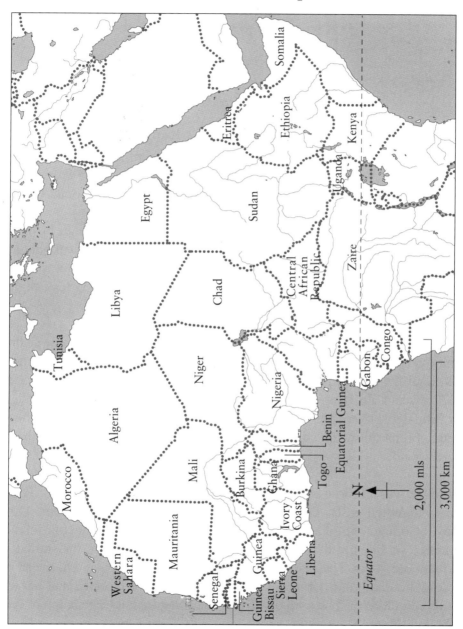

Chapter 2. A Colonial Servant in Nigeria

"If you were appointed which colony would you prefer to serve in?"

"Nigeria."

Dramatic pause. "'Did he say Nigeria?"

But I am getting ahead of myself. I must explain how I came to be a Colonial Servant in Nigeria. I graduated in 1948, full of self-confidence but short on wisdom, and surveyed the future. One door had closed and another was about to open on the third floor of the Colonial Office. The waiting room was dominated by a large map of Africa. Outside in Horseferry Road taxis hooted and post-war London went about its business on a grey autumn day. Beyond the yellow door a committee was shaping the destiny of Trevor - like me a newly hatched graduate geologist, with dreams of limitless horizons and glowing colours, velvet African nights and grave discourse with robed dignitaries in remote places.

Why did I choose to serve in the Colonies? The perception was that three years in the sun at £575 a year would be preferable to 18 months' National Service in post-war Britain at one shilling and sixpence a day (£29 a year). So I applied to become an Officer in the Colonial Service. In hindsight, character building on a barrack square might have been better preparation for sliding down the razor blade of life in the hard, hard world.

With me was a fellow applicant. Trevor and I had little in common. Three years together in the Dickensian lecture rooms of 'little Siberia' – the Royal College of Science - enduring the cacophony of the uncoordinated practice sessions at the Royal School of Music next door, had failed to cement our souls. The awful thought that we might be posted to the same colony floated into my mind just as he emerged to announce that he was to serve in Kenya. The map of Africa was consulted; a large patch of red, labelled 'Nigeria', seemed to be a long way from Kenya.

Portrait of a northern Nigerian chief

At the interview the long mahogany table supported the elbows of grey, wise men. The interview dragged on until the inevitable question came.

'Er, Mister er . . . hem . . . errhum . . . if you were appointed which colony would you prefer to serve in?'
'Nigeria.'

Dramatic pause.

'Did he say Nigeria?'

Few sane men had ever volunteered to go to the White Man's Grave. I was happily ignorant of the statistics. The life expectancy of a Colonial Servant in West Africa, following compulsory retirement at age 40, was then on average 18 months and the list of endemic diseases – had I consulted it – would have made gloomy reading. To a bachelor with no children to speak of, the intimations of mortality set out in the compulsory Widows and Orphans Pension scheme should have been discouraging. The premiums, deducted at source, very plainly reflected the mortality statistics.

The Secretary of State for the Colonies – no less - in a highly formal missive intimated that he personally had no objection to having me on the strength. Moreover, he had the honour to subscribe himself as my humble and obedient servant, a form of official epistolary farewell that has mercifully been overtaken by a simpler though less flattering format.

I once conducted a prolonged correspondence with the Nigerian Treasury; prolonged by me as I was curious to know how much time and money they were prepared to expend on a trivial matter. The difference of opinion concerned a halfpenny. The tone in the second month became somewhat terse, though the financial scribe was to the end my humble and obedient servant.

At the tropical outfitters in London, as I clutched the official list of Minimum Essential Kit and with the considerable help of a fatherly salesman, reality and fantasy were disentangled. Out went the saddle and curry comb; out, with reluctance, the Wolsey helmet, a khaki contraption like a fireman's helmet. Though they were rather splendid I found later that only sanitary inspectors wore them. The spine pad had recently been deleted from the list; medical opinion was coming round to the view that the actinic rays of the sun, suitably filtered through the material of a shirt (bush), would not harm the spinal column. The cholera belt was always a myth, though some were deceived. Trek boots, hideously uncomfortable, proved a mistake. My steward, previously a private in the West Africa Frontier Force, subsequently wore them with great pride but only in public. The crockery, cutlery, camp table and chair, canvas bath and washbasin, camp bed and net . . . the list went on and on. Finally, two tin trunks ('to be inscribed with the officer's name only'), all to be sent to the ship ('to be advised'). The bill 'to be deducted from the officer's pay in three monthly instalments'.

Two lines of epitaph in the local paper (Local Man Secures Post in Nigeria) lifted my soul for the farewell.

Learning the trade in the Dark Continent

Rising above the Liverpool wharves, beyond the customs sheds, were swathes of steel-clad hulls but none could I see that bore the title *SS Liberian.* Steered towards a gap, by advancing to the very edge and looking down through the gloom a very small, very elderly worn-out looking freighter could be discerned.

A hierarchy of passenger ships out of Liverpool existed in those days. Every fortnight a glamorous cruise liner, the *Andrea Dorea*, sailed for South America; and from the next berth sailed the Mail Boat, the *Elder Dempster* liner to West Africa, known to the cognoscenti as the Thursday Workman. There was no problem of identification; matching leather luggage went to the *Andrea Dorea*, scruffy holdalls and tin trunks to the *Aureole* (if you were lucky) or the *Apapa* or the *Accra*.

The coal-burning freighter *SS Liberian* was something else; owned by the United Africa Company, though never their flagship, it had survived the wartime convoys. Of the 12 passengers, eight were Old Coasters, veteran merchants of vast experience. The rest were one generation younger, with the prison pallor of academic halls not yet enriched to that complexion peculiar to Old Coasters, an intricate venous network on a rich mepacrine-induced yellow matrix. The best that could be said for mepacrine as a malaria prophylactic was that it was an improvement on quinine; the downside was the sombre, hepatitic hue of skin and eyeballs.

When blue sky appeared and the officers, metamorphosed in friendly white shorts, became individuals, fiercely competitive deck games broke out. Between times we beautiful people sprawled in the sun on the forehatch; the loudest sound was the hiss of the bow-wave, and without a hint of vibration the gentle steam engines pushed us southwards at a gentle ten knots. The Old Coasters had even less strenuous routines that we had yet to learn and were slow to appreciate. Off the Canaries, the steering broke down and for three days we made great circles, punctuated by Tenerife jutting at intervals above the horizon. We ate our way through all the permutations and combinations of a vast menu and recycled our wealth via the sweepstake on the ship's daily run. On half pay until we landed, and with debts to settle, the month that elapsed before we reached Takoradi on the Gold Coast seemed an eternity. The plan was then that the *SS Liberian* would take in tow a broken-down tug and plough on to Lagos but our new masters had other ideas and we were whisked off into the pursuing mail boat.

And so we arrived. In the next 13 years I learned how to ply my trade in a sheltered environment. We were housed, provided with transport, paid monthly. We had free medical attention; 18 weeks' paid leave after 18 months' service; our first class passages were paid; we had much freedom of movement and generous local leave. On the other hand, the pay was poor and the bureaucratic processes could be stifling. Tropical disease was rife and barely contained. We took all this for granted at the time and in retrospect it was a good apprenticeship.

Putting into Lagos was a self-contained travelogue. On the horizon appeared the low dark line of the coast then questing birds from the shore.

The water became muddy brown, fitting well with the equally muddy smell of the land. Quite abruptly we were gliding through Lagos Lagoon, past the palms and lawns of Ikoyi Island then Five Cowrie Creek and the gardens of Bishopscourt - the deserved haven of successive Anglican clergymen robust enough to survive to wear the purple. Mooring at Apapa island and the rush to the notice board to discover postings - no feigned indifference here, for 18 months in the Black Borgu Bush is much longer than 18 months in a regional secretariat. Passports stamped in the First Class lounge, down the gangway to the long customs shed and tin trunks whisked away to the boat train. Then three long days and nights as a veteran steam engine with a veteran white driver hauled us in wooden coaches (first class - of course) through the swamps and forests that gradually gave way to savannah, to Kaduna Junction.

Kaduna town, named after the river that ran through it, was created by the great Frederick (later Lord) Lugard who followed the river upstream from the old northern administrative centre of Zungeru in search of a less unhealthy location. Of all the diseases to die of in those early years, pneumonia seemed the least probable; yet the temperature in the Zungeru gorge can swing in December from near freezing to 40°C in a few hours.

Kaduna Junction was quite literally on the wrong side of the railway. To reach the dwelling places of the most high, the Administrative Officers, and attend polite society we queued at the end of a railway bridge over the river until a man with a green flag waved us through. The Junction was thought suitable for technical departments and needless to say we wore with pride our largely imagined second-class status.

Young geologists were not encouraged to stay in the Station during the touring season and certainly could not aspire to a house. For a few days I shared a cool and comfortable thatched hut with Jan van Coppenhagen, a famous marksman and seasoned geologist with a whole three years' post-graduate experience behind him. The first shared dinner was a greater bustard, common then but now rare and protected; we sat on either side of this magnificent bird and ate towards the middle. When our knives met, we stopped and meditated on our considerable achievement.

Cases of 'minimum essential kit' were made up into manageable boxes, a kit car and driver were allocated to me, a trader sold me a bow with lethal looking arrows. Archery back at home, with a state of the art laminated bow and well turned, well fletched arrows, had rather spoiled me for the local version. To test this deadly killing machine I set off at dusk into the orchard bush. A target soon presented itself – a brown, rounded hump which I was convinced was an antelope. As I fitted an arrow to the bow, the antelope translated into a farmer, who stood up and greeted me gravely. He did not appear one whit apprehensive; I imagined he had little confidence in my accuracy.

To engage a cook and steward (in those days regarded as essential staff for touring officers) I convened a committee of old hands adept in deciphering the nuances contained in character references. (Example: 'I trust he will do you as well as he has done me'), and settled on a rotund Ibo cook called Sam and a very tall very thin steward, Ali, from Bima hill, a rocky fastness beside the Gongola river.

The Bima tribe are tall, with heavy cicatrices. These facial scars originated as a means of identification so that children scattered during slave raids could be reunited with surviving relatives. The big northern rivers were trading arteries; slaves and ivory had been transported northwards through the dry Sahel region to the Mediterranean coast, salt came southwards. Later, at the time of the Fulani jihad in 1804, the Bima tribe made fortified camps at the top of Bima hill out of range of the arrows of the Fulani mounted cavalry. They are one of the few groups the Fulani never subdued.

Sam claimed to have served in the West Africa Frontier Force in Burma, the only tangible evidence being a battered bush hat of faintly military style. He probably made a better soldier than a cook. When a group of elephants stumbled one dark night through our camp near Jakura, he observed that these were the first African elephants he had seen. But elephants were not new to him; he claimed to have machine-gunned several Indian elephants in Burma.

At the beginning of December, 1948, I was 21 and at the bottom of the Staff List. But life was good and issues simple and uncomplicated. In this cheerful frame of mind I set off down a sandy track for the three-day drive to Kabba. Toward the end of a long, dusty day we swung back toward the Kaduna river. Here, just before Bida, the river flows wide, with sandbanks. We drove on to a ferry, which was a simple platform mounted on empty oil drums with barely enough space to open the cab doors and step outside. Four crewmen poled us across; the river was low and to avoid grounding - while dodging water too deep for poling - we covered about three times the direct distance from bank to bank. The kit car (nowadays called a pick-up) was an evil beast with a distorted chassis and a top speed of 40 m.p.h. It firmly decided when it needed a rest so it was dusk when we limped into Bida.

Rest houses for touring government officers were simple mud and straw rondavels, about seven metres in diameter, with a conical thatch sensibly reaching to about two and a half metres above ground level. An outer veranda led to a dark, inner bedroom. The routine of settling in was unfamiliar but was to be repeated countless times over the years. My camp bed was dragged from its bag and assembled, complete with mosquito net. A canvas camp chair, collapsible table, kerosene pressure lamp, straw mat and canvas bath were set out. Hot water appeared miraculously from a smoke-filled cavernous kitchen; bathed, dressed and mosquito booted, I awaited the arrival of dinner. It proved that Sam was very good at opening tins though not strong on fresh food but I was too tired to expostulate.

The rondavel next door was occupied by an expatriate teacher; I had not expected to meet her, as the male expatriate community had invited her out for drinks and dinner. In the middle of the night a timid voice called 'Can you help me?' It transpired that she had returned late, went to bed, and woke in the dark to find that her belongings – except for her bedding and pyjamas - had been stolen. There was no sleep for anyone after that. The police chief, in a grump, searched my kit, and was deeply suspicious of Sam the Ibo cook, but could find no stolen goods. In the morning we set off towards Ilorin. The next river crossing was the Niger at Jebba, near where the Bussa rapids swallowed up the explorer Mungo Park and his canoe. We had the luxury of a bridge shared between vehicles and trains. At Ilorin the RAF had a rest camp. We parked the kit car next to a truck carrying RAF roundels and labelled 'Jock's Trap' and I was given a room in a wooden barrack-style hut. After an invigorating morning shower and breakfast I found my team and we were preparing to set off for Kabba when Jock appeared; an irritable chap he was, complaining of some noisy fellow who sang fortissimo in the early hours. No sense of humour.

Lokoja

Lokoja was on the road to nowhere yet was far from being a ghost town, though haunted by its past. On the waterfront sacks of grain were being loaded into barges by elite stevedores with a great show of effortless strength, possibly influenced by the presence of the younger women at the market stalls. Drummers hired by the trading firm sustained the loaders with an urgent rhythm. A stern-wheeler would take the straddled barges down the Niger river to the railhead as it had done since the Royal Niger Company flag and later the Union flag were hoisted at the turn of the century; here where the Niger and Benue rivers join.

Years before that, the early white explorers tracing the source of the Niger ran the gauntlet of temperamental fulani slave raiders; this was *their* patch and they were ever unsure whether to entertain the white men or rob them. The presence of the Royal Niger Company garrison removed all doubt.

By the Forties roads had begun to achieve an ascendancy over the river and Lokoja was at the end of the road from the south and west. From the east access was across the river by ferry through several miles of dangerous currents and eddies. Though local trade flourished, government officers were increasingly isolated; indeed Lokoja was a punishment station and as a young and callow but blameless 'first tourer' I was lucky enough to be pitched among some highly original minds.

The doctor there, Douglas Quantrel, was about to uncover an unwholesome financial scandal in a northern emirate when he was transferred suddenly to Lokoja, for there was a genuine risk that he would be poisoned. His preferred style was Dr. Cointreau. The Admiral, a courtesy title for the Marine Superintendent, had sailed before the mast in windjammers; remnant stubs of fingernails bore testimony to his having taken in sail in bleak weather. The inland waterways must have been a poor substitute for the Roaring Forties. The representative of the United Africa Company was at the hub of a social whirl where parties went on for nights and days on end. And ruling us, somewhat tenuously, was the Resident, a private man whose sterling qualities were never completely revealed to us.

At river level the hot, humid air was enervating and air conditioning was an unattainable luxury. In the hot season sleep was fitful.

I was mapping far from base and visits to Lokoja were rare and blessed necessities: to collect stores and a bag of shillings, to enjoy a real bath, a cold beer and philosophical discourse. The intellectual battleground was undoubtedly the Lokoja Club and at 'sweeping up' time the more impassioned protagonists would drift across to the nearest bachelor quarters. To be frank I could never remember what was discussed and profanity probably had the edge over profundity but we must immensely have entertained each other. On one such occasion we gathered up-wind of the Residency and were made aware of this by the brief presence in the early hours of the Resident in a dressing gown and pyjamas. He made a terse statement to the effect that he was unable to sleep and whirled away into the night. An ad hoc committee formed, as the displeasure of the Resident could blight a young man's career, and it was resolved that:

> As many touring officers as possible would leave town.
> We would individually send courteous notes of apology
> tothe Resident before leaving.

The first resolution was executed with dispatch; the Forester went off to his forest, the Engineer to inspect his roads, the Admiral to repair a far-off slipway. Doctor Quantrel decided to open a new clinic far up the river. His decision was influenced by a hazy recollection of having told the Resident that it was a fine thing when a few friends could not gather to discuss the political situation and that he suspected the Resident was a communist. I went back to my patch of mapping and a month later at a subdued reunion it became disapprovingly apparent that I had sent the only apology, a solecism forgiven only because of my extreme youth.

A Resident administered an area typically the size of Wales and with inadequate funds but dedicated staff (district officers, assistant district officers) did a first class job. Some had their idiosyncrasies; others had idiosyncratic wives. One stalwart used to send round an expansive memorandum on a Saturday morning inviting everyone to a party that evening. He who was generally obeyed was invariably asleep when the guests arrived. Wakened, he would berate them for invading his privacy and unceremoniously eject them.

In my time the Resident at Abeokuta had a wife of commanding presence, she who *must* be obeyed. The Residency was at the crest of a steep conical hill and to reach it one drove round and round on a helical path that gave up near the top, whence one walked. Terrace upon terrace of rose beds protected the summit, where the house in glory was aproned by a splendid lawn. The Resident, bless him, had taken pity on us touring officers who were quartered in a cramped rest house and invited us to dinner. Everyone piled into my kit car and we set forth. At the road end, while yet sober, I manoeuvred the vehicle to face downhill, and we all trudged the rest of the way. Across the lawn into the expansive reception area, the Resident's wife called down from above that they were nearly ready and to make ourselves at home. At that moment I was sharply conscious of the need to 'see Africa' and strolled out into the darkness to what I thought was a rose border. It was not; and I tumbled 20 feet down to the next level, landing in a particularly thorny rose bush. Coated in mud and with twisted spectacles, I found my way up the wall and across the lawn just as the Resident's lady advanced majestically down the stairs. 'Oh, you got lost,' she exclaimed. 'I told the watchman to show you the way.' A miserable evening followed, with smeared, crooked glasses, a thumping headache and a bursting bladder.

Along the big rivers of Nigeria mosquitoes abound. Lokoja was founded before the cause of malaria was discovered. Prefabricated wooden houses from Wales were brought up the rivers by the stern-wheelers. The theory was that a house on stilts of brick (Welsh brick) improved circulation of air, inhibiting the 'mal-aria' feared by the Portuguese centuries before. In Lokoja these handsome houses, with broad verandahs, formed a horseshoe around a miniature golf course and their sheer elegance for many years inhibited any desire to move the government station up to a cooler level. Mount Patti looks down on Lokoja and the slopes were planted in the Fifties with white-painted government dwellings typifying the mediocre style of British post-war architecture. In later years the virtues of Italian designs were appreciated but the 'T63' and 'T64' models were totally unsuited to the West African climate, providing no shade for enjoyment of cool breezes created when the rocks cooled in the evening. The charitable view is that the designers foresaw the advent of air conditioners; if so, they certainly did not foresee the fickleness of the electricity supply in days to come.

One hundred years ago quinine was the only known cure for malaria and when the stern-wheeler could not reach Lokoja with quinine supplies untreated malaria could develop into blackwater fever, a ghastly disease when the liver liquefies and urine is black. Death follows swiftly and a little cemetery on a bluff overlooking the river is filled with sad tombstones. 'John Smith, Acting Resident, died of blackwater fever aged 23.' The tribespeople had a herbal remedy. They gathered leaves from a shrub, boiled them and drank the juice. We now know that the shrub is a species of Artemisia (wormwood, southernwood) and is an efficacious cure. To the early white men it was juju medicine which of its nature was unacceptable.

Mount Patti is one of many flat-topped hills technically known as buttes. These are the dissected remnants of the Tertiary African land surface. Because of its monotonous continuity in East Africa, travellers knew it as 'Mamba' (miles and miles of bloody Africa) but over much of central and southern Nigeria where the river tributaries have eroded deeply, groups of these buttes form an attractive landscape.

The African land surface developed during a long period of stagnation in the Miocene age when a crust of hard red laterite formed. Around Lokoja, this laterite and other odds and ends contain iron that briefly engaged the interest of post-war steel manufacturers. The process of digging a trench on mount Patti and taking samples for analysis was sufficient a spectacle to attract weekend visitors. A well-nourished accountant from Lagos had made what he perceived to be a perilous journey to stay with friends in Lokoja. He had firm ideas about self-protection in the hinterland; his principal armament was a magnificent Mauser rifle and my first sighting of this splendid warrior as I climbed out of a prospecting pit made a deep impression. We were entrusted with his packed lunch before he strode purposefully into the African bush. Despite assurances that so near town he would never see large wild animals, his grip on the Mauser never faltered. He reappeared soon after in some disorder and breathing deeply. We gathered that on rounding a patch of bush he had come upon a lion asleep on a rock and he stayed not upon the order of his going. Before returning thankfully to the dull and ordered life in Lagos he eagerly traded his rifle for my camera. To acquire an unused 9.3mm Mauser at a tender age was a mixed blessing but in the field seasons that followed my team grew strong on protein and I felt much safer.

To meet a lion unexpectedly is unnerving. The white hunters of fiction and tourist guides instinctively knew instantly whether the lion was sleepily replete or would 'turn nasty'. A shot would opportunely 'ring out' and the beast would fall within inches of its victim. I found the reality a little different. After a long and exhausting day I once took an evening stroll, unarmed, out of my camp down a dry river bed to watch birds. The birds I saw in the trees were vultures. Beneath by a dry waterhole lay a disembowelled hartebeest, and I can only plead fatigue to explain why I stood stupefied for several seconds wondering what had caused all the blood. A movement under a thorn tree resolved into a twitching tail. I was too frightened to run but rather waltzed slowly up the bank, figuratively whistling, gradually increasing speed as the distance widened. At dawn the following day I returned but only faint bloodstains in the sand and some spoor remained as evidence. I was to learn in time that a lone bull buffalo is much more dangerous to meet than a gorged lion.

A question of colour

Nowadays, in much of tropical Africa, the colour of one's skin is of no great importance. It was not always thus, though difficulties related more to lack of understanding of language and culture than innate prejudice. In my early African days, though, one unexpected colour crisis suddenly arose and was as suddenly dispersed.

My vehicle was bestowed about 25 miles from our camp under a shade tree by the Lokoja road, in the care of Maurice, the driver. Washing the car, he gashed his arm on a sharp edge and sliced through a vein. Having stemmed the flow of blood, he showed great and overvalued trust in my ability to patch him up by trekking to the camp clutching the arm in his spare hand.

With the confidence of youth I resolved to sew him up. The only anaesthetic was a bottle of brandy, and I dosed him liberally. This quickly dulled the pain though, being completely unused to alcohol, his mind entered a highly critical state. In deference to his skin colour I found in my sewing kit some black thread. He immediately objected on the ground that his skin was of a deep golden hue. The only other colours of thread available were bright green and white and he expressed forcefully a preference for white.

Bless him, he shortly lapsed into a muttering torpor while I boiled the needle and thread and stitched him up; first with tacking stitches around the vein, then bold gobble stitches, over and over, to pull the skin together. The operation was a complete success but after 24 trying hours complications set in. Trying, because the ardent spirit had taken a firm hold and he embarked on a singing marathon. His voice, though tuneful, was powerful and penetrating, thundering around the wakeful camp through the interminable night.

So we sent him off, under escort, with his surgeon's notes attached to a letter of referral to the doctor in Lokoja. A couple of weeks later he returned, proudly brandishing a cicatriced arm. He was reluctant to discuss his treatment, which a month later I heard all about - straight from Dr. Quantrell's mouth, crisp and to the point. Paraphrased and bowdlerised, it went like this:

"The trouble with you so-and-so field men is that you are adjectivally useless at stitching. Too many stitches, much too tight, much too adjectivally close together. I took them all out and prepared to do the job properly, whereupon he fled. Have a beer."

Touring in the north

"G-g-g-giwa."

Administrative officers of the Colonial Service came in for a lot of stick until the millennium but expressions of public opinion nowadays are more gentle. District Officers in Nigeria were hard working and poorly paid. They were burdened with office routine and the fair dispensation of justice. To go on tour was a relief; giving time to think and to plan - a new road or a dispensary or whatever - and to hear petitions and complaints. If the District Officer's kit car were in running order he would travel by road - if a road existed and was passable. After the rains, when washed-out culverts had not been repaired, the Emir would provide a horse and colourful retinue. A traditional Hausa saddle was agony for horse and rider, so the D.O. provided his own.

One wet day I traversed down a long, muddy path towards the Gongola river, having reluctantly left the hospitable village of Doho where the chief (the only English speaker) read Shakespeare to me with a gentle Edinburgh accent. Years before, a Scottish well-sinker had taught him from the only book he had. With no expectations of an enthusiastic welcome from the village in front, I was agreeably surprised to be met in the sorghum fields by a mounted reception committee with a spare horse. Mounted in some style we all swept into the village centre where a small guest hut was ready. The chief made me welcome and left me with a bowl of milk, a stick of sugar cane and honey to render palatable the inevitable pounded stodge. He returned later with the town band (a drummer) and a troupe of dancers - tall ladies of mature years, some with arms encased in long gourds. These kept in place cold henna poultices for dyeing their skin.

The next morning, despite my assurances that no help was needed to traverse the narrow valleys, close followers darted to the hill tops to signal my movements ahead. Days later on the way back on foot I met the District Officer well mounted with red and green-clad attendants from the Emir of Gombe. We chatted and the realisation dawned that I had for days been mistaken for the D.O. One of his less agreeable tasks was to assess cattle tax on the basis of the herds he could count and clearly all cattle had previously been manoeuvred from my path. Coming in my wake, his unexpected arrival had a highly unenthusiastic reception, though as compensation he scooped the pool for cattle tax.

On the Cross River, access to the administrative division of Obubra was by ferry and then by road - the only road in the Division, precisely 24 miles long - through primary forest to the government station. The District Officer had a passionate attachment to his Rover 90, and regularly drove to the ferry and back at high speed. One day he was early and a burial party was caught unawares. The coffin, suspended across two bicycles, was abruptly abandoned by the owners who heard the familiar snarl of a well-tuned engine, shouted 'Ah! D.O. Anderson' and dived into the bush. The coffin travelled for some distance on the bonnet of the Rover before order was restored. In this remote corner of the white man's grave, the D.O. was the magistrate and so instigated and heard the case brought against himself, of desecrating a corpse. He conducted his own defence, fined himself ten shillings and bound himself over to keep the peace.

An engineer on tour would be visiting an up-and-running project with his needs anticipated. A very tall District Engineer once fell ill with yellow fever and, as he was not a stock size, his coffin was custom-built. Against all probability he recovered and as the coffin would not suit any current terminal case he took it home and converted it to a touring bookcase.

To a geologist, setting out on tour usually meant driving a heavily laden kit car to the end of the road and taking on carriers. None could emulate the sheer style of a friend in East Africa, who travelled in a convoy of two Rolls-Royces. By contrast. our large American pick-ups were utilitarian, battle scarred relics with thin tyres and idiosyncratic engines. Loading the kit car was an art. The 20 officially sanctioned 'head loads' had to be fitted in, as well as a messenger, a cook and a steward. When this was ultimately achieved a bag of shillings was dropped on the floor of the cab and volunteers would push us off. Our vehicles suffered chronically from 'batteryitis'. On one occasion I sensed we were dragging a little and found that the steward had somehow lashed his very large wife and an iron cooking pot of comparable stature to the tailboard.

At the road's end the pick-up would be parked under a tree and the key left with the local chief. Carriers were easy to hire except at harvest time but choosing and matching them to loads that suited their capability was a long and tiring task, one of the many that fell to the messenger. A head load was 25 kilos on average paths, but less in broken terrain with ill-defined tracks. Loading up involved placing a halo of cloth on the head, tiara style, then with some help manoeuvring the load to a point of balance. The spine in engineering terms is a pole, capable of withstanding vertical thrust, but not a beam as back sufferers can testify. A line of children leaving a spring in the early morning carrying water pots back to the village on their heads is still a common sight and later, on the way to school, an ink pot or a book in the same fashion. What splendid carriage these people had, putting in the shade the drooping stance of Europeans

Once when rations were low and I had shot a buffalo we could not muster enough help to carry all the butchered carcass back to camp and on my head I carried the buffalo head. I soon realised that a buffalo head is very heavy and that head loading is an art to be nurtured from infancy and not taken up casually by a dilettante. My neck was extremely sore for days.

Standard technique was to set off ahead of the caravan and march maybe a dozen miles to choose a camp site. Life was easier if a village could be reached with the headman forewarned and grass shelters already erected. More often, in the heat of the afternoon, as soon as the weary carriers were paid, thanked and gone, we turned to and built the skeleton of the camp. I had a gift for supervising, though my suggestions were not always put into practice. Sam the messenger and two labourers brought poles and grass for thatching, the tin trunks were complementary furniture to the camp bed, chair and table.

In the kitchen Sam the cook assembled his stove. Two empty kerosene tins with detachable lids, placed on their sides served as ovens, flanking the fire. These supported a grid of expanded metal mesh on which the cooking pots fizzled away. With this basic unit, a cook could prepare a three-course meal. Without a refrigerator it was not possible to keep meat fresh except on the hoof and chicken of rubbery texture often dominated the menu. Palm wine used for leavening dough was effective but imparted a sweet taste to bread.

The further the camp was from a village with a market, the greater the cook's required ingenuity; equally, the more chance there was of obtaining 'bush meat' - any wild animal or bird. 'Bush fowl' (francolins) were prized above guinea fowl for flavour; both were easily located, as they had not the sense to keep quiet. Possessing only a rifle, I hunted antelope. An annual game licence cost £25 and the quota of various species in theory allowed plenty of choice. The smaller antelope - harnessed antelope, duiker, oribi - were delicious to eat and easy to carry but remarkably absent when meat ran short. Herds of hartebeest (four allowed per year), great heavy creatures the size of horses, were plentiful and because of their curious nature would run a little way then stop and look round to remind themselves what they were running from. This made them quite literally easy meat. The meat of the west African buffalo, the famous 'bush cow', is tough by any standards, and I found only the tongue and tail attractive but a single bush cow fed hungry labourers for days, fresh at first then smoked. Visitors to game reserves often comment on the plenitude of water buck; the reason is simple - the meat is so tough and fibrous that poachers leave them alone. Wart hog, too, is an acquired taste.

The head man of my trenching team was the acknowledged expert at skinning animals. Skinning a buffalo was almost ceremonial in nature. An ugly west African buffalo with its short horns and heavy barrel of a body is not improved by death; at close quarters its lower body is seen to be coated with huge ticks. An antelope lying dead often triggered a regret that such beauty was destroyed for ever but a dead buffalo triggered off a calculation as to how much the hide would fetch; bullets were expensive. The head man always briskly sliced off the scrotum and presented it to me. No doubt I should have followed some ritualistic act but lacked the curiosity to find out. Over two field seasons I finished up with eight dried buffalo scrota in a box. At some stage I tackled a friendly expert on local custom who assured me that it was *de rigeur* to keep these gruesome mementos. After several beers the idea germinated that as they each had a capacity of about a pint they could be fashioned into a set of rather elegant drinking vessels, suitably trimmed with silver.

Later, on leave in London, I took them in to a famous firm of taxidermists in Piccadilly with the intention of putting this plan into effect. An assistant in a wing collar glared down at me frostily and called for the manager, also in a wing collar and even taller; falteringly I repeated the request. The manager stared and stared and uttered not; generations of experience in the art of putting down went into that stare. Had he spoken, I imagine something like: 'It would not have done for the Duke, Sir, it would never have done for his Grace.' So muttering something about calling again I repacked the goods and slunk out. A shameful retreat altogether. Back in Nigeria I let these unattractive objects lie in a box where they grew progressively wizened until the resident termites solved the disposal problem by eating them.

In one camp a slab of rock beside my grass shelter was of convenient size and shape for stretching animal skins to dry. Visiting jackals loved to chew at the edges and when we remembered we took in the skins at dusk like washing. Buffalo skins were too tough to suffer damage and I became used to being lulled to sleep by the roar of distant lions and, a few yards away, the scuffling and scrabbling of jackals. One night some predator, probably a hyena, took a jackal that screamed and screamed into the distance. I have seldom been so frightened. A mosquito net is a wonderful psychological barrier against the idea of attack but the reality of the scream shattered the dream of immunity forever.

A mentor of my earliest days was a South African who, apart from being a superb field geologist, was an expert in the art of making biltong. Antelope meat was cut into strips shaped like tuning forks and steeped in brine overnight (in the canvas bath); then hung in the shade until rock hard and black and looking like plug tobacco. Biltong keeps for ever and, cut thin is delicious, especially if you are really hungry and you chance to find a piece among the fluff of a little used bush jacket pocket.

In the dry season, when the harmattan wind blows dry dusty air from the north east as it whirls round the desert edge, the meat dried too quickly for the flies to do much harm. In April, when the damp Atlantic air dominated, the biltong dried slowly and soon seethed with maggots; whereupon the ants homed in on the maggots and we were left with honeycomb biltong, the flavour unimpaired.

The wind from the Sahara carries fine dust almost as far south as the gulf of Guinea. When the air falls still in the evening the dust settles and ultimately it is washed down into the sub-soil by the end-of-season storms. In the meantime the dry leaves on the ground and the dry branches and stems of vegetation are covered with rust coloured dust. Stalking antelope requires great concentration to avoid treading on crackling leaves. Brushing against branches releases a cloud of dust and pollen and brings on a sneezing fit. When the tall dry grass catches fire a long, high line of flame advances (against the wind) leaving a smudge of black smoke and an evocative semi-sweet acrid smell. These grass fires do little immediate damage: at the first substantial gully they peter out; the antelope easily out-run the flames; and after about ten days the dew triggers a new growth of grass. The losers are villagers, who rely on a grass harvest for thatching.

It is time to describe the sort of work we did. The Department of Geological Survey was just that. The emphasis up to the mid-Fifties was on creating geological maps and before air photographs became available we also mapped the topography. The first 4x4 vehicles (Land Rovers) were available in the UK but not in Africa where mapping was done on foot. The biltong expert taught me how to walk on a compass course, blazing the trees to simplify the exhausting return journey. Distances were measured in paces that, with a little practice, were standardised to suit the individual. Twelve miles out, then a rest, then 12 miles back, noting every feature - rock outcrop, loose boulder, stream, gully, ridge, vegetation change. Each day we swung across 10 degrees from the previous day's course and from one camp a circle 24 miles in diameter would be mapped. Then to the next camp 24 miles away, then a third camp, so that each camp was at the apex of a triangle, the length of each side being 24 miles. It sounds hopelessly inaccurate but errors cancel out and the closing error was normally around 0.3 per cent.

It was traditional at the end of a 12-mile traverse, before turning back towards camp, to sit under a tree for 20 minutes and cool off. Glass bottles of water, each wrapped in a wet sock and cooled by evaporation, were a delicious luxury. One very hot day, when it was time to start off I asked old Garuba, the messenger, to chip off a sample from a grey rock in the middle distance. Garuba's sight was poor – he wore thick glasses – and he stuttered when excited. He was within a few feet of the rock when it erupted and charged off in a cloud of dust. I have an abiding visual image of Garuba, shaking and stuttering 'G-g-g-giwa! G-g-g-giwa!' (No! Elephant! Elephant!')

From the early Seventies, mapping in the field became subordinate to interpreting satellite images and air photos. Image 'signatures' are identified by 'ground truthing' but nowadays field geologists rarely stray far from their all-terrain vehicles. The gain is that the big rock units are quickly mapped; the loss is that detailed textures and structures are often overlooked.

MATT

Discourse on buffalo

The great herds of grazing buffalo constituted the biggest single hazard during field mapping. Though they have a keen sense of smell, their sight and hearing are poor and it is possible to cross down-wind of a grazing herd without disturbing them. In a draft field map an offset in a traverse was, to the initiated, a sign that evasive action was taken. Before meeting my first buffalo I had heard gruesome stories of those who came off second best after an encounter with lone bull buffalo. These grouchy creatures, supplanted from the herd by a younger bull, are unpredictable. A grazing herd when disturbed stampede downhill and it is not difficult to manoeuvre into a safe zone - though I have a keen memory of a difference of opinion with a labourer called Yusufu in such a situation. Tramping uphill, we unexpectedly met a herd. I had marked down a young tree that I could shin up; Yusufu had marked down the same tree. He won. I managed an undignified scramble past his shoulders, and my feet dangled just, only just, above the herd as they thundered down in a whirl of dust. In anger I sacked him on the spot but by the time we reached camp he had been reinstated.

However, a lone bull charges without warning and either has forgotten the downhill rule or reckons it does not apply to him. Bill Ferris, a desk-bound District Officer, trekked to my camp one Friday afternoon for a recreational weekend armed with his father's ancient Martini Henry rifle, which took one cartridge at a time. The 24-mile hike to my camp from the road left him within a mile of my camp when darkness fell. Late that evening I woke to the sound of a rifle shot; half an hour later his messenger staggered into camp to say 'master, he lie down for path; he suffer from no water.' I lit the pressure lamp and – laden with bottles of water - stumbled up the long hill to where he lay. He rehydrated but was exhausted and slept there on the ground till dawn, when he turned up for breakfast and waxed lyrical about the outdoor life. He had brought with him Suzy, a puppy a few months old, and this unfortunate creature was bleeding from cuts in her paws and in exhaustion slept for hours.

Possibly the heavy armour Bill brought along (an ancient family heirloom) scared the game off for he saw nothing bigger than a hornbill until on his long walk back late on Sunday when he met a lone bull buffalo. He dropped his unloaded rifle and sprang up a very thorny acacia tree. The buffalo snorted around the tree for an age, excited by the smell of blood from Bill's torn shins, before giving up in disgust.

Bill left with me the puppy, which I fed with raw antelope meat for a few weeks; by the time I returned her to her owner she had grown into a veritable Baskerville. However, she gave us all a nasty fright one day when she came out with the field mapping party. Lured by a troupe of baboons barking from a hilltop, she ran happily towards them. Had she reached them they would have torn her to shreds and, reluctantly, I had to shoot two of them before they retreated.

First steps into water

The Geological Survey of Nigeria shouldered responsibility, among other matters, for rural water supply. Finding water was at first a chore but gradually became a delight. Water underground is a mineral resource. Like oil and gas it is renewable but vastly more abundant and vastly cheaper to find and to exploit. Operating in an evolving science, I was too close to the subject to perceive the scale of developing hydrogeology. Recently I was able to write an account of the history of British hydrogeologists in West Africa and the record is impressive. When the perception in the United States was of the British ruthlessly plundering colonial mineral resources, often almost the entire staff of the Geological Survey of Nigeria was engaged in water supply work.

By today's standards our methods were primitive. We did not call ourselves hydrogeologists in those days. Only two useful books on groundwater existed and a deal of common sense went into our approach. When we could find no recommended course of action we invented our own. In fact, the first hydrogeologist in history was probably Moses in biblical times when he struck a rock (probably fissured limestone) with his staff and out flowed water. Much, much later, at Lourdes, Saint Bernadette scratched the floor of a cave and achieved a similar result. Indeed we have illustrious forebears.

In West Africa of the Forties drilled wells were few, as the level of technology was out of scale with the infrastructure, the well sinkers' experience and the money available. A design for dug wells, perfected by a Colonial Servant called Cochran in 1929, proved highly successful and almost 2,000 have since been constructed in Nigeria and many more in francophone and anglophone states.

A group of well-sinking teams was typically controlled by an expatriate supervisor; always comfortably built with a red nose under a wide straw hat, of rock-like immobility when the job was going smoothly. He managed several teams of well-sinkers, each of four alpha males directed by a head man. They were the elite. Physically very tough, they luxuriated in the hospitality of the village. At the bottom of the well, two men hacked and shovelled the spoil into a vast bucket called a kibble. Two winch operators at the top wound the kibble to the surface. As the well became deeper the air below ground grew hotter and more stifling. Periodically, a little sand was sprinkled down the well; the trapped air helped the diggers to breathe, but 20 minutes was about the endurance limit before they were hoisted up and replaced by the other two men. When they met water they dug on between intervals of baling until the inflow of water made progress impossible. The deepest dug well on record in Nigeria is 113m (370ft.)

By descending a well in a big bucket during construction we had a three-dimensional view of the disposition of water-bearing beds – a view denied to later generations of water geologists. They are obliged to rely on churned-up sludge samples from a drilled well to work out intricate textures in the parent rock. This is akin to tasting a soup to identify and describe the ingredients.

Near the village of Doho a group of dug wells met a coal seam and work was halted so that I could take samples. Lowered in the kibble, I was about to climb out on to the floor when, by the light of my lamp, I saw that it was populated by snakes and scorpions that had fallen from above during the night. With the kibble slung a little above the floor, I tried to hack off lumps of coal by the glow of the lamp. However, the action of swinging the hammer sent the kibble lurching to the other side of the well and the rebound was too slow for me to rescue the lumps of coal before they crashed on to the infuriated reptiles. Etched in my memory is of looking up to see a very small disk of light far above, while listening to the hissing of snakes below and only a few miserable fragments of coal to show for it all.

The basic principles of groundwater occurrence and movement are simple but applying them adequately in the field called for a depth of knowledge that, as a youngster, I did not have. Much later in life there are blushful memories of overconfidence and under-performance. Usually alone and far from the support of our elder brethren we made mistakes but by and large learned from them. We listened to the well-sinkers' accounts of successes and failures and gradually worked out the 'whys' of these.

Government drillers were rare and of variable quality. In Britain skilled drillers were scarce and competent ones were understandably reluctant to work overseas. Water drillers generally were not highly rated, were recruited from the labour exchange, used out-dated technology and design, and compared poorly with their opposite numbers in the United States. In Nigeria there was a leisurely approach to drilling; it was not uncommon for a driller to go on leave with a partly drilled well mothballed and to complete it on return. Nowadays a drilled and tested borehole would be completed within a week. As a result, young geologists learned more from well sinkers than from drillers.

Water gets into the ground in a deceptively simple way. Some rain and dew evaporates or tops up the soil moisture, the rest sinks straight down through permeable beds until it can go no further. It reaches either a body already saturated, or an impervious layer. So it goes sideways until it reaches the surface somewhere and flows out as springs and seeps. Our job is to find out the groundwater's depth and how much is available. We work out how much water is needed and whether the money available will be enough to make a borehole and to pump the water up. We also need to know whether the water is pure enough to drink. Where water has been in contact for a long time with 'nasties' in the rock it becomes undrinkable.

Water is a liquid mineral, and so is petroleum oil. But oil usually lies deeper than groundwater, occurs only in places where it can be formed from old, dead bugs and usually travels upwards rather than down. Finding petroleum is more difficult and expensive than finding water. When oil exploration boreholes are drilled if one in every five strikes oil the searchers are content. In drilling for water, if more than one hole in five is dry there is trouble. In the field of economic geology, the very best brains are found in petroleum geology.

Spot the Elephant

Chapter 3. Ancestors: Past Perfect and Imperfect

*"My father set about finding his roots. Undeterred by Victorian
rectors' propensity to use tombstones in garden design,
he dug up their rock gardens until restrained."*

I understand that I was born at an early age, but the first coherent report
concerning the next few years was that at the age of four I had 'golden
curls and a silvery tinkling laugh.' Thank heaven these traits were
transient.

Being a normal youngster I was aware only of close relatives; the usual
complement of uncles, aunts, grandparents. Facts about ancestors of the
distant past emerged much later when my father, in his prime, set about
finding his roots. He had a tidy mind and his researches took him to the
Public Record Office in Somerset House; to put some flesh on the bones
of the dates of birth, marriage and death he haunted parish registers and
graveyards. He really did very well. Undeterred by Victorian rectors'
propensity to use tombstones in garden design, he dug up their rock
gardens until restrained.

In my father's time the family name was a happy hybrid, 'Temple Hazell'.
The Hazell side descended from Robert, a disreputable half-brother of
William Duke of Normandy (William the Conqueror, who was no saint
either). Further back, some collaterals were exciting, some eccentric. A
Cumberland sheriff, Edward Hasell of Dalmain was granted a coat of
arms in 1699 described thus:

> 'Or, on a fess azure between three hazel nuts proper, husks,
> stalks and leaves vert, as many crescents argent. Mantling
> azure and or. Crest: a wreath of the colours, squirrel sejant
> argent cracking a hazel nut proper and encircled with two
> hazel branches crossing each other at the top vert.
> Motto: "Qui nucleum vult nucem frangat"

Someone, presumably the sheriff, had a sense of humour: 'Who wishes the kernel must first crack the nut' can be interpreted in many subtle ways.

The nineteenth century Hazells were extensively documented; they would have described themselves variously as solid upper middle class and middle class professional gentry.

To counterbalance the Norman side, the first Temple was the son of Leofric the Saxon and Lady Godiva. William the Conqueror, 'wishing to placate the family of Leofric the Saxon granted to Leofric's son Henry the manor of Temple, Com, Leicester. He then became Henry del Temple.'

Four centuries later the Temples sided with the Roundheads and two Temples added their signatures to the death warrant for King Charles I. This did not do them a lot of good when the Royalists bounced back. Later descendants settled in Stowe in the Cotswolds and a Temple became the Third Viscount Palmerston, who as Prime Minister was a high Tory and in the aftermath of the French Revolution the scourge of the French. Much later two other Temples became Archbishops of Canterbury.

At the start of the Great War my father was just old enough to fight. The rather grand sounding Honourable Artillery Company taught him how to be a signaller and off he went to the trenches in Flanders. For four years Lieutenant Hazell endured the beastliness of the very wet trenches in the Ypres salient; when it was all over he put it out of his mind as much as he could and rarely spoke of it. At the Honourable Artillery Company's base just north of the City of London, the survivors of the battle of Hoogh used to meet and dine once a year and once my father took me along. The battle was a small one, part of the first battle of Ypres; and there never were many survivors. Very ancient and craggy and fierce they looked.

An early memory is of my father on every Armistice Day anniversary, November 11th, taking down his sword from over the mantelpiece and going off to the cenotaph. When I was older and saw the cenotaph for myself every man who passed on foot doffed his hat; nowadays few folk bother.

Chapter 4. A Manner of Speaking

"The seed wey we d'plant 'em never 'gree come up."

It has been asserted that geologists are accustomed to hitting rocks that don't retaliate and that they project this principle to humans. There may be an element of truth in this. However, to achieve a useful degree of contact with real people, away from the big towns, even rock bashing geologists need a smattering, a few words, of the local language. To overlook this precept is to invite disaster.

Long ago I had occasion to travel to Milan in company with a driller call Sid, a Royal Navy veteran who, being vertically challenged, was suited to life in submarine engine rooms and had risen to the rank of Chief Petty Officer. A true product of Portsmouth, Sid was stoutly of the opinion that:

'The English, the English, the English are best,
I wouldn't give tuppence for all of the rest.'

Our appointment in Milan was with the adjudicating committee of a well known Italian company. Sid was technically suited to argue the suitability of his company to drill for uranium in West Africa but was far from successful in communicating his intrinsic charm. In a fairly short time it was indicated to us that the meeting had broken into their lunch break and that doubtless we knew our way back into town. By the time we reached the restaurant area of the city Sid was sulphurously xenophobic. His rage could be appeased only by a really good meal. He homed in on an arcade beside the Duomo, an elegant and ruinously expensive establishment, which I later discovered was world famous.

The head waiter was at first courteous but after the initial exchange of views he became sad and pensive. It was time to intervene and I asked what he recommended for lunch. "Feesh" said he.

"**!!**" exclaimed Sid. He added, very slowly, fortissimo and in basic English, that Portsmouth was famous for mobile fish restaurants which must by definition be superior to any Eyetalian dump. I at length persuaded him to relax and resumed negotiations with the Head Waiter.

With a sigh and a shrug, "Ees Friday, ees dorado". Having explained to Sid that dorado was a great delicacy it was a relief to hear him command: "We'll 'ave some of that. o ne each.

The head waiter sighed, even more deeply and some time later a vast silver dish was uncovered with a flourish to reveal a single magnificent fish weighing in at about two kilos. A kilo of fish is quite a load to the system and progress was slow. The desert that followed, unwisely commanded, was a huge duomo of melba studded with strawberries, and progress was even slower. Then of course there was the row about the bill . . . .

As we staggered away to rest, Sid delivered an epitaph that stays with me to this day: "We might have died for these buggers during the war - and some of them don't even speak English.

In any language, even in Italian, there are magic words and phrases that help the traveller and are passwords for strangers dealing with local people. One wet day in Lincolnshire my gravel survey strayed from its valid path and I was assailed by an irate farmer with two slavering hounds. With great presence of mind, brought on by fear, I blurted out, "It's a bit thin." In the fens this means that it is raining. This fragment of local knowledge saved my skin and in the ensuing instant peace came civilised dialogue.
A geologist assessing clay deposits in north Portugal once strayed through ignorance into the lady's toilet at a parador. The indignant occupant was instantly pacified when he bowed gravely and murmured "obrigado."

In our blessed land the standard greeting used to be "how are you", then "hiya", and now "hi". This phrase neither seeks nor welcomes a reply describing one's current state of health. Except in parts of Wales where, when acquaintances meet, an entire conversation is encapsulated in one sentence: "Good morning how are you I am sorry to hear it." Or so the story goes.

In Africa, however, overconfidence breeds puzzlement, especially as many Bantu languages are tonal. In Hausa, gishiri means salt if the accent is on the first syllable but on the second it means short.

Along the coast of British West Africa, where many tribes each had their own language, a trading language developed. English words dominated, though fragments of Portugese and Spanish from earlier times persisted. This form of basic English was named Pidgin – from the Chinese version of 'Business'. In Sierra Leone a similar language is Creo. Using West African Pidgin, the tenses of a verb are roughly the same as in English: *I go* (I am going). *I done go* (I went), *I pass go* (I went long ago), *I go go* (I will go), *I fit go* (I can go).

And distance: '*E near* (close by) '*E near small* (fairly close) '*E far small*' (fairly far) '*E far*' and '*E too far*' (a long way off). Willingness and ability share one term, which is '*gree*' i.e. agree. So 'E gree' means either he is willing or he (or a thing) can. If in Britain a gap is too small to accept an object, we would say 'It won't fit in'. Pidgin equivalent is 'E no gree enter.'

The French and Portuguese in Africa taught standard French and Portuguese, as they had tacitly - though rashly - assumed they were there to stay. Indeed, the Portuguese produced appropriately titled maps, such as the 'Mozambique Province of Portugal'. Moreover, in French speaking colonies traders would literally live 'over the shop', which in British colonies was rare.

During the Fifties, in Iboland in eastern Nigeria, schooling was far from universal. We employed a 'garden boy' called Gabriel who was one day brooding over a bald seed bed and I ventured to say 'The seed wey we d' plant em never gree come up.' Gabriel replied solemnly: 'No sir, they do not appear to have germinated.' Collapse of stout party. The management was convulsed with mirth. Said she: 'I told you he had been to school.'

Later, following the massacres of the Biafran war, when tens of thousands of Ibos fled from the north to their homeland, Iboland seethed with intelligent, educated, articulate folk, reduced to great poverty, and the use of pidgin declined. Looking for an abandoned borehole once, I greeted a ragged farmer carrying a hoe, and (unthinkingly) continued in pidgin: 'Which side borehole dey?'

With a smile, he replied 'Take the next track on your left, about 100 metres on, it's on your right. It was constructed in 1977 but the pump was not fitted.'

In northern Nigeria there are only three major tribes, Hausa, and Kanuri, which are relatively easy to learn, and Fulani, which is not. Administrators and missionaries were thicker on the ground than traders and were obliged to learn the languages and pidgin never flourished. The average geologist or forester was not linguistically gifted but learned the necessary key words.

In Hausaland the most important is "lafiya". This means 'health' and is a component of many greetings in the language. There are many, many greetings and friendly exclamations in Hausa, some invoking the name of Allah, a few concerned with work and weariness, but 'lafiya' transcends them all. A bature (white man) with a very limited Hausa vocabulary can maintain a reasonably good relationship by exclaiming 'lafiya' or even, on a good day, with 'ina gajiya' ('where is your weariness') on meeting a Hausaman.

In the course of our water supply work, as we drove around in the far north or walked over cultivated land where maps were obsolete and villages ephemeral, we often needed to find someone who knew where our target villages were. We spy two lean lanky fulani herdsmen, straw hatted, with staffs, and the exchange (translated) goes like this:

'Greetings.' - 'Greetings.'

'I have a question.' - 'Oh!'
'Where is Garin Isa?' - long pause and interchange of glances between the herdsmen.
'We do not know'.
'What is the name of this village?' - 'It may be Garin Isa.'

They play dumb but they are not. They have been working out why we want to know and whether or not it is advantageous to tell. They have guessed that we are not tax gatherers and that something good is coming.

Though their village is not Garin Isa it is worth a try. Towards the end of a hot day it is tempting to site a borehole and christen the village Garin Isa!

Investigating groundwater in the field, the usefulness of geophysics comes a close second behind common sense. It would be tempting to assume that it would be beyond the scope of local sons of the soil to work as a geophysical survey team. In most developing countries a team leader can draw from an abundant pool of local men with time to spare and the need for a bit of cash. These men are accustomed to repetitive rhythmic work, be it hoeing the land, planting seed, cutting sugar cane or whatever and work that to a sophisticated European can be boring is to them perfectly acceptable.

The team leader needs to treat these folk as friends and equally to be able to communicate with them. Many do not speak English, some do not speak the regional language, but it doesn't take long to learn how, in their own mother tongue, to greet them, use the words for 'stop', 'go on', east, north, south and west, and the numbers from one to ten. And most importantly, to laugh with them.

Chapter 5. Coal, crabs and conversion

"Imagine the sense of betrayal birds must have felt when, after a long migration, surviving Spanish shotguns and Saharan birds of prey, they alighted on the arms of St. Francis' statue to be peppered with shot by a Franciscan brother."

The great paradox: delta and desert

Some of the wettest places on earth are short of useful groundwater; and some of the driest places have more than is needed. In southern Algeria years may pass between rainfall events and quantities are measured in millimetres. The Algerian government was at one time intent on proving a uranium deposit at Tim el Gwain in a remote area south west of Tamanrasset. Brilliant yellow fragments of uranium oxide littered the surface – the Tuareg tribesmen did not steal it, having discovered long ago that carrying a lump around for any length of time made them very sick indeed. A water supply was needed for the projected mine and there is ample groundwater below – but so radioactive as to be undrinkable. Some 200 kilometres to the east, just over the border with the state of Niger, lies a huge reservoir of underground water. This is 'fossil' water, with origins in the distant past when up to Roman times rain was abundant. Except in the centre of the Sahara, fields of wheat provided grain for the Roman empire. Murals in ruined Roman cities along the Mediterranean depict elephants, hippos and crocodiles and clearly the Sahara desert was not then a formidable barrier to travel. The groundwater lies in a great sandy basin, too deep for the Tuareg to reach by digging wells. The Algerian government planned to create a field of drilled wells along the border with Niger, and pump it westwards in a pipeline to the mine site. Had this been done, it is possible that a few holes would inadvertently have sloped eastwards into Niger, where most of the groundwater lay. This would have pulled out water belonging to Niger. Perish the thought!

Our team prospected a route for the pipeline avoiding the high dunes and finding where ribs of rock would need cutting through. A water pipeline in this thirsty part of the world needs to be deep to prevent enterprising

Touareg from opening it up with a hammer and chisel. We left camp with three vehicles – two for the field party, the other laden with drums of water – and worked our way eastwards. Before the days of global positioning systems we relied on our Touareg guides who knew every inch of the terrain. We rested during the hottest part of the day, seeking the shade of overhanging rocks where the drivers brewed very bitter tea sweetened with sugar. Conversation with the Touareg was patchy; they refused to speak Arabic or French but we managed to communicate in Hausa, the lingua franca of the southern Sahel.

Gossip over tea ranged widely, designed in duration to last until it was cool enough to continue work. Our traverse from west to east crossed the trans-Sahara piste, a mesh of tyre tracks several kilometres wide. This gave a misleading impression of heavy and frequent traffic, though in fact tyre tracks last for years. Some tracks were created by intrepid contestants in the Algiers to Agadez rally; our guides hated these travellers and said so at length. As a people who scraped a living from the desert, the use of this silent wilderness as a racetrack for the rich was repugnant to them. A Touareg mounted on a camel is a majestic and photogenic sight, though they strongly disliked being photographed.

Among the high dunes we ate our supper and drank our tea then, near the dying embers of our cooking fire, drifted towards sleep in a huddle of blankets. The silence was intense, the stars blazed in the sky. This was profoundly satisfying. Often enough, flying southwards over the Sahara in a big jet I braved the afternoon wrath of devotees of the silver screen by opening the blind. Peering down I could discern tiny black dots in the wadis – the skin tents of the bedou - and knew where I would rather be.

By contrast, in the Niger delta rainfall is measured in feet rather than inches. Abundant freshwater creeks are filthy and water-borne disease is rife. Though groundwater lies only one or two metres down it is often too salty to drink. Buried far down, great tongues of ancient sand slope downwards from far inland. These can contain huge quantities of good, sweet water beneath clay bands that exclude salty groundwater from above. The palm oil traders used to anchor their sailing ships above springs of fresh water that bubbled up from these deep sands and using canvas hoses and pumps would replenish their water casks.

In 1960 I directed a water supply programme in part of the Niger delta where tribal animosity had always been rife. In 1935 there had been a major bust up when an expedition of Kalabaris in war canoes from Buguma set upon the peaceful Okrikas. The District Officer fined the Kalabaris a substantial sum, which was handed over to the Okrikas as reparation. With this fund the Okrikas built a town hall and erected a statue of King George V. By 1960 both had all but vanished into the mud and of the statue the only visible feature was the top of the regal head. Some years later a borehole at Okrika yielded a copious supply of good water. But there appeared to be an enduring curse on the Kalabari. I supervised test drilling on Buguma island, coinciding with a prolonged and continual period of heavy rain; the drillers living on a leaky barge ran out of dry clothes. On day 21 the drill reached its maximum reach – in salty water. The people watching in stolid wonder during daylight hours were anticipating great success and their warlike tendency made it inappropriate to break the news to them. Being nominally in charge of the operation, though in years the youngest, I was enjoined to leave the area stealthily in a skimmer (a flat bottomed power boat) to bring higher authority to keep the peace. That night a particularly heavy downpour drove the vigilantes into cover and the drill crew were able to escape in the barge.

The oil rivers

For several hundred years mariners from Europe traded and settled in West Africa, mostly along the coast but also into the riverine hinterland. From the 13th century onwards the seafaring Portuguese predominated. Their early traces survive in several forms. Along the coast they are mainly the names of places and of rivers. However, near navigable rivers far inland are their styles in building and decoration, grave goods, pottery, plants and settlements. They brought from their own land blue glazed ceramics, ecclesiastical robes and black umbrellas and installed ambassadors to the courts of the empires of Ashanti and Benin. From

India and Malaysia they brought trees and plants. They went home with ivory, palm oil, peppers and slaves.

British traders arrived later and early in the 19th century established posts under the umbrella of the great kings, trading mainly in slaves. When the British banned the trade in slaves that lucrative trade gradually gave way to palm oil. The delta of the river Niger, with a humid tropical climate, was possibly the biggest source of this golden liquid rich in vitamins. In forest clearings, the copper-coloured red nuts of the oil palm were stewed up, the oil was skimmed off and used for cooking.

On the western edge of the delta is Benin City, heart of the Edo empire, which until the end of the 19th century dominated a belt several hundred miles wide. The Oba held court at the heart of an elegant city that early travellers compared favourably with similar cities in Europe. In style the Portuguese influence was strong and until comparatively recently the court language was an amalgam of basic Portuguese and Edo. The sophistication of their culture is evident in the famous Benin bronzes in the British Museum.

The delta's rough and ready British traders contributed little to the cultural and artistic development of the people. They brought in utilitarian items such as copper and firearms. The nearest they came to introducing culture was the importation of black bowler hats that became immensely popular and to this day are traditionally worn on formal occasions by local statesmen. In the process of making money they wrought a boom in the palm oil industry and the network of navigable creeks became known as the oil rivers.

The hulks were converted into 'factories' and the traders became known as 'palm oil ruffians'. Many died of malaria, the toughest survived and grew rich. At weekends they foregathered to eat 'palm oil chop', a delicious stew that had evolved its own ritual. With the stew was served pounded yam (fufu) and the mess president tested its consistency ceremonially by loading a knife blade with a dollop and flicking it up to the ceiling. If it stuck it was ready; otherwise it was sent back for more pounding. Beer brewed from maize or millet was served in great quantity. Each man wore a protective jacket, a 'palm oil waistcoat', which was never washed. The wearer of the waistcoat of deepest yellow hue was the equivalent of the mess president.

One successful trader used to amass a heavy bank balance over several years then sail off to London, where he hired a wing of the Dorchester hotel and invited his cronies for a prolonged party. When his money ran out he sailed back to the delta and started another cycle.

It is ironic that following the discovery of petroleum oil in the delta, the term 'oil rivers' acquired a new significance. Little of the oil revenue trickled back to the local population. An inevitable consequence was that the oil pipelines carrying the crude oil inland were sabotaged with enthusiasm – a hammer and chisel being the sophisticated tools used. The resulting 'own goal' spills polluted the creeks and seriously harmed the fisheries.

Hard rock men

In the post-war years the Colonial geological surveys, for a variety of reasons, were under considerable pressure to step up the search for economically useful minerals. The spotlight was on columbite and tantalite, previously the Cinderella of metal ores. Among many other things, they were needed in the manufacture of hard-wearing spare parts such as hip joints. On the Jos plateau these minerals overtook tin in demand and price. One prospector with some sacks of columbite made a very good profit by putting them in a shed for a year as the price soared. A useful by-product of the mineral hunt was the creation of first class geological maps - the directors of Geological Survey having had the wisdom to insist that only by thorough knowledge of the geology could the valuable minerals be located systematically.

Before our activities became dominated by water supply, the lower and middle echelons of the Geological Survey comprised (with increasing age):

- hard rock men, young and peripatetic bachelors, lean and wild bearded, who made maps and sought valuable useful minerals;

- soft rock men, also young and peripatetic, lean and wild bearded but less spectacular, given to eating and sleeping in comfort.

- Senior Geologists, fairly young men but softened in contour by the demands of desk navigation.

I progressed through all three categories and, elsewhere in this strange, eventful history, have rendered a fragmentary account of my involvement in the wilder youthful shores. In more mature years, as a Senior Geologist, in intervals between battles with mountains of files, I had the doubtful pleasure of briefing hard rock men. I was not much older than they were, but protocol demanded that I adopt a sedentary, studious pose, the hard rock man standing, like a coiled spring in eagerness to get away and relieve his feelings by hammering inoffensive boulders.

The Great Gold Rush.

Two mineral investigations came about completely incidentally in the course of a youthful foray into water supply. One was unsuccessful but had unexpected repercussions.

In a remote area north of Benin I was charged with inculcating elements of water supply investigation into a newly hatched geologist. The fact that he was older than I was, with two years in the Royal Navy under his belt, did not bother either of us. I told him that he was not obliged to call me 'sir', and he replied that he would not fail to keep me up to date with his opinion of me. We got on very well.

We were based in the very dry village of Ukpilla high up on a granitic ridge. From the rest house we could look down on the bed of a dry river with scattered pools of water winding through a broad sandy alluvial flat. The object was fairly simple, which was just as well as I knew only a little more about the disposition of groundwater than did the naval veteran. Working out how to get the water to the village, by pulling it out of the alluvial sand and pumping it up the steep slope, was thankfully not within our brief.

In the course of completing our survey I read some detail from a dusty, dog-eared file I had brought, which recorded that someone had once applied for a licence to 'mine' gold from the river. In itself that was not remarkable as small occurrences of gold were known in quartz veins among the older rocks. Much later I found that one-man operations in some northern rivers were common. Though the yields were only marginally economic it was a useful occupation for local folk.

Consumed with curiosity, we took a day off to pan the alluvium using prospecting pans of standard issue backed up with boundless confidence. The results were predictably negative: not one grain of gold did we find.

So back to work, and we completed our task and moved on to pastures new. Soon after this, the Inspector of Mines in Ibadan heard that two Europeans had been extracting gold illicitly, and with full pomp and panoply of office came to effect an arrest. He did not find us but found and arrested several dozen local men who had waited till we left before imprudently resuming their activities.

A meeting of cultures

An interesting interlude followed the great gold rush. My colleague Hugh and I stopped off for the weekend in Auchi, an adminstrative centre, where the Assistant District Officer was a young man of about my age. Despite the disapproval of his senior, he had brought a piano to what was a very remote location; soirees were unknown and music was very much of the hearty vocal type.

Our visit coincided with that of the circuit judge, His Honour Justice Bola, a very civilised Nigerian who could play the piano, preferring the classics. We were invited to a recital by the judge and, indeed, it was delightful. At the end, with a sigh of content, His Honour rested his hands and asked if there were any other pieces we would like to hear.

Hugh awoke at this moment and in his Oxford drawl, slightly blurred by the pressure of the evening, asked 'Do you know the Harry Lime (hic!) theme', and relapsed into slumber. I seldom had cause to feel ashamed of my countrymen, but this was the exception.

A game of marbles

An unexpectedly successful facet of our work in the 'gold rush area' was that I found the river wended through the outcrop of a major marble deposit. These old marbles are part of a succession of old sedimentary rocks that started life as siltstone, shale, sandstone and limestone. These had been metamorphosed, baked and squeezed, to form belts of schist, gneiss, quartzite and marble. I had discovered a similar marble way off to the north at Jakura, which was why I recognised it down near Ukpilla. Having started life as a very pure calcium carbonate limestone, from the ground-up remains of ancient shellfish, they were transformed into interlocking, dazzling white calcite crystals. Two curious features are that the surface of the outcrops are jet black and among the calcite crystals are tiny black blebs of carbon. These I reckon to be the relics of soft organic tissue. Over the millennia the surfaces of the outcrops had dissolved away in acid rain, leaving the carbon to spread and smudge over the face.

Inevitably, I had orders to go back and map this new marble. We set up camp by the river on marble pavements, whence we could look down on deep pools. The first night I looked forward to a good sleep under the stars but suffered invasion by a silent, secret enemy. A horde of minute red ants had climbed up and easily crawled through the mesh of the mosquito net. While in itching terror I tore off my clothes and jumped into the water, the team slept with no mosquito nets, protected by smoke from a dying fire.

Soft rock men

Soft rock men earned their place in the scheme of things when a sensible decision was made by those in high places to create a cement industry and the search was on to locate suitable component minerals - rarely in wild craggy uplands, usually in humid sedimentary lowlands.

In my lean years on the Cross River plain I mapped a belt of limestone that stretched interminably northwards across rivers and swamps in 'pristine terrain', a term not yet coined. High rainfall and humidity made working conditions difficult; the local delicacy was a stew made from giant catfish with pounded yam. The palm wine, however, was excellent. It was important to intercept the wine-tapper coming away from the tree and buy a gourd full before it had been diluted with local swamp water. Apart from its soothing quality, palm wine was an important source of vitamin B and the older and wiser government doctors prescribed it.

As in many rural areas in those days, remote hamlets were populated with folk who had little contact with the outside world and maintained a strict code of morals and basic village administration that had evolved long before the advent of missionaries and politicians. Theft was unheard of and one could safely leave coins and valuables lying anywhere. Sexual activity before marriage was banned. Maidens, who were not allowed to wear clothes until they were married, carried their dowry with them in the form of brass bracelets on arms and legs. A wealthy family added on bracelet after bracelet, forming inverted cones, until movement was impeded. The distracting proximity of these young ladies was heralded afar by the jingling, clanking sound - possibly the original heavy metal.

An obsolete custom of Iboland was the fattening pen, where betrothed brides were incarcerated for several weeks before marriage and gorged with starch and oil to increase their livestock value.

Use of spring water was controlled in a simple and effective way. The stream flowing away from the spring was sectioned off. The spring pool was populated with scavenging fish; downstream a log heralded a water dipping zone bordered by flat stones. Further downstream was the washing area for bodies and laundry, and near it an area for soaking cassava roots, to rett out the prussic acid. There were health hazards (guinea worm, schistosomiasis, onchoceriasis) but human to human contact diseases were rare.

The impact of a quarry and a cement plant on these remote hamlets was brutal. The simple and practical code of living, previously ensured by the council of village elders, was swamped and disappeared forever. I unwittingly became a part of its destruction and made a sub-conscious decision: to spend more time looking for groundwater - a much more valuable mineral.

A rewarding experience, when a borehole neared completion, was to see children watching in joyful anticipation for the moment when, with a blast of compressed air, a fountain of water sprayed and drenched them. No one was the worse for the sudden change. Indeed the only complaint I ever received was from an ancient Obi who used to send his wives off each morning with empty pots to a spring ten kilometres distant and enjoyed silent contemplation until hours later they returned. With a working borehole on his doorstep, his tranquillity was destroyed forever.

With the introduction of English as the working language in the new primary schools, the use of the classic Ibo language became debased. Grey haired elders no longer depended on Ibo in formal discourse at council meetings. These meetings were held in the shade of huge trees in small amphitheatres made of logs, highly polished by the dignified posteriors of elders over the centuries. I knew an ancient priest from Alsace, fluent in classical Ibo. He once averred that, with a vast vocabulary achieved by using multiple variations in the vowel sounds of short words, Ibo elders debated complex matters. He lamented the incursion of English which, imperfectly understood, inhibited nuances of meaning.

Father Treich left Marseilles during the flu epidemic of 1918, attributing his survival to 'ze red wine', and became one of a select band of missionaries, travelling his vast parish at first by bicycle then, when roads improved, in a battered Citroen. With a heavy white beard, resembling a latter day Johannes Brahms, a more humble and devout soul never lived. He treasured the memory of a journey through Awka when, in the troubled Fifties, sporting his Wolsey helmet, in his 2CV, a youngster shook his fist and shouted 'imperialist.'

Slavery and the Aros

At the beginning of the 20th century a Royal Naval detachment stationed in the delta travelled northwards in a steam launch to chart the main channel of the Niger river. The appointed leader, a lieutenant, fell sick with fever and the expedition was led by a Scot, Surgeon Lieutenant Baikie. His name became history; in most of southern Iboland the white man was called 'onyeocha', a direct transliteration. In the riverine lowlands south of Onitsha, the white man is for ever called 'bakaye'. At Onitsha, where high ground forms a bluff overlooking the river, shots were fired at the launch. This had nothing to do with resistance to colonialism. It had everything to do with the fact that Onitsha was a staging point for the middle-men supplying the slavers and they feared that the white men would sever a profitable link in the illegal slave trade.

Before the logging industry made serious inroads, south eastern Nigeria was covered by primary forest. The great highways were the two big rivers, the Niger and the Cross, carrying traders and disease. In the adjoining lowlands people dwelt in hamlets, seldom travelling beyond the larger rivers and swamps that bred malarial mosquitoes. Of the high forest little remains except in the villages where stands of hardwood survive, usually near the local shrine.

Bordering the lowlands are long, often sinuous sandstone ridges and well-defined trails follow each watershed. Down the slopes are large springs of clean water. With assured supplies of clean water from springs along the flanks, large villages existed that later developed into townships. These were the great overland trade routes. Along them it was possible to travel for hundreds of miles without getting one's feet wet. Just as the Touareg controlled the movement of desert caravans crossing the Sahara, so the Aro tribe controlled the movement of trade in Iboland and played a part in the profitable trade in slaves and ivory. Their power base was at Arochukwu; 'Chukwu' means 'god' and appropriately the town once sported a notorious oracle where many vulnerable people visiting to pray and supplicate simply disappeared. The British sent an expedition to destroy it. Arochukwu lies at the jutting knee of the main sandstone ridge, not far from the navigable Cross river, which reaches the coast not far from the historic slave market of Old Calabar.

The landing beach below Arochukwu is the site of one of the bloodiest battles of the Nigerian civil war. Over and over again the federal troops in landing craft tried to land; the Biafrans waited until they were close in and mowed them down with automatic fire. The beach is to this day littered with rusting weapons, cartridges and bullets.

Juju and fetish

The simplest forms of mystic token gave protection against harm and theft. A worker who left his shovel by the track would protect it with a tuft of grass twisted into a knot. Our house in Enugu was never burgled, though surrounded by many less fortunate households. This puzzled us; until a colleague pointed out that our daughters had scribbled graffiti with coloured crayons on an outside corner of the building. In addition, I normally hired labourers from Abakpa, a village that I later discovered was notorious as a nest of thieves; maybe they had loyalties.

In the more remote settlements reached only on foot, small shrines were common. One village sported a beautifully thatched shrine over a block of coal; understandably a rock which would burn like firewood was an object of superstition. Trekking through another remote hamlet, I saw a human skull enshrined, though on my return journey it had disappeared. In the eastern mountains gorilla skulls were commonly perched on pallisades protecting farmland. These were not mystical; they were scarecrows. I remonstrated with a farmer who courteously pointed out that they could not afford the luxury of protecting gorillas; their need was to scrape a living from the soil.

Most superstitions evoke tales of medieval Europe when pagan gods – mostly harmless - competed with Christianity. A modern equivalent of the scapegoat (originally a human, later a goat, beaten in expiation of guilt) survived as a horse beating ceremony. Worn-out nags from the north were driven into trenches and beaten to death with iron rods. This custom was observed on the northern edge of Iboland, where distant memories of raiding fulani cavalry persist.

Most forest tribes observe rituals connected with life, death and fertility. The masquerade, where the participants dance completely covered with decorated straw costume, has lately modified to a social occasion, though strangers are not encouraged. I attended one where, identified as an onyeocha (white man) and a Christian, my presence was tolerated but none would shake my hand. In Cornwall similar rituals are observed and flourish at the Helston flurry dance and the Padstow 'Obby 'Oss.

The sacred spring of Achi

The village of Achi Isikiwe is on the crest of a high sandstone ridge, and the people draw water from a mighty spring far below. Hans, a Danish water engineer, and I visited the council of elders who wanted to improve their water supply. First we were warned that the spring was the property of the juju and protected all wild creatures. We were conducted down the steep path to the spring, totally unprepared for what we saw. Above a lush grove of trees a spring bubbled from the foot of a cliff into a pool. From the tree tops noisy monkeys showered twigs upon us. A young crocodile slept in the shade nurtured, we were told, by hens' eggs from the village. A long snake slithered away, birds screeched. After Hans had (cautiously) gauged the flow from the pool, I inched my way along a ledge to a shallow cave behind the spring and posed for one of many photographs. Our escorts were uneasy; it was improper to disturb the juju and I was encouraged to climb down.

The scheme we suggested was to feed the flow into a tank and pump it up through a pipe to the village. This was agreed, though the elders asked us to wait until the site was deconsecrated. This, by the way, would cost the village £200.

The spool of film we developed on the first cold night when the air temperature was down to 70° F and the following night we printed from our negatives. It was clear that there was something very odd about some of the shots Hans had taken. A complete halo surrounded the cave mouth and in those shots where I was heroically posed the halo was interrupted. This scarcely troubled me; I have always held that supernatural manifestations are not all fiction and trickery; indeed as a Catholic I hold fast to tenets that would puzzle the veriest pagan. Hans, a staunch rationalist, took the whole matter very seriously. With a new spool of film he returned to take more photos, with the same result. His trusty light meter showed no anomalies. And sure enough after the elders had paid £200 and the grotto was deconsecrated, Hans made a final photo shoot and the halo had vanished. But the people had their piped water.

One of my pet aphorisms is 'never go back' – but much later I did. Gone were the trees and the grass, barren loose sand had drifted across the pool, a ruined shed held the twisted relics of a pump.

Brandy galore

On a loop of the Cross River, in a remote part of eastern Nigeria, is the town of Afikpo. Here I lived for some weeks prospecting for coal and met with much kindness from the expatriate community.

Historically it was an inland trading port, exporting mainly timber shipped down to Calabar. In the early Fifties the town, though in decline, was still an administrative centre. It was classified as a 'difficult' area. The British raj was represented by a Senior District Officer, of medium stature. His second in command, as District Officer, was the honourable Hugh from an old Cornish estate, a delightful and modest man. Gerry Hennessy, the Assistant District Officer completed the trio, and it was he who carried out the humdrum routine work.

In Achara M'bom the local worthies could not understand why I was digging pits and the explanation - that the object was to see if there was enough coal to found a local industry - was automatically disbelieved. These dignitaries were wildly and effectively obstructive and I asked the raj for assistance. So one fine day these big fish were summoned from their small pond to appear before the court to give an account of themselves. In due course Authority, the Senior District Officer, effected his entrance. Clad in immaculate white complete with regulation pith helmet and platform soles, he was flanked by uniformed messengers and an interpreter. I brought up a reluctant rear in modest, well worn, field khaki clothing contrasting strongly with the glorious robes of the dignitaries of Achara M'bom. These dignitaries were lambasted by Authority, accused of 'humbugging the geologist' and, suitably deflated, were sent packing. Field work subsequently progressed peacefully but, like most prospecting programmes, humdrum to the inventive, poetic soul.

More interesting was the discovery by the river of a rich bed of large fossil crabs. They had weathered out of shale in the riverbank and tumbled on to the beach, looking remarkably similar to modern crabs though about 180 million years older. So well were they preserved that the females still had their eggs tucked under their tummies. When a healthy colony of creatures suddenly dies, not of old age or disease, some catastrophic event must have killed them. As clay (which later was compressed into shale) had covered them and thus preserved them, they must have been 'dead on arrival' as healthy crabs are happy in the silts and clays of a near-shore environment.

The most lucrative trade in this part of the Cross River plain was in Spanish brandy smuggled in from the island of Fernando Po. This was known locally as Genuine Okposi after a village of that name on a tidal creek, served by 'the Okposi ferry', a commodious canoe. The landing stage was conveniently near a Catholic mission. In the diocese of Ogoja were two Fathers called O'Sullivan, conveniently labelled 'the holy one' and 'the hairy one'. The hairy priest was stationed at Okposi and to him fell the task of exerting quality control on the trade. Enrichment of the brandy with creek water, using a hypodermic borrowed by the smugglers from the local dispensary, was simple and cost effective. Thus Father O'Sullivan, in addition to normal duties, carried out the onerous task of exerting quality control. Needless to emphasise that this was purely to ensure the health and well being of the community. In addition he was able to keep the discerning though scattered British community supplied with a guaranteed product. An acceptable product labelled 'Terry' cost five shillings a bottle. The premium quality Pedro Domecque cost seven shillings and six pence. The Hairy father, cut off by distance from his brother priests, endured these duties with devotion and fortitude.

Inevitably there were hiccups in the flow of trade. The most serious followed a visit from a young and zealous police officer. Unappreciative of the universal benefit of the flow of golden fluid, he used the police launch to intercept and confiscate a major consignment of brandy. He lodged the cases in Afikpo prison and Gerry Hennessy was instructed to pour it all away down the prison drains which, with tears in his eyes, he did. Outside the prison walls a multitude of enterprising volunteers caught the precious fluid in calabashes and rejoicing carried most of it away in four-gallon tins.

The high spot of this Afikpo sojourn was, for me, becoming a Catholic. This was brought about for a combination of reasons and feelings and I do not propose to wax on about them. Enough to say that after 60 years I have had no regrets.

A visit to the Holy Ghost Fathers' mission station in Afikpo to buy brandy developed into agreeable social contacts with the team of Irish mission priests. At the back of the mission is a spring-fed rock pool where the priests splashed around and cooled off after the day's work. For me, a pleasant routine developed: a dip in a big rock pool followed by cold lager. Inevitably discussion became serious. A young priest was detailed to be my mentor and I would drive him out to the riverbank looking down on the fossil crabs for argument sessions. He was an intelligent and unprejudiced man and presented a fair picture of the Roman Catholic church, warts and all. So I took the plunge and 'went over', which in the early Fifties was a serious matter. Reactions from family and friends varied: many were hostile, a significant few were sympathetic. Oddly enough my Anglican godfather, by then the Bishop of Peterborough, wished me well.

Locally, up and down the Cross River, the word went round that a Government Officer was to be received into the Church of Rome. A great feast was planned by the nuns and the newsletter of their parent organisation in Britain gave the event banner headlines. Monsignor McGettrick, a muscular prelate, travelled 100 miles to officiate. The run-up was relaxed. Had I been baptised? Yes, by an Anglican bishop. Better baptise you again to make sure of it. So they asked Gerry Hennessy to be my Godfather. Then I was confirmed and after some bewildering formalities we all went off to the feast.

Before I reluctantly left Afikpo, three more blessings were showered on me by kind expatriate friends. First, the wife of the medium sized Senior District Officer, who had previous nursing training, realised that my recurring fevers were not malarial. She insisted on sending me, in a very uncomfortable ambulance, to a distant hospital where a disease called microfalaria was diagnosed. Added to my existing impressive list of previous tropical afflictions, I wondered afresh how the soft machine of the human body survived.

Back in Afikpo, the Honourable Hugh heard the sounds emerging from my venerable wind-up portable gramophone. He winced at the scratchy impact of sharp needles on warped shellac '78' records and gave me a fibre needle from his thin supply.

Finally my new Godfather introduced me to the rich beauty of the Bristol wurzle dialect. He later retired from the Service and trained to become an income tax inspector in the UK. Over the years he attended to my welfare and phoned me annually to give me counsel, albeit on matters fiscal rather than spiritual.

Cameroon Highlands, 1954

Apart from the generous home leave provision Colonial servants were entitled to a week's 'local leave'. In March 1954 we set off for the Cameroon highlands, my wife Kath and I, with a mountain of baggage in the pick-up. Balanced on top, exposed to all perils, our nurse girl and carry cot; and on the nurse girl's knee our first-born daughter, Cecily, a few months old. Our first staging post was on the Cross River near Ikom, where we met up with the District Officer. His house stood on a bluff overlooking a pool where hippos cavorted. On his crackly radio we listened to the Boat Race. Then on Maundy Thursday up the steep winding narrow track to the Bamenda plateau. Traffic could pass uphill on Monday, Wednesday and Friday, downhill on Tuesday, Thursday and Saturday. We glanced anxiously back to make sure we still had our precious cargo and forward in case someone had mistaken the date. For on our left there was a plunge of hundreds of feet into the forest. After the humid heat of Enugu, and the Cross River plain, the mountain air was invigorating.

After the First World War Cameroon was annexed from Germany and split lengthways. The western half became a protectorate as British Cameroon, administered from Nigeria. The eastern half came under

Juju masquerade

French protection' The Rest House at Bamenda was an old German fort; a truly teutonic structure with watch towers at each corner. The German colonists imposed a hard disciplinary regime. In the Fifties, some 40 years after the Germans left, old men stood to attention and saluted when a white man drove past. In former times, if they did not do so they were shot.

In the mountains there was little contact between clans; each has its own language. The lingua franca used by traders and missionaries was 'classic' pidgin English. A few words of French, Spanish and Portuguese survive but most are English. The mainly Catholic missionaries of necessity used pidgin and at the Easter services the Bible readings and prayers at first sounded incongruous but we quickly came to appreciate the deeper understanding that came to us.

North of Bamenda was a Fransiscan monastery and college, heralded by a huge statue of St. Francis. Over all this presided a Dutch priest, Father Samuel Untervater, affectionately known as Submarine Sam. A previous brother had made a splendid collection of stuffed birds and in the entrance hall was a second, smaller statue of St. Francis with plaster birds on his outstretched arms, surrounded by cabinet after cabinet of stuffed, real birds. Imagine the sense of betrayal birds must have felt when, after a long migration from Scandinavia, surviving the shotguns of Spanish hunters and Saharan birds of prey, they alighted on the arms of St. Francis to be peppered with shot by a Franciscan brother.

From Bamenda to French-speaking Cameroons (now called Cameroun) is a short drive and here was a magnificent restaurant. This was when the realisation dawned that meat from humped cattle is not intrinsically tough and the difference between the 'Hausa cow' of Nigeria and the Francophone equivalent was due to skill in maturing and cooking. The British were bachelors in the white man's grave and could not cook, so could not teach their servants to cook.

In later years I often bought a steer from a fulani market at the end of the dry season when they were cheap. We fattened each gentle, trusting beast for a few weeks on the nutritious tops of groundnut plants before slaughter in a stress-free environment. The meat, hung in the air-conditioned container that housed our computer and telex machine, was exquisitely tender.

Royal Visits

Cecily was three years old when Queen Elizabeth toured Nigeria in 1956. I was 'Geologist in Charge, Eastern Region' which stretched eastwards from the Niger river to the Cameroun border, and from the Benue to the ocean - an area of about 150,000 square kilometres. My office was a row of wooden hutches by the road from the airport and on the day the Queen was to arrive we assembled under a shady tree with Union flags to wave. In advance came two policemen on motor-cycles complete with sirens. At the age of three, Cecily was understandably confused and for years referred to all black policemen on motor-cycles as 'queens', which potentially led to some awkward confrontations. While the stately black Rolls Royce whispered past we cheered and waved our flags. The local Ibo bystanders did not know what all the fuss was about and looked on silently.

The Governor of the Eastern Region at the time was Sir Clem Pleass, moved from the relative peace of Lagos to restless Iboland. Lady Sybil Pleass was a vigorous and commanding presence who had battled with game fish offshore from Lagos and conquered colossal barracuda. The garden at Government Lodge was splendid. For the royal visit a wing of the house was surrendered to the Queen and the Duke of Edinburgh. At the banquet the traditions of the Coast were observed. Before dinner, by hallowed ritual the ladies went upstairs to 'powder their noses' while the gentlemen, headed by the Duke, trooped outside into the velvet night to 'see Africa'. And incidentally to water the flower beds.

The deliberations were interrupted by an authoritative voice from the balcony above: 'Clem, don't forget the hydrangeas'.

The garden was home to some introduced plants. A striking addition was an attractive shrub with small powder blue flowers, a variety of eupatorium. It thrived and spread and within a few years had seeded 60 miles in every direction. At Onitsha, seeds were carried by the winds across the Niger and westwards to Benin and Togo hundreds of miles away. An evergreen, it could not be burnt by farmers and was cut down each season before crop planting. The clay soils were thus enriched. This delightful little plant is known in the southern languages as 'new weed' and is the most enduring memorial to the days of Sir Clem and Lady Pleas.

Before the arrival of this plant I mapped sand and clay boundaries by traversing the dirt roads and recording where the dust cloud behind our truck began and ended. 'New weed' was a more precise marker – it thrived on clay but died on sand.

For us, the big event of the visit to Enugu was the appearance of the Queen at the House of Assembly. Dressed in our best, we followed the crowds down to the reception area – rows and rows of collapsible chairs beneath an arcuate pattern of four huge concrete elephant tusks, the whimsy of an architect. The royal cortege appeared on time, the BBC film crew wound up their gear and somewhere inside the building the Queen was on hold while out at Government Lodge a search was made for a steel trunk containing the insignia and the 'gongs' to be awarded. When the Queen emerged finally, an acoustic quirk carried to everybody her aside to an aide - 'It's all right, they were under Philip's bed.'

The following year, in 1957, Princes Alexandra visited Nigeria and I had a brief unplanned encounter with royalty. On a very wet day I had driven a colleague to Port Harcourt on the edge of the Niger delta to see him on to a flight to the north. Leaving the airport I became aware of the princess's visit when I was politely but firmly asked not to leave the area until the royal cortege had set off for the city. So after a quarter of an hour I splashed back down the road. Through the rain I could see hordes of drenched school children lining the road and, remarkably, they were waving Union flags at me. Flattered, I held my course, singing a little song and looking forward to lunch at the rest house. Then, through the rain and 20 yards ahead, a large square black shape . . . .

From the viewpoint of the cheering, flag-waving children it must have been confusing. The glittering motor-cycle escort, then the Royal Standard fluttering from the bonnet of a stately black Rolls, and then a mud-spattered blue truck driven by a grimy European in ancient shirt and khaki shorts, skidding to a crawl just in time to avoid a lese majeste shunt. After a rapid assessment of the situation it was clear that the only course of action was to keep station, waving to the children (the royal micro-wave) and sitting very straight and grand until an opportunity arose to slither off on to a side road and resume normal activities. I have been an ardent royalist ever since.

Food and endurance

Before the advent of effective anti-malarial drugs in the early Forties, colonial servants in West Africa were predominantly male, as wives were discouraged from joining them. This ruling was not unreasonable; mortality from fever was high and life expectancy short. But social life in Nigeria was unbalanced. Grumpy young men endured boring evenings and execrable food, as they knew not - and hence could not - teach Nigerians how to cook.

Routine eating in the earlier days could be, for bachelors, dull and monotonous. We endured 'Hausa cow' in various forms, tough and overcooked. Chicken cooked during rigor mortis was equally tough. Our cooks used recipes passed down by indefatigable British pioneers. With our own rudimentary knowledge of cookery we could not improve their work and carried on the practice of stern, masochistic chewing.

One problem was the need to eat meat before it rotted in the hot humid air. In the market cattle were slaughtered at dawn. Joints bought and carried away while still warm were cooked and eaten the same day. The humped cattle carried on their shoulders a lump of allegedly more tender meat known as 'homp'. It was well down on the scale of toughness but still pretty chewy.

Throughout much of black Africa the Bantu people traditionally prefer tough meat associated, I imagine, with power. Even today, fillet steak bought in Botswana is much cheaper than the more challenging cuts. During the great oil boom in Nigeria the federal government remedied a shortage of meat by importing Brazilian frozen beef carcasses, sold locally at heavily subsidised prices. Well matured and tender, they were largely shunned by Nigerians but relished by expatriates.

So in bachelor-dominated expatriate society there were only a few special meals for high days and holidays. Chicken curry, the most popular, was laden with side dishes called gauges. The more side dishes the higher was the curry rated - there could be more than 20. Fierce chillies, moderate chillies, roast groundnuts, boiled groundnuts, tomato, paw-paw, pineapple, orange fragments, tiny dried shrimps and many other items combined to create a spicy fruit salad with fragments of meat. Curries were Far Eastern introductions with Nigerian bits grafted on. By contrast, groundnut stew is a truly West African food item. Meat served in a sauce based on groundnut oil was enriched with crushed roast groundnuts and accompanied by the same vast proliferation of side dishes.

But the king of the three regal dishes is 'palm oil chop.' In Iboland, I had for some years by my front door an oil palm bush. I kept a keen eye on the maturing clusters of palm nuts called 'bangers'. As soon as the first nut fell to the ground friends were invited to the feast. Preparations began two days before. First, the cook chopped out the banger, boiled the nuts in water then pounded them to release the fresh deep red oil. This superb cooking medium was used, by prolonged simmering, to make bits of meat palatable. In parallel with this activity the many side dishes were assembled and the silver polished. By lunchtime on Saturday cold lager from the long-suffering fridge gave way to tepid. But by this time a contemplative mood would have set in, conversation languished and serious eating began.

Chapter 6. War and peace

An Australian, once asked if he played the violin, replied:
'I don't know - pass me one and I'll see.'

Undertones of war

In the summer of 1938 my sister Denise and I used to cycle to Bickley junction to see the great steam locomotives thunder through. Then came the rumblings of a coming war and during the Munich crisis that autumn we looked out at the night sky, this time to watch searchlights illuminating aircraft in an exercise. This, Heaven forgive us, was exciting.

At grammar school we played what I now know to be Rugby Football, though we called it rugger, a game in which finer feelings are largely subdued. This was mock warfare, followed the next year by the real thing. What was happening in Europe was not real to me at the age of 12. Coming home from school one day I found my mother in tears; the Belgians had capitulated to the Germans. 'Is that all?' said I. 'Isn't that enough?' said mama. With the German army pouring towards the Channel coast we in Kent abruptly became vulnerable. Suddenly it became real. The British Expeditionary Force was evacuated from Dunkirk and train spotting at Bickley now meant watching train loads of exhausted Tommies being whisked northwards to rest. My sister and I heard that King George was due to visit the local anti-aircraft post and we cycled there to see a parchment faced, uniformed monarch with many ribbons in an open staff car. He looked utterly weary.

Our father joined the Local Defence Volunteers and was issued with an armband and a rifle - a Lee Enfield .303 that was propped fully loaded in a corner of the drawing room. He quickly became a Captain and formed a bombing squad. I was recruited as a messenger – fortunately unarmed. On summer evenings in 1940 we threw petrol bombs (known as Molotov cocktails) at a tank painted on a wall.

A friend of my father was Archie Hamilton, an eminent engineer and an inventor. He invented an explosive called ammonal and a pipe bomb – a piece of water pipe filled with ammonal. A derelict building was used for our warlike games. We stormed it and Archie threw a pipe bomb through the empty window. The damage exceeded even Archie's expectations and left me deaf for hours. We made sticky bombs consisting of a cloth bag full of explosive, dipped in gooey rat poison and fastened to a throwing handle. Dummies only were we allowed to throw and they stuck fast to the tank painted on the wall. Whether we would have stopped the German invasion I do not know but we were full of steely resolve. When our name was changed from 'LDV' to 'Home Guard' (an inspiration of Churchill) our pride was the greater.

In the Thirties Archie had built a road through Kurdistan in northern Iraq and wrote a book about it. He invented the Callender Hamilton Bridge, a forerunner of the Bailey Bridge, pre-fabricated like Meccano. His assistant was a young Kurdish engineer called Barzani who later formed and led the Kurdish separatist movement, spending much of his life as a fugitive at the head of his tribe in Kurdistan. When Archie died – of old age I am thankful to say – the sons of Barzani made the long and dangerous journey in disguise across Europe to his funeral in Kent.

Years later, as part of a team advising the Iraqi government on rural water supplies I toured Kurdistan. From the Mesopotamian plain the road wound up to Erbil, the capital, then on through wild limestone terrain to the Turkish border. At Ruwanduz one of Archie's bridges still stood. While I was admiring it a horseman rode down from high above and courteously introduced himself as Barzani. Hearing I was English he casually asked if I had known Archie Hamilton and was delighted to hear that Archie was my childhood hero. I was loaned a horse to ride and given much hospitality.

The story does not end there. Months later I was in Lagos drinking a beer with a Scottish driller called Bill Brett, who was intrigued to hear of my Kurdistan trip. He recalled drilling water boreholes at Ruwanduz, and being accosted by Barzani who asked if he knew a man called Archie Hamilton. 'Weel, I kenned one Erchie Hamilton frae the Gorbals, a desperate character he was, but I owned tae it; and afterr that he aye lent me a horse tae ride.'

Adventure in the Antipodes

The summer of 1940 brought German bombers droning over us towards London, protected by Messerschmitt fighters. We watched the dogfights far above us when our Spitfires arrived; glittering shapes suddenly wheeled overhead, a rattle of machine guns and just as suddenly were gone. If my sister and I heard of an aircraft shot down we would race our bikes to the spot and join the great circle of spectators gazing silently at the smoking wreck. At school the playing field was dug up, with air raid shelters round the edge and potatoes planted in between. 'Dig for victory' was the word.

My father was convinced that invasion was imminent and heard of a scheme to evacuate children to the Colonies. What followed is an account set out in schoolboy style that I wrote on board the *RMS Rangitata* in August 1940:

In 1940, when things in Europe looked bad, and the Home Guard was preparing for invasion, the Government evolved a scheme which altered the whole course of my life – together with the lives of several hundred other children. It was, in fact, to evacuate British children to the Dominions and to U.S.A. for the duration.

We applied at once – my elder sister Denise, aged 15, my brother Tony, 10 and I at 13 – and after much excitement and fuss, and medical examination and filling in of forms, we were informed that we were accepted.

For several weeks nothing happened. Then there appeared a letter, full of official documents. At 13, I was not greatly impressed by the content of this and subsequent messages, but I was impressed by the effect these letters had on our parents.

They knew very well that they might never see us again, that our parting was to be of many years' duration. Filled as we were with the excitement of it all, the prospect of going overseas to a strange land, and the thrill of strange languages and customs, we gave little thought to the effect on our parents of all this.

Early on in the proceedings we had to decide which country it was to be. USA? No they were sitting on the fence. Besides, father didn't like the Americans.

Canada? 'Too near U.S.' said he.

Australia? No, the Aussies were a wild crowd.

South Africa? No he didn't like them.

New Zealand? 'Ah! There is a country! . . . . in the last war' and so on for some time we heard a monologue on the achievements of that Dominion which left no doubt in our minds that it was the finest country on earth. And New Zealand it was to be. Before we knew what had happened almost, we were whisked away in an atmosphere of tremendous secrecy. Very few people knew of our going – five people outside the family, to be exact. And they were on trust not to talk. On our way to London our parents were very silent and for the first time we realised the thoughts they had been thinking for weeks. Our exuberance was checked and the rest of the journey was a very thoughtful one.

At Kings Cross came the parting – which remains as a painful memory. The other two had been hurried away under escort. Unfortunately, I remained for a few seconds and my mother broke down completely.

This breaking down had a saddening effect on me for several months. The thought of my mother's face, with grief stamped on it tragically, gave me many sleepless hours.

Liverpool was reached at last and we were driven out in buses to a school in the suburbs and there we endured life for two days. Two days, in a strange environment, with nothing to do, surrounded by woebegone kids, while in the Mersey river the convoy slowly assembled.

On both nights, we experienced several air raids. The older among us were given charge of the younger ones. My charge was a child of six and keeping him happy was my lot during all the long hours we spent in the brick air raid shelter. One lad was very, very homesick. He came from Yorkshire and we used to try to draw him out with questions about his home. Poor lad – at the last moment the authorities decided that it would be better to leave him behind. And so he went back to Yorkshire among the cows and chickens he had told us all about.

On Sunday we were marshalled to the local parish church, where a benign clergyman with rosy cheeks and peripheral white hair preached at us from a lofty pulpit. We were all miserable at the start but when the dear old boy hoped – at length – that we were thinking of our parents as, said he, we might never see them again most of us shed furtive tears. I was not weeping, I was silently furious and wanted to cry out 'do you really think we don't know'

At last, all was ready for sailing, and we went aboard the Rangitata – a wonderful old boat of 17,000 tons. It was to be our home for 37 days.

That night we were again badly raided as we lay in the Mersey and we didn't sleep much. We were immediately below the gun mounted in the very stern of the boat and we knew all about it. What we didn't know till next day was the fact that a bomb had nearly eliminated everyone in the boat. It fell with a mighty splash below the stern.

Next morning we were much more like a normal, healthy mob of children; we were all up on deck early, watching the land disappear behind us. The following days were the most exciting I have known. In those days there was only one channel open to shipping – round the north coast of Ireland. Every four hours we had lifeboat drill. This involved struggling into life belts, helping the little ones with theirs and pelting up to our boat which was promptly run out by the crew ready to be lowered. In view of all these exercises we were not at all surprised when the alarm bell went at 10pm on the third night out. Quickly we leapt out of bed, donned life belts and bolted up on deck in our groups.
There was no panic. We had little imagination and did not think of the possible consequences. Very soon we were at the boat station. It was very

dark and over the surface of the sea we could see dim shapes scurrying to and fro – this was the convoy scattering.

Far astern, with all its lights blazing, was a large liner, heeling over in the water, and looking very much the worse for a torpedo. Apparently, the torpedo had been intended for us. It missed our stern by 15 yards and hit our neighbour instead. The victim was the Volendam – a Dutch boat taking British children to Canada. Many weeks afterwards we learned that there was only one casualty. All of the children got away in boats but one of the officers got his foot stuck in the lifeboat falls and was killed.

I suppose some kid had boasted of the journey he was going to make. This, overheard in a bus, and passed on, was just what the enemy was waiting for – the enemy within.

Our captain, rather glad of this opportunity to get away, immediately "whacked up" the engines till the old Rangitata logged 18 knots – a record for her. For several days we steered a zigzag course, with an ingenious gadget behind us to break up our wake – a small cup-like affair, trailed along by a rope. With the increased speed the fun began. Figures began to line up at the rail and for some time the fishes were well and truly fed.

For several nights we slept on the boat-deck, dressed in overcoats and life jackets. And we were heartily glad when at last the danger zone was passed and we could sleep in our bunks. For several days the line of figures leaning over the rail was augmented and some half dozen of us were spared to partake of meals. And we were pleased when the rolling motion finally steadied up and we approached warmer, flatter seas. At last sea-sickness was cast off and prickly heat was taken on. The thought of prickly heat still makes me want to scratch my arms and legs, so penetrating was the irritation of the merciless rash which overtook so many of us.

The orders to the captain had been that in the event of a torpedo attack he could break convoy and make off at full speed. So Instead of plugging on to Halifax and creeping down the eastern American seaboard to the

Panama canal we were free to make a direct line and until we reached Panama two weeks later we saw only the sea and the sky and the gulls.

The *Rangitata* was a handsome vessel with two yellow funnels; high up were spacious staterooms looking onto the sunny boat deck. In the depths of the stern were steerage cabins allocated to us children. Each cabin held six bunks. Tony and I were in the rearmost starboard cabin. As the oldest I was the appointed and self-important leader. We had one porthole, which was often submerged. A little patch of the lowest after deck was our playground. We swayed and lurched and watched the sea swoop up to the sky and the sky plunge to the sea and loved it. As the ship was provisioned overseas, food was not rationed and in the vast dining room we ate hungrily and vastly.

In the Panama canal we were taken ashore by lovely American ladies with big gold teeth and were fed gallons of ice cream while the ship was warped through the locks escorted by armed US sailors. When we had left England an invasion seemed imminent and I eagerly asked an American sailor for any news. He scratched his head, and said 'Waal, there's been a big fire in Noo Jersey.' Clearly events in Europe meant nothing to him.

The Pacific was much like the Atlantic only it seemed to go on for ever and the albatrosses and flying fish appeared. At Pitcairn Island we hove to and saw our first 'natives', small swarthy descendants of Fletcher Christian. Lines secured to our railings were thrown down to the canoes far below and baskets of fruit and carvings hauled up; I suppose they were paid for I don't remember.

Then no more land till one dull morning after a month at sea we reached Wellington and a welcoming group of Very Important Citizens came aboard and made speeches while we dutifully gathered around for a press photographer. They departed, the adult passengers went ashore and suddenly our little dynamic world fell apart. Travelling hopefully was definitely much better than arriving. We drifted aimlessly and dismally about the ship, stared at the great ropes and the walls of the dock, for what seemed for ever. At last we were escorted ashore and taken to an orphanage on the outskirts of the city while transport arrangements were made. The overwhelming impression of this strange city was of steep hills, slightly rusty red tin roofs and great hedges of gorse. Ahead of us, though we did not know it, was a five year-long experience of growing up in a young, raw, pioneering country.

Growing up in New Zealand

Growing up is good in parts. The whole business is a deal easier if you have parents to talk to when times are tough. We enjoyed New Zealand but we did miss our parents. The southbound contingent of evacuees made a rough, tumbly journey from Wellington in a ferry called the *Wahine* (maori for Maiden, pronounced 'Wuheenay' but 'Worhine' to us). We rolled heavily across the Cook Straight toward Christchurch. A dozen of us then went on southwards by train to Dunedin. Half way, at Oamaru, all the passengers trooped into the station restaurant and sat down to a hot meal (the cost was two shillings - now 10 pence). At Dunedin town hall, heavily attended by press photographers, we sat down to high tea and ate as only children can. Denise then went off to one family while Tony and I drove off with our new guardians to another huge meal. Gabriel and Amy Luke, good-hearted Presbyterians, and their two daughters Eileen and Florence, lived in a wooden house in a street built entirely of kauri – a beautiful rot-proof timber nowadays growing only in a few protected forests.

Gabriel's family had come from Australia where his forebears were gold miners. Amy was descended from the Early Settlers. In the early 19th century the Established Church of Scotland was riven by dissent and some members broke away to form the Free Kirk, or 'Wee Frees'. In 1848 some of these adventurous souls took passage on the *Philip Laing* to a small settlement in Otago harbour that they called Dunedin (the gaelic form of Edinburgh). These Early Settlers bought plots of land, worked hard and prospered. Their transient neighbours were whalers on the Otakou peninsula and later an influx of roughneck gold prospectors of Central Otago.

Our guardians for five years were immensely kind to us. As they had two daughters in their early teens it must have needed courage to take in two complete strangers with unfamiliar ways. We were young enough to adapt to a single storey timber house, with meals cooked on a coal range and taken in an old-fashioned kitchen. We had been brought up to accept that a glass of wine or beer was harmless; to Wee Free Presbyterians alcohol was anathema. Our English culture accepted patent medicines as a necessity of life; the words headache and aspirin were synonymous. Our guardians accepted sickness as part of the discipline of life; if you were really ill you saw a doctor; otherwise you took a dose of Dr. J. Collis Brown's Pain Killer. I once read the small print on the label, and found that it was 90% proof spirit. A great rejoicing seized me inwardly but I had just enough good sense to keep quiet.

The young men were in north Africa fighting the Germans so schoolboys worked on the land 'up Central' during the long summer school holidays. Melt water from the glaciers of the Southern Alps of Central Otago feeds the great rivers flowing through bare, treeless hill country. Thousands upon thousands of sheep ranged fairly freely in great sheep stations. They were mustered once a year. Children and dogs raced round the gulleys driving all before them. The sheep were penned and shorn and the lambs sent off to the cities to feed the carnivores. A gang of peripatetic Australian shearers moved in and enlarged our vocabulary. The top Aussies could shear 400 sheep in a day. Child labour (willing child labour) was used to pull the sheep out of the pen and half drag, half carry them to the shearers, sit them down on their woolly bottoms and struggle back for another. The fleeces we folded and carried away to be baled. Most shearers were gentle with the sheep. A weary man, or one with a grouch or a hangover, might cut too deep with the electric shears and puncture the skin; then would roar 'Tar!' and we would run up with the pot of Stockholm tar to paste on the wound.

We slept in bunkhouses; the bunks were hard but we were too tired to notice. We ate ravenously. For breakfast, porridge, then two mutton chops each topped with a fried egg, much bread and butter and mugs of strong tea. Mid-morning brought 'Morning tea' – scones with mugs of strong tea. At midday we had a hot dinner with mugs of strong tea. Mid-afternoon brought 'Afternoon tea' - scones with mugs of strong tea; early evening meant supper, a hot meal with (yes!) mugs of strong tea. New Zealanders were the world's greatest tea drinkers.

When the shearing was finished and a great silence descended upon the valley off we went to the paddocks to thin and weed turnips. For weeks we pushed and pulled our hoes, with breaks for boiling the billy on a wood fire, stirring in tea, boiling it again, slurping it down to ease the way for descending wodges of buttered scones. This was living and we felt very manly.

Forty years later we went to New Zealand for the wedding of our niece, Denise's daughter Trish. I warned our party that New Zealand was a pioneering country and that for breakfast there was no alternative to a pair of mutton chops topped out with fried eggs and strong tea. To my chagrin we stayed in a dainty motel, ate dainty food and could opt for coffee.

Another summer I thinned turnips in vast silty fields in Glendhu Bay on the western shore of Lake Wanaka. It was hot and weary work, on hands and knees up and down row after row, but the setting was glorious. To the west is snowy Mount Aspiring, near the pass leading to Milford Sound on the west coast, and melt water from the snows flowed in a stony river past the carrot fields and discharged into the lake. The farmer's son, Lloyd, was constrained to work on the farm when his heart was set on fighting with the New Zealand Division in the Libyan desert. His dog and I followed at his heels one evening as he set forth with his gun to seek a wild Christmas goose. A great skein of Canada geese streamed overhead and with a left and right he shot the leaders. The remaining 11 birds, accustomed to following their venerable parents, became disorientated and landed in the grass all around us. There we charged them down and pinioned them. So we corralled and fattened these fine young birds. We ate the rather tough leaders at Christmas and thereafter alternated between goose and mutton until mid January.

On another farm further south, in the Hakataramea valley, I was taught to ride the hard way: if you fell off you climbed back on and tried again. Then for several days my job was to ride a pony around thousands of acres checking for sheep that had rolled over on their backs. Before they were shorn the great heavy fleeces of merino sheep made them unstable; if a sheep rolled over it needed help to regain its feet. To cover all the land took a full day; my mount was blind in one eye and would shy violently at any lateral movement, such as a darting hare, and I was pitched off into the tussock too often for peace of mind. There was a drought, the sheep were listless and thirsty and by the end of the day so was I.

On Sundays everyone went off to the tiny school for a service conducted by the travelling Methodist minister. There was one classroom with 14 desks ranging in size from moderately small to small. Being the youngest I was jammed into the smallest. We prayed for rain, following up with a supporting hymn called 'Showers of blessing' (Moody and Sankey.) The chorus goes:

> *'Showers of blessing, beautiful showers we need Mercy*
> *drops round us are falling, but for our showers we plead.'*

The Minister decreed that we had not put enough energy into the rendering so we sang it all over again. A few days later when I was on the train back to Dunedin and the new school term the rain came. It rained and it rained, the grass turned green and the run-off ruined the flax harvest further down the valley. Such is the power of prayer.

Before the war, we were nurtured in the Nominal Anglican tradition, and cycled three miles to Matins in Dartford, partly because Denise (then aged 14) had taken a shine to the curate. Poor man; he had red hair and his sermons were awful. Once he climbed very slowly into the pulpit and stood swaying for some moments before admitting with a burst of candour that he could think of nothing to say. Fortunately, Denise's affection was transient and never declared. Just as the Scots overseas become ultra Scottish, so we in Dunedin became ultra Anglican and on Sunday evenings attended evensong at All Saint's Church. When my voice broke I joined the choir and to this day I know the base line of about 400 hymns ancient and modern, with only a sketchy notion of the melody line.

Sunday mornings, however, were in the domain of our guardians' Presbyterian leaning. Sunday school at ten o'clock was devoted largely to memorising chunks of the Pauline epistles; this was a Good Thing for two reasons. The prize for reciting a chapter of St. Paul's epistle to the Romans was a great clutch of books. Though at the time I had only a foggy notion of what St Paul was banging on about, the words stuck and I can now pull them out of the deeper recesses of memory and mull them over at leisure, like a cow chewing the cud. We then trooped across to Knox Church where on the dot of 11 o'clock the Rev. David Heron (DD, MA Edinburgh) would appear through a little door into a sort of small throne room opening out on to the congregation. We all stood and sang:

> 'The Lord is in his Holy Temple
> The Lord is in his Holy Temple
> Let all the earth bow down before him.'

The very few who appreciated the irony of the timing and the words had the sense not to laugh. Worship with the Wee Frees was not a laughing matter. Only one prayer was said but it went on and on. The sermon was closely reasoned, no doubt, but soporific. The whole service lasted only an hour, no longer than the Anglican evensong but it seemed longer.

There are in New Zealand more sheep than there are people. Fortunately sheep are exceedingly stupid, otherwise they would some time ago have wiped us out, or at least would have pulled the wool over our eyes. Chickens may be marginally more stupid than sheep but only by a whisker. Cattle are by comparison almost Einsteinean in intellect. I once saw a cow standing on its own udder but after some minutes it reasoned where the problem was, moved its hoof and stopped bellowing. From an ovine standpoint, that is pretty bright. It is almost impossible to get into the mind of a sheep: there isn't room.

Slugs are different. Slugs are neither graceful nor beautiful but they have a discriminating taste. Old Charlie Bicknell lived out his days in bliss, matched with an aged wife, in a cottage near our home in Cornwall. He grew magnificent lettuce; one day he was asked how he kept the slugs away.

'Well', said he, 'you gotter get into the moind of the slug, see. Three weeks afore I sows me lettuce seed, I sows any old brassica seed, and it comes up first so slugs eat un. By the time the lettuces sprout, the slugs is fed up with brassicas so they let un alone.'

With the coming of electricity and television, Charlie's eyes grew big and square until, full of years, he passed away; and we miss his rustic wisdom.

And there were, probably still are even nowadays, more rabbits than sheep. New Zealanders are good marksmen, partly due to adolescent rabbit shooting. Not for sport but because a rabbit skin fetched two shillings - a lot of money in those days. We turned the skins inside out, that is fur side in, and stretched them on a bent wire like a giant hairpin, hung them in the sun till they were dry and sold them.

Victorian slang for a sheep was, in New Zealand, 'colonial goose'; and a rabbit was 'underground mutton.' To add to the confusion, the local name for the sooty shearwater is 'mutton bird'. These breed in burrows and are prized as a delicacy by the Maoris.

Another holiday job was working in a wool store. As a probationer, I started sorting rabbit skins. We tipped them out of bales and the sorter juggled them according to quality and size. Then we baled them up again. This was not intellectually demanding work; equally, not for the squeamish. There were thousands upon thousands of maggots that wriggled towards the light. The big windows in the roof pointed north, towards the sun, so the maggots wriggled northwards, off the table to the floor, and wriggled their way as far as the north wall of the sorting shed where they banked up and were shovelled into sacks.

Promotion came rapidly - to the wool sorting shed. There are 117 grades of wool and a good sorter can grade a fleece in a few seconds. We carried fleeces from the sorting table to the bins for hour after hour, stopping only for morning and afternoon tea.

The next rung on the ladder was the baling gang; out came the bales from the bins, thrown up to the gaffer who stood within a huge sacking bag in the baler and tucked the fleeces round him as he caught them. Then we compressed the bales down with levers and ratchets, and sewed them up. Ultimately, the sturdiest survivors were promoted to the elite stacking gang, a team of four with hooks who carried the bales weighing about 200 kilos, one to each corner, to a depot for export. I grew muscles till my shoulders and arms split my shirt yet my hands were soft with the lanolin from the fleeces.

The great lakes of Central Otago were ready-made adventure playgrounds. Uncle Gabe and his old friend Stevo took me on a fishing trip to Lake Hawea, staying in a batch - a small cabin. He caught great rainbow trout weighing three, sometimes four, kilos, while I caught the huge silver-belly lake eels, a metre long and as thick as a man's leg. The technique was to tie the head of a rabbit to a cord and throw it in into the water, then when an eel sank its teeth into it pull it smartly out. We smoked the trout and slices of eel in a canvas smoker, fed by smouldering manuka brush and sawdust. Long after the eel is dead the flesh twitches, even after hours in the smoker.

In the evenings Stevo taught me to play cribbage. During one game, the cabin started to tremble, then shake. We rushed outside in time to see the manuka scrub whipping wildly as the shock wave of a small earthquake passed. A line of steep little waves marked its progress across the lake.
The Water of Leith flows through the University grounds in Dunedin and migratory salmon on their way up river to spawn gathered in a pool, below a metal grill designed to halt them. Periodically the fisheries people stripped the fish of roe and milt, for hatching baby fish in stocking ponds. One frosty November morning on my way to church I saw a big fish wedged in the grill and liberated it, held it under my raincoat (to keep it warm maybe) and during the service lodged it on a shelf under a pew. The central heating pipe ran under the ledge and soon a distracting aroma of cooking salmon filled the nostrils and hearts of the faithful.

The Otago Boys' High School in 1940, though I did not know it then, had just become non-fee paying. The school uniform was very uniform indeed – dark grey – the cloth quality varied with the means of the parents. Some jackets were immaculately tailored while others were very shaggy. In my perception the only suit I possessed, of pale grey flannels, made me conspicuous. The image of the English was of dandies wearing monocles and my new schoolmates would screw a penny into one eye and swagger past me; this fell rather flat for I don't suppose I had ever seen a monocle before. But I had to live with my standard English accent and its clipped short vowels. Dictation was full of pitfalls: by writing what I heard I scored low! Shakespeare's "This seat of Mars" became "This seat of Myers." Luckily the English master was tolerant and my accent gradually broadened to approximate with the local diction, largely as an unconscious form of camouflage.

As the war years slowly passed we adopted happily and with enthusiasm the thought processes and habits of New Zealanders and this was probably good for us. Our previous upbringing between the wars had been moulded to a long established way of life in the highly organised society of our crowded islands. In Britain there were then 50 million people. New Zealand was mostly empty spaces and there were a million and a half souls in much the same area. The concepts of improvisation and inventiveness entered our way of thinking. An Australian, once asked if he played the violin, replied: 'I don't know - pass me one and I'll see.' The average New Zealander had no time for the Aussies (though only 1,300 miles away they were held to be a wild bunch) but they had, and still have, a similar elastic spirit. The down-side of our new environment was that the social graces were not given much priority.

Twilight of the war

We followed events in Europe and the Far East through heavily censored newspaper articles and faint crackly broadcasts relayed from Wellington. Weekly letters home took an hour or more each to write; frankly we hadn't much to say. The image of our parents grew faint. Then our parents travelled to London to record a message to us; forewarned, we clustered round Uncle Gabe's wireless set, waited and waited while other parents spoke and at last heard our parents' voices after a three-year gap. A few days later we walked to the Chief Post Office to hear the recording over again. The voices, faint but clear, were for me reassuringly unchanged and the experience was comforting; how the others felt I do not know but they were silent and subdued. Our weekly letters were no more inspired, but we had a fresher image of whom we were writing to.

As a student at Otago University from 1944 on, I joined a bunch of enthusiastic amateurs playing at soldiers, known as the New Zealand Independent Mounted Rifles, though I doubt whether our existence was recorded. With .303 rifles and borrowed mounts, at weekends we scoured the Otago Peninsula diligently for Japanese invaders. Many rabbits were obliterated – a .303 bullet causes some overkill. After a matter of weeks we disbanded. In later years no one ever asked 'What did you do in the war daddy?' but the answer was ready: 'Weeded turnips, thinned carrots, stacked wool bales, shot rabbits, made fruit cases, served in an antique shop'. No wonder the enemy shook in their shoes.

Antique shop, I hear you ask. With shop assistants away fighting, bright, numerate scholars were called for; three of us were directed to what to us was a junk shop. As a sideline, the proprietor bought empty fruit cases from Chinese greengrocers. These we collected and repaired in a dingy cavern at the back of the shop, carted them to a railway siding and loaded them in trucks destined for the orchards of Central Otago. Vocalists all, we sang lusty choruses while hanging on the back of hired lorries rumbling around the back streets of Dunedin. Only one of us had a true musical vocation; he became a professional singer of international repute and it is good to think that in some small way we set him on his path to greatness.

Rarely, a bell signalled the entry of a customer, possibly attracted by our window display. We had unearthed and set out a collection of what I later came to know as silver tea strainers; not knowing their purpose, we enterprisingly labelled them 'soup showers'. Mystifyingly, they sold well.

We had been taught not to interrupt a promising customer but one such came in and asked for an item just as a noisy tram passed outside. As the racket subsided she continued thus:

'. . of spun glass (I nodded sagely) tapering at each end (another nod) twisted like coloured barley sugar (nod) about 18 inches long ('of course'I murmured). Have you one in stock?'

'We've just sold the last one.' In hindsight, this was unwise but seemed a good idea at the time. And to this day no one knows what this mysterious object was.

An elderly widow wished to sell her late husband's police whistle and I gave her two shillings for it. The proprietor disapproved so I bought it from him and have it still.

In 1944 Otago University, which had welcomed Denise (who proposed to read domestic science), swept me in. It had a motto that puzzled me then and still does. *"Sapere aude"* bad us to dare to be wise - a strange association of wisdom with daring. I had a vague vision of becoming a physicist or mathematician, or possibly an organic chemist but the following year came VE day, the end of the war in Europe, and we were summoned home. It should have been a difficult parting but the anticipated excitement of further travel dulled the separation from so many friends. My father had suggested that I did not really want to be a physicist and what about geology? (He was right.) If I hurried home, there was a place at the Royal College of Science. So in a little, miserable huddle we all stood on the dock at Port Chalmers, avoiding each others' eyes and muttering platitudes. Above us towered the *Port Jackson*, a passenger-cargo boat, calling at Dunedin's port on the way from Australia. Carrying a well-travelled suitcase with a tennis racket strapped to it I tottered up the gangplank. There was less rush for Denise (who definitely would have preferred to stay behind) and Tony; they followed in a big liner. Eleven of the 12 passengers were in the VIP bracket: an admiral, a commodore, the family of a senior army officer, a Norwegian ship-owner and his wife, a few high-powered businessmen. They were all immensely kind and made easy for me the transition from a simple calvinistic household to a relatively sophisticated environment.

Japan had not yet surrendered but our north-eastward journey across the Pacific was carefree and vastly different from the journey southwards in 1940. At the equator the 'crossing the line' ceremony was duly held, with King Neptune being piped aboard and passengers brought up for judgment on all manner of frivolous charges. King Neptune disappeared, surreptitiously changed back into his uniform as Captain, and ordered the First Mate to run out a lifeboat and test the survival kit. Passengers who had survived being ducked in the canvas swimming pool by King Neptune were invited to join in. The kit included a patent device for distilling sea water, which included some damp 'firelighters' but no other fuel, and no matches. The Chief Engineer eventually located some splinters of wood in the bowels of the ship and three hours later the first drips of drinkable water emerged. How fortunate, murmured the Mate, that the Japanese navy stayed away.

At Panama, a committee formed to show me the sights ashore. The ship's doctor was a Harley Street specialist on prolonged recuperation from a close encounter with a flying bomb and was a trifle eccentric. It was he who led our group round the night clubs of Colon. We drank beer amid hundreds of boisterous American sailors and were tremendously entertained by the glittering floor shows, a smooth band playing South American rhythms. To an 18-year-old coming from five years in a calvinistic household, this was immensely, joyfully exciting.

At Liverpool the river Mersey was littered with semi-submerged wrecks and delay was expected before a pilot could arrive to navigate us to the docks. The Admiral, however, was expected and his barge arrived alongside. All the passengers were invited to go with him, our baggage was speedily loaded and off we sped, bypassing customs and immigration. Soon we were in a train rolling to London through the soft summer night under the harvest moon.

London after the war

Enduring the post-war years around London was hard going. The prevailing atmosphere was gloomy and stressful. A neighbour stopped me in the street to say in sepulchral tones 'Welcome back; we've had a lot of flying bombs round here.' The background austerity and war neurosis has coloured my memories of this period and even 60 years on it is not easy to present a balanced sketch. I was lucky that a place was available to study geology at the Royal College of Science. For Denise, who most keenly missed the company of her close friends, there was no place at university and she was very unhappy. On top of this she contracted polio. On recovering, she saved her wages and returned to New Zealand to study Karitane nursing, a form of infant care. Tony, at the age of 15, was out of phase with the education system. He secured an interview at the Dartford Grammar School. The headmaster offered him a cigar, which he was too polite to refuse - surely a most unfair test of character. Dartford Grammar had a few distinguished alumni, nearly all were Victorian warriors long dead. The one exception was Mick Jagger. My limited pre-war experience of the regime made me in later years profoundly thankful that this school and I had avoided a closer acquaintance. After three years at a technical college Tony carried out his compulsory two-year National Service, became a trainee electrical engineer and rose by sheer ability to run the South African branch of a very large engineering company.

Meanwhile we made the most of the social scene in London, albeit within slender budgets. One November evening, never to be forgotten, Tony and I went off to the Royal Commonwealth Society's fancy dress event. Tony dressed as a Maori warrior, with grass skirt and swirling Polynesian designs and little else. I went more decorously dressed as the 'Order of the Bath', plastered in bath towels that made dancing a sweat-drenched experience. When the time came to catch the last train home Tony announced that he was escorting a new-found girlfriend to her home in Kilburn. Festooned with sweaty bath towels, and further burdened by Tony's overcoat (which he disdained to wear) I slunk off to Charing Cross to wait for him. He did not arrive and, not relishing the prospect of spending the night in a rapidly chilling waiting room, I took the last train complete with Tony's overcoat.

In Kilburn, Tony bade a cuddly farewell to his lady and set off towards the underground station. The euphoria evaporated and the horrible truth dawned that there were no pockets in the grass skirt and his money was in his abandoned overcoat. He spent a miserable shivering night roaming up and down Kilburn High Street. In desperation he tried to beg a free cup of coffee from a stall. The owner, confronted by an authentic looking tattooed Maori face grimacing over the counter, took fright and bolted. In the grey dawn Tony hobbled across London to our father's office on the Embankment and on a chilly doorstep awaited his arrival and an infusion of funds. Fortunately papa saw the joke. Though the joke wore off, the tattoos lingered for months.

To one accustomed to a true university environment in Otago, the Royal College of Science seemed a technical sweatshop. The department of geology lived up to its pseudonym of Little Siberia. Building materials were in short supply and if a window was broken it was boarded up. We also endured the inability of most lecturers to communicate audibly, if at all. As compensation, the professor, the great H H Read, had a first class brain and a gift of exposition. In our first year he reached out to us and imparted an enduring enthusiasm for the study of the earth. He pioneered the study of transformation of rocks in the solid state and his lectures on granitisation were sheer joy. Dr. Gilbert Wilson, a dapper eccentric artist of South Kensington, lectured us on landscape development. He tried, with limited success, to relate mature profiles in the chalk to mathematical formulae. By contrast, structural geology was the preserve of RRM Shackleton, nephew of the polar explorer: a gruff, inaudible giant with no sartorial taste but great charm. 'Shack' had immense physical stamina and could walk the fittest of us off our feet. In east Africa, alone in the bush, he was once bitten by a puff adder; with a pocket knife he slashed open the wound and walked on, allowing a steady trickle of blood to carry away the venom.

The College was indeed a sweatshop but an efficient one. We became proficient surveyors; indeed Kensington Gardens must surely be the most frequently and intensively mapped bit of London. We lugged around noble brass instruments of great antiquity and weight but of high accuracy; terms like sidereal and azimuth held no terrors for us. We studied hundreds of hand specimens of fossils, rocks and minerals. The mineral collection, in chest upon chest of trays, was displayed book fashion from the simple (top left) to the complex (bottom right). Cubic crystals of common salt, like huge sugar lumps (top left - halite to us) suffered severe degradation, as it was a time honoured custom to pop them into one's cheek and suck them while memorising the difficult ones (plagioclase, triclinic as no doubt you may recall). Every few months the rounded relics of halite were replaced. We dissected dogfish pickled in formalin one day, carved up pickled strawberries the next (they made wonderful missiles). We learned the names of hundreds of microscopic fossils from the huge cartwheels of ammonites to the microscopic foramenifera.

When Irish eyes are flashing

Shackleton took us on field trip to Connemara. This changed my life for ever – brought on not by a sudden passion for rocks but by human attraction. It fell about upon this wise. On Kylemore lough is a pseudo castle built in Victorian times by the Duke of Manchester, a cotton manufacturer, and converted into a school by Belgian nuns. As a sideline the nuns ran a posh guest house. In the vast dining hall our heavily booted geological party sat at a long table along the starboard side. To port, separated from us by sundry honeymoon couples, at a long table sat a party of bonny botany students from Galway University. Their keeper was the elegant Maureen De Valera, daughter of the then Teoiseach (prime minister) of Eire. The two parties, between the soup and the stewed mutton, eyed each other nervously. Maureen decided to establish an entente cordial. Summoning a timorous little Belgian nun she commanded that we should all meet up for a wholesome social evening and despatched her to acquaint Shack with the ultimatum.

In the stress of the moment the nun's English faltered and she spoke thus: 'Ze girls would like ze boys to play wiz zem in ze school hall after supper.' So we clumped across to the school wing, left our boots outside the door and were inculcated into the mysteries of Irish dancing and the singing of heroic ballads. In turn we taught the girls some of the more wholesome songs from the English countryside and much fun was had by all. The dominant botanist, Kathleen Maguire, all dark hair and flashing eyes, invoked my admiration; so much so that in 1952 we wed and were together until 53 years on Kath, God rest her, went ahead of me into heaven.

As a field project I was given an area to map near Ballyshannon in the south of Donegal. The border between Eire and the Six Counties almost coincided with a major unconformity, limestones to the south and metamorphic rocks, older by some 200 million years, to the north. The work entailed traversing to and fro across the border almost daily, through very prickly hedges. One day, being tired, I crossed by the main road and had my rucksack searched by HM customs. I was asked: was I importing these rock specimens? Some of them, I replied. The awful truth came out that I had apparently been crossing the border illegally and I was severely admonished.

In Ballyshannon I lodged at Curran's Select Bar, full board and lodging £4 a week. Frank Curran and his family were friendly and hospitable but common topics of interest were few and conversation languished. The local doctor also felt the lack of convivial company and he invited me to supper - a magnificent salmon of unknown origin - and lamented that he had a long time to go before retirement.

Evenings were monotonously dull until one day a large, battered American style saloon car erupted. The two occupants, who proposed to stay the night, were aggressively boisterous and Frank Curran muttered furtively to me that they were IRA, which at that time was a dormant organisation.

The evening was interminably long but very exciting. We were assembled in the parlour and taught revolutionary songs, which were rendered so often that I can repeat them from memory so many years on. The daughters found it necessary to catch up on their homework elsewhere but poor Frank had a miserable time, very nervous and anxious that I should not be put into the firing line of political conversation.

At last the two broths of boys, soggy with Guinness, reeled off to slumber and left early next day. The relief was tangible. The local Guarda, who had kept well out of the way, called to make sure that all was well and life returned to normal.

Shack paid a fleeting visit before taking off to Rosguill Island in north Antrim, where fellow students were working, and soon after the time came for me to leave and make my way through Donegal to Rosguill Island. I hitchhiked part of the way, then took off across the Bluestack Mountains on foot. Here is a note I made at the time:

A Night in the Blue Stacks

With a last longing look at the retreating tail of the lorry I had hitched, I turned my face towards the north west and, settling my pack on my shoulders, set off up the foothills. By nightfall I hoped to be at the top of the main range of the Croaghgorms (The Blue Stack Mountains) – a rugged, bleak mass of granite north of Donegal town. It was late afternoon, and travelling was pleasant. A following wind and plenty of interesting geology among the foothills to give me an excuse to stop and mop the brow, ostensibly of course to take notes and tap rocks. My map was useless, so I resorted to my compass, going on a NW bearing as much as possible and tramping up riverbanks whenever they went in the right direction.

Soon I was well above the trees and bushes, in land of heather and bog, stretching for miles round the hills into the darkening distance; the gradient grew steadily steeper until, tacking to and fro on the steeper parts I had cause to reflect on that peculiar agency which causes a pack weighing 45 pounds at the bottom of a mountain to weigh 60 pounds at the approaches to the summit.

Gradually, the dusk came on and ragged cloud brushed the hillside as the air chilled. Hastily lighting a fire of heather roots I had a billy boiling while I could yet see, and ere it was quite dark I was snuggled in a sleeping bag amongst the heather in the lea of a huge boulder.

I watched the Loughs gradually lose their gleam. I saw the twinkling lights appear in the few scattered cottages in the valley. And then tired eyelids fell upon tired eye, and I knew nothing till one o'clock when I was awakened by a smart hail shower. Drawing my cape over my head I dozed off again.

At 2.30am I woke again.
At 3.40am I woke again.
At 5.00am I woke again and each time it was raining.

When at 7.00am I recovered consciousness I was delighted to feel warm rays of sun beating upon me. And I scrambled out into the air to witness that beautiful rosy flush of dawn lighting up the tops, and transforming wisps of cloud which still clung to the gullies in patches.

I lost no time in taking photos and getting underway once more.

It was as well that I did so, as very soon the mist reappeared, condensing from nowhere, and reducing visibility to a few yards. So long as I kept to the ridges I was safe, as I could take bearings from rock to rock almost, but the time came when I had to descend into a valley. It is a terrifying experience to be scrambling down a rocky slope into a pool of mist, when precipices probably lay ahead, and I was very glad to reach the valley bottom.

At this stage this snapshot breaks off; perhaps the mist made a mush of the note pad.

Chapter 7. Goin' Fishing

'Sir, I have put a lady in your bed.'

Methods employed to catch fish are limited only by the ingenuity of the angler. During the Munich Crisis of 1938, my brother and I were packed off to Bedford, which in the event of war was deemed to be safer than Kent. A stoic aunt and uncle met us, with forced jollity, and looked after us for many long idle days. The novelty of watching barrage balloons bobbing up and down at Cardington airfield soon paled, as did watching Wellington bombers on training circuits over our heads. So, with most of our limited resources we invested in a fishing line complete with hooks. Our remaining cash went on six pennyworth of maggots, and we set off for the Greater Ouse River. In the clear water were shoals of fish with unattractive names like rudd and tench. These restless creatures cruised languidly in the clear water, as visible to us as were our wriggling maggots on their appointed hooks. With great excitement we awaited results and were deeply disappointed when the bait was regularly tugged off the hook and taken away to a place of safety.

Clearly we needed more robust bait, and in the orderly flower beds around the house we dug for worms; but these astute creatures had evolved an exit strategy even before our long suffering aunt showed signs of tension. So we fashioned from plasticine some bright orange worms, long and voluptuously curved, that glowed enticingly in the sparkling water. With the patience of seasoned anglers we watched for hours those same fish as they swam by with contemptuously curled lip.

Sad, empty handed and late we returned to base where we endured the added sorrow of being informed, tersely, by a hollow eyed aunt that the police had been hunting for us for hours. This was the climax of a week which neither we nor our hosts enjoyed and it was a relief to all parties when Neville Chamberlain returned from Munich to announce 'Peace in our time' ('our time' being as it turned out precisely one year), and we could go home.

In New Zealand I raised my game. The waters around Stuart Island abounded in blue cod, red cod, trumpeter and butterfish and these uneducated fish, a rich prize for a youngster, succumbed to my clumsy attempts.

I never achieved any great degree of co-ordination of hand and eye. A friendly Dubliner took me fishing on a 'soft' windy day in Connemara. Fishing for small very wild brown trout in a tarn half way up a mountain involved casting a fly from the shore against the wind with the idea of getting it to land gently among a bank of feeding fish. At the close of play the score was:

Dubliner: 20

Me: 1

So, to more exciting fishing in Nigeria. At the end of a day making a geological traverse along a barren quartzite ridge I turned back towards camp, hoping to shoot an antelope to feed my hungry workers. Instead I stumbled upon a deep narrow pool fed from a fissure in the quartzite. In the clear water about a dozen fair sized fish cruised actively, simply asking to be caught. Two questions floated to my consciousness, one theoretical: where on earth did those fish or their spawn come from, so far from a river? The other practical: without the help of a fishing line, or a tame fish eagle, how to get hold of this valuable source of protein?

It is considered most unsporting to shoot a fish and my heavy 9.3mm bullets would not leave anything recognisable to collect. But I reasoned that the shock wave would stun them all for long enough for retrieval. The best laid schemes of mice and men . . . . .

The fish swam on laughing but I had an immediate lesson in hydro-dynamics. The track of the bullet left a vacuum that was instantly filled by a high pressure, backtracking jet of water. Some vanished up the barrel of the rifle but most of it continued, to land in my eye.

Later a little older, not much wiser, but better equipped with a casting rod, I worked in the south east of Nigeria where in the uplands were fast flowing sandy-bedded streams abounding in fish. Alestes was the firm favourite; to them a grasshopper on a hook was irresistible as *they* were to us, fried with chips. They have a delicate flavour and once one became accustomed to the unpredictable location of small bones these half-pounders were greatly preferable to tough cow meat. So I contrived to visit suitable rivers in the course of my work.

Near my favourite river was a township on a sandy plateau, Igbo Ukwu. Here lay the site of the capital of the 9th century kingdom of Iboland. I had been enjoined to liaise with Thurstan Shaw, an eminent archaeologist excavating the ancient tomb of an early king. Screened by high iroko forest, this small township had once enjoyed a culture comparable with two other centres of civilisation, Benin and Ife. Like most of earth's great kingdoms this one, the 'Igbo of igbo', had passed away almost without trace.

Thurston Shaw had dug a great pit and there he was, two or three metres below ground, in deep concentration whittling away with a brush. This was the first of several burial sites. He subsequently recovered bronzes of great elegance cast using the lost wax process with partly detached ornamental panels. Dating placed them in the 9th century. Younger Egyptian glass beads indicated that the dynasty had persisted for a further 700 years.

I called down to him and out of the depths he cried unto me to the effect that he was busy and what did I want. I sweetened the pill of my incursion on his thoughts by telling him that under a tree by his jacket I was leaving two fish for his bodily sustenance - and left him to his labours. Later that day I trekked through the village on the way to the road; still in the depths, Thurston Shaw gave me a response greeting. Somewhat nettled I rejoined that I wanted for nought and did he enjoy the fish. His true spirituality and dedication were revealed when he gave me to understand that there were things more important to him than food.

A cousin to alestes is the tiger fish. This fierce creature also abounds in bones and tastes like blotting paper but, like salmon (a distant cousin), is a fine fighting creature. It sports rows of outward jutting fangs like those of a barracuda. The national record weight for one of these splendid fish is 12.4 kilos, held by a District Officer called Laurence. Fifty years later, leaning on the railing of a bridge by a Somerset reservoir, I chanced to meet for the first time this intrepid fisherman. The years had used him well, and in his eyes still danced the embers of piscatorial passion.

To catch these fish with a rod and line, a wire trace with a swivel was essential, trailing a 'spoon' or a 'devon'. These are glittery devices that wobble on the end of the wire trace like a wounded fish. Among the fast flowing lowland tributaries of the lower Niger these tiger fish were abundant partly, I suspect, because locally contrived vegetable poisons cannot maintain sufficient volume to be effective and partly because those fierce teeth would do great damage to cast nets.

Working by Oguta Lake down by the lower Niger river, I stayed once in a comfortable stilted old timber rest house. Taking a day off, I engaged a local boatman to paddle me along the shallows and had some success in landing a couple of tiger fish, though they fell far short of record weight. In later years the cruelty of the sport put me off game fishing but at the time there was always a great thrill when, by routine, the silvery fish leapt high in the air and twisted in an attempt to dislodge the hook. Alas, my last surviving lure was lost in some water weed but I reasoned that anything lashed to a hook that wobbled would serve,. By hacking a white tab from my shorts, complete with glittering buckle, I concocted a lure that proved effective enough to secure a third fish.

On the far side of Oguta Lake two idealistic Irish volunteers taught in a school. A tatty note arrived at the rest house one day inviting me to dine that evening, and the same boatman was engaged to paddle me across and enjoined to return later to take me back.

The evening passed without incident; the cuisine was Irish modified by local constraints and I was escorted, lamp lit, to the landing place. Thunder rolled and the darkness was deafening. Then down came the warm torrential rain. So black the night that I could not see the boatman, only the phosphorescent spray from his paddle; yet unerringly he bore us, or I assumed he bore us, across towards the rest house. After a while his stroke faltered and he finally shipped his paddle and crawled across towards me. It seemed inevitable that he was lost and I did not relish the thought of drifting, soaking wet, round the lake through the long night.

Cupping his hands, he bellowed conspiratorially into my ear: 'Sir, I have put a lady in your bed.' Followed by a gleeful chuckle.

I seldom lose my cool, but the puzzled boatman was left in no doubt that the lady should leave the premises forthwith. He was puzzled, I later discovered, because a touring education officer of amorous bent used regularly to stay in Oguta rest house and this was the service to which he was accustomed. Yuck!

Mudfish, also known as catfish, look with their huge shield-like heads and whiskers like prehistoric relics and are great survivors. In the dry season, they hibernate, buried in damp clay. After the first rains when they come to life and wriggle out they are vulnerable until they slither into the river channel.

Rather muddy in flavour, with roasted yams they are nevertheless acceptable as protein in hard times, but only accidentally did I ever hook one and with a sigh prepared to reel it in. This was more easily said than done, as I realised when a head the size of a dinner plate appeared above water. No landing net would have served, and none would have held this enormous fish. Before the line inevitably snapped I was able to take a photo of the glistening head, otherwise no one would have believed me.

Niger perch, known in East Africa as Nile Perch, are without doubt the tastiest and largest freshwater fish in Africa. Known as 'giwan ruwa' (elephant of the water) they can weigh over 100 kilos. Great, slow moving deep water feeders, catching them involves towing a hook attached to a bit of gaily painted broom handle, all on the end of a strong line. Much patience is needed, which ruled me out, but the occasional catch is worth the many fruitless hours paddling to and fro. Hauling them in is hard work for the angler but no fun at all for the fish. Its weight makes it difficult to bring to the surface, and the standard technique is to wrap a twist of tobacco round a lead ring that slides down the line and encounters the poor creatures nose. Being non-tobacco chewers, they become irritated and in rage come to the surface.

At the other end of the size range is the small tilapia, known throughout southern Africa as bream. Allegedly they spend much of their time sucking minute insects off leaves and for a true sportsman the prescribed way to catch them is to impale a cassava leaf on a small hook, and let it drift around in the shallows. Up to my calves in water on the fringe of a young lake I once spent boring hours in this far from exciting exercise. Finally I glanced downwards and espied, perched on the toes of my wellington boots, a fine specimen peacefully relaxing. I gave up.

Catamaran Adventures

In the big rivers the local fishermen use light canoes made from umbrella wood, which is as light and as soft as balsa. Carved from single tree trunks, these are just over three and a half metres long and 30 centimetres wide, elegantly hollowed to a thickness of about two centimetres, and are called bicycle canoes. There is room only for a man who casts the net and a boy. The man directs events standing up, requiring a fine sense of balance. The small boy crouches in the stern, to keep the centre of gravity low, and paddles. The man points to a shoal of fish, the youngster paddles like fury towards it, the man twirls a weighted net round his head and, graceful as a ballerina, casts it ahead. It billows out like an umbrella, and when the weights hit the water the disturbed fish dart inwards, to be imprisoned by the closing net.

Visited by a vision of using these craft to fish in a less exacting sedentary posture, I bought two of these craft. Made by eye in the Niger delta, they were of identical width and within one centimetre of the same length. Treating them as floats I spent many hours fashioning a mini catamaran around them. Secured cunningly to a robust, rigid frame, I topped the structure with minimal cross-ways decking. There was enough room for one, perched nautically and only fairly uncomfortably aft of the beam. It looked like a primitive pedallo without the pedals. The potential problem was propulsion; paddling was not an option as the beam was 1.2 metres.

Returning from leave a few months later I brought in a very small outboard motor called (Heaven knows why) 'the Skylark'. A Customs officer in the Lagos arrival hall, unaccustomed to seeing such a device, and in an officer's baggage to boot, sought enlightenment. To fasten to a sort of canoe to push it along said I. He latched on to the word with relief and chalked the packet saying, grandly, 'No duty on canoe!'

At the end of working days there followed many practice runs in placid waters learning, by trial and a deal of error, how to steer the craft with the outboard using one hand while towing a fishing line with the other. In the process I acquired a new respect for the versatility of one-man band musicians.

Trained at last up to the standard of expertise required, or so I thought, I journeyed to the Niger river. The craft sat uneasily, upside down, on the roof rack of my state of the art Standard Vanguard saloon car.

Anticipating the strength of the main current, I resolved to creep along the river's edge, and was unprepared for the multitude of capricious whirling eddies in the shallows. It was easy to achieve a working relationship with more effective fishing folk, who rightly regarded me as being no threat to their operations. I even managed to land a few unwary fish but soon settled for more peaceful hours at the head of a small body of water miles from anywhere.

This pond, upstream from Nike lake near Enugu, was inaccessible except by water. Humans were blissfully absent. With the motor cut, it was possible to drift into a new time frame. The variety of wild life was spectacular. It was a special joy to see the blue lightning flash of a malachite kingfisher diving from a perch to bring back a flapping fingerling fish.

Chapter 8. Goodbye To All That

"To kill an elephant is easy; to turn it over is very difficult."

The sheltered life in the Colonial Service was not conducive to planning but with the advent of Nigerian Independence came an opportunity to leave the Colonial Service for pastures new.

The assumption was that as colonial servants we would climb slowly up a pre-ordained path until retirement at the age of 45. We would assist in the 'Nigerianisation' process, of training local Nigerian staff to do the work that British staff had carried out and in due course Nigeria would attain independence and white men would continue to work alongside Nigerians. Indeed, back in 1921 the great administrator Lord Lugard saw independence for Nigeria as the ultimate goal. We did not appreciate the strength of resentment and influence of the United States. In the aid package offered to European countries after the war was a condition that independence throughout all African colonies must be brought forward dramatically. The result was predictably dismal, with half-trained staff promoted to positions for which they were not ready.

A spin-off was that the Colonial Office could not guarantee that our pensionable contracts could be honoured. They offered lump sum compensation (affectionately called 'lumpers') to staff wanting to leave. Neither the local education system nor the medical service were adequate to the needs of children, Nigeria being still one of the least healthy countries in Africa. We decided to move on. I was, at the age of 34, the youngest pensioner in the Colonial Service so my lumpers was a modest £2,000 but this enabled us to buy a home in Cornwall. The spring of 1961 found us with two small daughters in Little Margate Cottage under the lee of Bodmin Moor. Our assets were the cottage, furniture brought back with us, abundant hardwood planks that encased the furniture, some modest savings, a pension of £100 a year and boundless optimism.

In the Colonial Service our lives were largely sheltered from roguery, deceit and harsh competition. I had resolved not to become part of a big organisation but soon found I was not ready to cope with living outside a cocoon. I lived a joyous summer with the family naively expecting that something would show up. Nothing happened so I rattled the bars of my soul and went on to the attack. My younger sister, Janet, worked for an airline run by Freddie Laker and one of the perks was cheap travel for her immediate kin. So I hitched a cheapo on an Airworks Vickers Viscount that pottered down to a stopover in Las Palmas, drifted on the next day to Freetown in Sierra Leone and then to Accra in Ghana. Refreshed by a night staying with friends I hopped on a short haul local airline across to Lagos. From there on I was among friends. In Kaduna a former colleague generously guided me in a search for clients.

The going was tough at first but I discovered I was known as an 'Expert' on Nigerian water. In the early Sixties the component regions of Nigeria decided, one by one, to review their potential water resources. I was asked by Tahal, an Israeli consultancy, to make a synthesis of the groundwater resources of the Eastern Region, then the Mid West, then the Benue-Plateau. Other work snowballed in and for much of the Sixties I was shuttling to and from West Africa, with nail-biting gaps between periods of plenty.

A gap opened up in Nigerian work due to the Biafra war. What came to the rescue, was a niche market in proving gravel deposits in the fens when a shortage of this raw material loomed. We possessed ourselves of a Mini and a Bentley, which cost £600 each. Petrol was cheap and Bentleys held their value. Deciding which vehicle to use for field work needed keen judgement as it depended on the type of client. A farmer would take one look at the Bentley and decide he could not afford me; a glossy young executive reckoned that to own a Bentley we must be very competent.

Being overseas for weeks at a time was not good for domestic harmony. Cecily and Jennie found it difficult to adjust to sporadic absences. We decided to send them to boarding school, where life was regulated, on the understanding that I would be home for their holidays and for visiting weekends. In later years they told me, independently, that this was a mistake. Indeed, the partings were hard for them and hard for us too. It was heartbreaking to take them tearfully back to school in the leaky Bentley. I invented mythical characters, Dutch Doll and Fairy, around which to weave stories and this helped. By popular demand, I'd also related anecdotes concerning odd adventures I had with Bob Aitken, a New Zealand scouting friend. These 'Bobbie Aitken' stories acquired formalised and almost mythical status and any deviations from the standard text were pounced on.

Bringing them home for holidays was joyful and needed no diversions. Long after, we visited Bob Aitken in Auckland where he had by then acquired a wife and sons. The sons were duly introduced and they immediately asked if the 'Robin Hazell' stories were true.

So well fed were the girls at Mayfield school that the mandatory homecoming feast was baked beans with a poached egg on top.

Chad Basin 1964-5

The Chad Basin is huge, about 1,000 miles across. Rivers rising in Nigeria, Chad Republic and Cameroun flow into a shallow lake where these states meet. When the climate was wetter, at the time of Noah, the lake was known as 'Mega-Chad' and rivers in a fourth territory, Niger, contributed. As recently as 2,000 years ago the Romans grew wheat around the lake; some wheat fields survived into the 20th century.

In the Sixties I was involved in a small way in an investigation of Chad basin water resources, first in north east Nigeria where artesian water was already being over-exploited, and later when a survey of the entire basin was carried out. Fort Lamy, now called Ndjamena, near the mouth of the Logon Chari river, the capital of Chad Republic, is the gateway to the vast empty spaces beyond and was the headquarters for this project. It was there I learned some of the great truths of Africa. Small truths in retrospect but they loomed large then. Melons grown near a septic tank derive nourishment and bacteria leading to unpleasant consequences. At dawn, just when the air has cooled to allow a snatch of sleep, peacocks scream in chorus. And if one treads on an acacia twig, inevitably a three inch-long thorn penetrates sandal, sock and foot.

I operated a large and expensive machine designed to record what goes on down a borehole. It was manufactured in the wilds of Oklahoma and had an uneven journey to Chad, surviving a sojourn of three months on a waterfront in the United States during a stevedores' strike. This brought about my introduction to another great truth known as Sod's Law: if something can go wrong, it will go wrong. So when the machine on its maiden voyage into the wastelands refused to work, I radioed base camp where contact was made with Enid, Oklahoma and the symptoms made known. The reply filled our hearts with joy. Take the machine to your nearest radio workshop and instruct them to replace a spigilic grofflehook. Simple!

The Biafra war

Much has been written about the civil war of 1967-70 that ravaged south eastern Nigeria. For the Ibos, it was two and a half years of misery and starvation. It is easy to make judgments on the protagonists, particularly the Ibos. The trigger was pulled in 1966 when junior Ibo officers assassinated northern leaders. This attempted coup was put down by General Ironsi, the leading Federal statesman, who was also an Ibo man. The northerners bided their time; little animosity appeared on the surface but the first phrase of a Hausa proverb was often quietly quoted: 'To kill an elephant . . .' The full proverb is to the effect that it is easy to kill an elephant but very difficult to turn it over. Some two months later, throughout the north, thousands of Ibos living and working in the north were without warning massacred. A British driller told me that he watched with mounting horror while in his workshop Hausa and Kanuri workers suddenly turned on Ibos with whom they had until then worked harmoniously.

That afternoon I drove westwards from Kano to Gusau, wondering unwittingly why so many folk were carrying rocks. In the Catholic mission in Gusau I came upon an American priest, silent on a bench in his church and in deep shock, the floor slippery with blood. I can never forget the desolation on his face and the smell of blood.

Further west, at Talata Mafara, a little kiosk where I had often bought staple groceries in the past was empty, the door swinging on one hinge. The Ibo proprietor had made the mistake of being provocative, displaying a picture of a coup plotter and declaiming 'this is the man who killed your leader.' When the mob arrived, he and his family barricaded themselves in the kiosk. At the last moment he shot his family, then shot himself.

In Gusau the Emir gathered surviving Ibos into his compound to protect them from the mob, with the help of a grim-faced Swiss official of the Red Cross. When I exclaimed at the savagery, the Swiss said sadly that he had been through it all in Germany 25 years earlier. I volunteered to 'ride herd' on a lorry load of refugees through to Zaria, as in those days a white man still carried some sort of authority. Here they were loaded into a train heading south. Once they crossed the Benue rail bridge at Makurdi they would be safe if the train was not boarded by the mob.

Comedy and tragedy go together. I headed out to Samaru, where the Catering Rest House still functioned. With remarkable speed I was booked in, given dinner, and escorted to my room. A dusk to dawn curfew was in operation; anyone in the open was liable to be shot. A penetrating whisper from the adjoining room 'Do you play bridge?' 'Yes'. 'Come through and join us.' 'I'll be shot if I go outside.' 'Idiot! Climb through the ceiling hatch, crawl along to ours, and jump.' And we played bridge far into the night.

After the massacre (the euphemism 'ethnic cleansing' had not yet been invented) the Ibos who had settled in the north and who formed much of the infrastructure straggled southwards to the Ibo heartland. Thanks to the extended family system of Bantu society, they were absorbed into their own clans. Months passed and in 1967 the south east proclaimed itself as Biafra and seceded from the federation.

At the time I was commuting to Biafra from Lagos, to keep in contact with clients in Enugu, crossing at Onitsha the only bridge for hundreds of miles. Though the federal troops on the west bank were friendly, the Ibos guarding the east end of the bridge, in their new Biafran uniforms, were increasingly hostile as tension mounted. On one trip, I waited at the bridge while a salesman in the car in front had his many bags searched by federal troops. The diligent searchers discovered a curious gadget that looked a bit like a machine pistol, though it was in fact a device for printing labels on a sticky metal strip. The soldiery were completely won over when he printed for each man his name to stick on his helmet. A man called Audu was so taken with this machine that the rep gave it to him. When later I was cleared to cross the bridge I came up with the salesman standing by his car looking very worried indeed. Having heard a rattling sound emanating from his car boot he had pulled over and discovered Audu's automatic rifle. In his joy, Audu had dumped it on the nearest available ledge. He decided to go back. I learned subsequently that the guards were in equal measure delighted to retrieve the weapon and embarrassingly eager to forget the whole episode and there was no problem.

When the Biafrans blew up one span of the bridge I made a final trip, leaving my car under a tree and hiring a canoe to cross. As usual I was searched but not as rigorously as were the many Ibos returning home. After their perilous journey from the west they suffered the final indignity of having their savings impounded. I walked up to the Onitsha Catering Resthouse and managed to phone Bob Scobie who was 70 miles away in Enugu. At that time the phones in Biafra, maintained by returned refugees, were the only ones functioning properly in Nigeria.

A solid Scot, Bob was a good friend and stout colleague and we embarked on a relaxed chat. A voice cut in to interrupt our conversation. 'Who are you?' I gave my name and explained that I was a visiting water expert. 'You are a northern spy.' Bob hastily interjected: 'I'll meet you at Awka' and rang off. A taxi took me to Awka half way to Enugu and I sat on a culvert and peacefully await Bob's arrival. The rest of the journey was uneventful until we reached a road block manned by a very nervous and hostile squad. A red-eyed corporal shouted 'You can go on.' Some 50 yards on the sergeant in charge shouted 'Stop! Go back.' So back we went, and the red-eyed warrior unshipped his rifle and shouted 'I said you go on!' So we stopped half way, until the warring parties agreed that we could pass.

In Bob's office a small man in a very natty suit glared at me. 'Who are you?' When I told him he snapped 'I was expecting a northern spy,' and stalked out.

The next evening, a Thursday, was the weekly duplicate bridge match at the Enugu Sports Club. Only a major emergency would disrupt a regular fixture at this club. Even the cinema entertainment had survived; imperfect though it was. Reels of film were often out of order and on one splendid occasion the villain was chasing a fair damsel into peril when the (British) national anthem cut in and with conditioned reflex we all shot to our feet, though some resentful rumblings broke out. The operator, a Lebanese called Soloman ultimately fled with his equipment northwards to Gboko and later I attended the first cinema show ever staged there. The screen was a white section of a concrete wall. The Tivs, of warrior stock, were entranced by the adventures of St George and the dragon. When the heroine was in mortal danger many of the audience drew knives and charged at the screen intent on slaying the dragon.

Most of the British High Commission regional staff were bridge players, possibly the only serious exercise their brains ever experienced. Much excited they gathered round.

'Oh Wobbin, can you tell us what is happening?'

'Surely you have a radio transceiver on the roof?'

'Yes, but we don't like to use it in case we upset the Biafrans.'

Bob spluttered and stalked off to the bar to relish a glass or two of excellent cognac and I tersely brought our country's representatives up to date with events beyond Biafra before the serious business of the evening. That

Sunday I made ready to return to Lagos. We hatched a plan. To avoid the brutal Biafran border formalities we drove several miles northwards to a creek by the main river. Bob handed over to me a great wad of money he wanted taken to a place of safety and we hailed a canoe. As I stepped aboard a splendid platoon of Biafrans appeared. Fortunately the lieutenant in charge was friendly and civilised but inevitably spotted my bulging pocket. Almost apologetically he made me hand over the money to Bob. 'Now you can go! Safe journey.' Bob came forward: 'I must say goodbye to my friend. We may never meet again.' We embraced as he shook my hand – and skilfully, surreptitiously and successfully secreted into it the wad of money. With tears in our eyes, we swore eternal friendship and all of us were affected: the lieutenant by the emotion of the moment, Bob and I by the virtuosity of our act.

My next visit to Enugu was in the following year, 1967. The battle for Enugu was over, federal troops were in charge and with a drilling colleague I drove down from the north to see what could be salvaged. As soon as we entered Iboland, near Nsukka, we had to weave our way for 40 miles past hundreds of burnt out vehicles – lorries, tankers, even tanks shoved to the sides of the road. Every few miles was an army road block; we were well prepared, holding a letter signed by Colonel Danjuma authorising our visit. A more effective aid was our strategic stock of Star beer, much enjoyed by the troops who became visibly relaxed. Naturally, we as the hosts were expected to drink level with them. At a place called 'nine mile corner' came the supreme test of capacity. We were flagged down by a vast major, with a pistol in his belt. Said he, 'Europeans, you will drink beer with me.' Bloated with beer, we demurred - but not for long. It is wonderful what degree of stimulus to co-operation is afforded by the jab of a pistol in the midriff.

Weary and soggy, we found the drilling company's apartment in Enugu thoroughly looted though the beds were still there. Among filth and squalor we slept for 12 hours. In the morning our first port of call was police headquarters, one of the few buildings in town not looted. The Biafran police had left hastily eastwards and within a few hours the federal police had moved in. The police commissioner was genial and anxious to help. Whereupon my colleague brought out a list of vehicles he wished to reclaim. 'By the way', he said 'the Ford Cortina outside your office is one of ours.' On the face of the Commissioner good humour no longer triumphed and the atmosphere became troubled. He delivered with sadness the news that for administrative reasons the car could not be released.

When the fall of Enugu to the federal troops was imminent two Catholic priests, both Irish, had decided to stay behind. With our remaining beer we visited Father Coleman, whom I knew well, in the spartan wooden presbytery in Ogui. While the street fighting had roared around them they had literally kept their heads down. One morning they woke to a hush and looked out into the street to see a federal patrol marching towards their veranda. Fortunately the lieutenant in charge was a Christian and arranged that they be left in peace. There were scores of ownerless chickens around them and the Fathers lived day after day on eggs and rainwater.

That evening with Father Coleman I will never forget; he related sickening stories of starvation and brutality. Most survivors were women and children. The principal enemy, oddly enough, were baboons that had invaded the town. Children weakened by hunger were at their mercy and some were torn to pieces. Father Coleman described how he tried to scare the baboons away by throwing stones at them. With lightning timing they caught the stones and hurled them back.

Driving back in the dark from St. Michael's presbytery we used my detailed knowledge of the town and thus came face to face with a very nervous sentry in the middle of the road. Appearing from the direction of the Biafran-held territory we disturbed him greatly. With a racking tension headache I stuttered out a greeting in Hausa. I imagine my English accent helped to soothe him for his rifle - which had been wavering around towards our heads – was lowered and after some negotiation we passed on as friends.

The next day we resolved to visit the drillers' workshop at Eke, a dozen miles west of the Enugu, again unaware that we were outside the defended perimeter. The compound was deserted, the only sound was the rustle of the wind in the shade trees and all seemed peaceful. Nothing had been taken as the federal looters had not yet moved in. We rescued some diamonds – industrial stones studded in a drilling bit - and were about to leave when we were assailed by a federal patrol. Though the officer was unimpressed with our letter from Colonel Danjuma he gallantly undertook to 'retake' the compound from the rebels. His men stormed through the houses, kicking down the doors, and puzzled over a tray loaded with a thermos of hot tea and two mugs. This was taken to be evidence that the Biafrans were not far away. It would have been indelicate to explain that we had been enjoying our morning tea before the eruption. We sensed that we were not overly welcome to hang around and went back to town.

In the town looting was systematic. Hausa entrepreneurs had organised teams to strip houses of every useful item and collection points were visited by a stream of lorries which, when laden, set off for the northern markets.

Coming and going from the flat we had reluctantly been stepping over what we had thought was the body of a small child. On the third morning, disturbed by the absence of putrefaction, we forced ourselves to look harder; the realisation that it was a large moulting teddy bear occasioned strained, semi-hysterical mirth and we decided to leave town before we succumbed to deep depression.

For the journey back northwards we subsisted on bananas bought from haggard old women who emerged from the bush and eggs cooked for ages in rusty hot radiator water. This episode ended for ever my fondness for hard boiled eggs.

Chapter 9. Geologist to the 'stars'

*'It's like flying along a radar beam: when his left
testicle twitches he turns left and similarly with his right.'*

Ibiza and the Costa Brava

In the late Sixties, a friend invited me to visit him in Ibiza where his
son, Tony Pargeter, ran a water drilling company. In the Balearic Islands
groundwater lies in narrow fractures not easy to find. On my first visit I
found I could achieve good success by using a black box, stereoscopic
pairs of air photos and some common sense.

This mystical box in those days was a state of the art geophysical device
that simply located fracture lines full of water; these lines conduct
electricity while the dry barren rocks on either side do not. Ten years
later an electromagnetic device became available, easier to use and more
accurate. Of this, more anon.

Moving electrodes around was tiring in hot weather and we conceived
the notion of bringing in our daughters, Cecily and Jennie, to help during
boarding school holidays. Tony assembled a list of clients and arranged
sufficient work to pay for each holiday. We enjoyed some very happy
times in the sun. Between surveys we ate good Ibizencan food and drank
good Andalucian wines and there was plenty of time for bathing and
sunbathing.

Our base was in Santa Eulalia, then a quiet village on the east coast. The
cultural centre was Sandy's Bar where the British artistic colony gathered.
Sandy was a delightful homosexual Dubliner who displayed paintings of
varying merit by aspiring artists and served sherry and bottled San Miguel
beer. Nearby in a back alley was a small restaurant called La Bota (The
Boat) that mercifully was too scruffy from the outside to attract tourists.
Here we enjoyed local cuisine at its best.

Among the British residents were stars of the silver screen. We sited water boreholes for them all. Those I remember are John Pertwee, Nigel Davenport, Denholm Elliott, Diana Rigg and Terry Thomas. We came to know them well.

Terry Thomas was a true gentleman. Somewhere I have a photo of us both sitting up to our waists in the sea wearing identical floppy hats and discoursing gently on every subject, literally under the sun. He lived with his wife Belinda and adorable children on the slope of a mountain where I succeeded in locating a site for a very successful borehole. He died some years later, alone and in poverty. One of his endearing traits was that he was unpretentious. Sunny and good humoured, he claimed to know only one joke; I heard it many times.

The singing duo, Nina and Frederick (a Danish Count) who had been all the rage, had sadly drifted apart. Frederick owned a finca (small farm) on a young mountain and wished to build a meditation chamber on the crest where he could find his soul without distraction. This was to be a tetrahedron, with three doorways, one pointing to the east, one to Mecca and one aligned parallel to the axis of water bearing fracture All this was explained to me by Frederick's Norwegian architect as we sat in the farmhouse in the soft light of paraffin lamps daintily sipping single malt whisky from silver tastevins. The architect had an uncle whose leg was bitten off by a bear, which impressed Cecily and Jennie far more deeply than did the meditation chamber.

We learned about the megalithic yard, the pyramids and the importance of the geometric centre of a tetrahedral chamber where meat allegedly does not rot but keeps indefinitely. Not having sipped enough whisky to attain a state of credulity, I may have registered doubt. The Norwegian architect was stoutly defended by his young children who indignantly exclaimed 'It works!' At school they had fashioned cardboard into the required shape and suspended a lump of meat at the centre; for how long I never knew – possibly till the neighbours complained.

Diana Rigg owned a finca in a remote valley. She was away, avenging or something, when one hot day we turned up complete with magic black box and electrodes. We were greeted by her current pink shirted escort, who from a shady patio waved a languid arm, heavy with gleaming bullion. The high point of this visit was finding an orange tree growing proudly on one of the steep sided terraces, heavy with fruit. It was my introduction to bitter oranges and to this day I remember the cringing bitterness. In later years I discovered that every small farm in southern Spain sported a single bitter orange tree. A fat pig was slaughtered annually and salted down and the juice of several oranges used to wash clean the edible bits of gut. The local legend had it that when in the 19th century the English aristocracy discovered Seville they were determined to make the fruit palatable, hence orange marmalade. A more prosaic, possibly more likely theory, is that marmalade was invented by a Scots lady from Dundee who sought to use a consignment of fast-deteriorating oranges by boiling them and turning them into marmalade.

The local night life was called The Owl and the Pussycat. Our daughters loved shaking a shoulder at the disco and so did I; but they resented being shepherded back to our quarters at what I reckoned to be a normal bed time. 'The girls need an early night' became a catch phrase and an enduring source of gentle nostalgic irritation.

The gentle civilised atmosphere of Santa Eulalia is on the opposite side of the island from the frenetic San Antonio, about 20 kilometres away but a world apart in any other way. Brash tourist traps attracted brash tourists. British visitors here were not a good advertisement for their country. Given to drinking sangria in the hot afternoons, often in the hot sun with inadequate knotted handkerchiefs for headgear, they were unattractive and were treated by local people with veiled contempt. Heaven alone knows what they were like in the neon-lit early hours.

Less professionally successful was my work in the Costa Brava on the Spanish mainland, where serious irrigation was needed for agriculture. From the great orange groves of Valencia down the coast to the tomato and paprika farms of Alicante and Murcia, a blanket of young silty rocks attenuates any geophysical signals bounced back from below. The guessing factor here loomed large.

A black box has ever been a source of mysterious respect but like any tool is only as useful as the competence of the operator. Tony Pargeter had a mischievous streak. One day he visited Sandy's Bar for a quiet beer and was drawn into conversation with the usual covey of film actors. They were curious to know what was my water finding secret, the black box being discounted as mere showmanship. With apparent reluctance to divulge my secret technique he gave the impression that I homed in thus: 'It's like flying along a radar beam; when his left testicle twitches he turns left, and similarly with his right.' Incredibly this was accepted. The repercussion was that next time I called at Sandy's I was met unaccountably with deference and respect. 'Is it true about your secret gift?' they asked. In total ignorance but with a notion that mischief was afoot I decided to be non-committal and the matter rested, though for some days drinks were pressed on me by credulous stars.

In Ibiza a few surveys were done for local farmers, who always had a dowser in beforehand to find a site. His peg was cannily removed and replaced only after my peg was planted. It was not surprising that usually the pegs were not far apart; but it was surprising that the distance between the two was usually one metre.

The scepticism of scientists is ill founded, for dowsing does work. An aquifer is an electric conductor and so are buried metal pipes. The dowser simply locates the conductor. For some reason not revealed to us, physicists - notably American - have not worked out the simple link. Their profoundly unscientific reasoning goes like this: 'We have searched but have not found a scientific basis for dowsing therefore there is no basis.' This is unscientific arrogance on a princely scale. They should climb down and search a bit harder.

Conductors generate electromagnetic fields. Some racial groups are susceptible to these fields, notably the Celts. The sticks, or whatever, held are simply tools clasped in a stressful position. They magnify any twitch of the wrist muscles.

Dowsers are defensive and so tend to overstate their ability. This inevitably ends in tears. A few years back a dowser in Bangor using an improvised whippy whalebone device worked in parallel with a geophysicist who used an electromagnetic meter. Each ran a traverse and independently plotted the measured reactions. The two plots were similar and the field trial was judged to be strikingly successful. Sad to say, the dowser then attempted to demonstrate his method in a television studio fitted with live cables. The result was disastrous.

In megalithic times, Cornwall and Brittany were inhabited entirely by Celts. These intelligent and underrated people used their dowsing gift to locate the major fracture lines called ley lines and at their intersections erected stone pillars. Allegedly they used these markers as a basis for a triangulation survey of west Britain. Much later on dowsers used reverse reasoning to ascribe to the pillars magic powers.

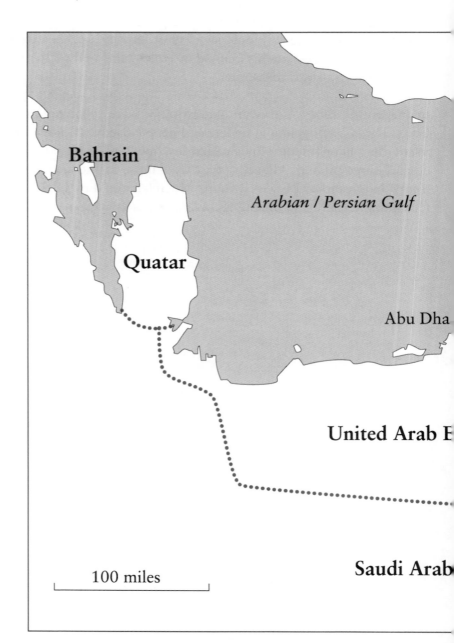

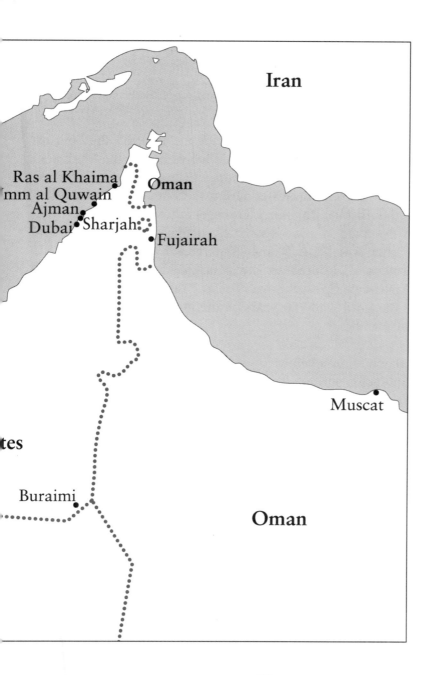

Iran

Ras al Khaima

Øman

mm al Quwain

Ajman

Dubai Sharjah

Fujairah

tes

Muscat

Buraimi

Oman

Chapter 10. Pakistan and Abu Dhabi

*The old Sheikh Shakhbut, a crusty conservative, deplored
the sudden influx of oil money and stored the revenues in
a great tin trunk under his bed.*

The Wali of Swat and all that

The North West Frontier of Pakistan was for me in 1965 the land of
Kipling and Empire and (poetically) of pale hands beside the Shalimar.
In 1850 engineers of the British East Indian Company built a system
of canals discharging irrigation water across the Punjab plain from the
Indus. During the British Raj army engineers further developed the
system so that the plain is criss-crossed by irrigation canals fed from
the five rivers after which the Punjab is named. Everyone prospered,
not least the crowds of children we saw splashing happily in the water
after school. However, a Spanish proverb says: 'Take what you want and
pay for it, says the Lord' and 150 years on the groundwater in the fields
started to become saline.

Great and grand irrigation schemes inevitably end in tears. The Sumerian
civilisation 6,500 years ago prospered from a great pattern of irrigation
canals feeding water from the Tigris and Euphrates to the Mesopotamian
plain. River water carries a few hundred parts per million of dissolved
salts - so dilute that it is tasteless. But spread on the land this irrigation
water evaporates and the dissolved salts stay behind. Over thousands of
years more and more water enters the region, very little leaves it and
the ground becomes saltier and saltier. Today that plain is coated with
sparkling salt crystals and much of the land is sterile.

Fast forward to Mozambique, where 50 years ago the Chinese converted
the lower Limpopo river by irrigation into a 'rice bowl'. As a bonus the
irrigation canals gave villagers their drinking water and they abandoned
their dug wells. When disastrous floods destroyed the canals and the
irrigation scheme the people returned to dug wells and discovered that
the groundwater had become saline. I tried to help Oxfam to pick up

the pieces but deep boreholes revealed the awful truth that there was no potable water underground.

Back to Pakistan. From Rawalpindi a must for tourists was a trip up the winding road westwards from Peshawar to the Afghan border, overlooked by cliffs decorated with painted insignia of the various regiments that had fought the Afghan tribes.

Our destination was to the north, to the edge of Pakistan's tribal territory, where nowadays an infidel geologist would not venture. The area is inhabited by Pashto farmers whose hobby and profitable sideline was the manufacture of magnificent copies of Lee Enfield rifles. Our unromantic mission was to discover and quantify limestone for a possible cement factory. This would have been welcomed as the only local industry apart from the very unofficial arms manufacture was a distant plant that turned sugar cane into alcohol. Though this was for industrial use potable alcohol was discreetly made sufficient to satisfy the needs of the elite.

On we went following the road northwards from the plain of the five rivers and up the Malakand pass to Swat, where relics of Empire abounded. On the way a high granite obelisk commemorates General Nicholson, who met his death while storming Delhi in the Indian Mutiny. It is said that he gave rise to the phrase 'in the nick of time' as he rolled up at the gates of Delhi with an East India Company regiment very opportunely. According to the inscription a 'terrorist' fired the fatal shot. A more recent tablet beside it commemorates the 'freedom fighter' who fired the shot. Away to the west stands Chakdara Fort, where half a century later Lieutenant Winston Churchill was stationed.

Though the authorities found it necessary to give me an escort of sepoys while I roamed the hills, I met only kindness. One hot day a farmer paused while winnowing corn to offer me a gourd of buffalo's milk. In a village on the plain while striving to master a few words of Pushtu I was offered a delightful curry.

The limestone occurs on a steep ridge that rises from the plain. At the foot of the ridge is a jumble of fallen chunks of limestone. As I was unfamiliar with the habits of the people my guide kindly warned me not to pick up any pebble or cobble that weighted less than a kilo, since in this area toilet paper was unheard of.

Transport from the main road at Dargai was by pony and trap; that was the easy bit! Daily, heavily booted and panting in the heat, I scrambled and slithered upwards, collecting samples from the rocks followed by my file of friendly sepoys. One of them explained that I should wear sandals ('No slip, sahib, no slip'). A demonstration failed to convince me when the lad lost his footing and slid down a scree slide for about 20 metres. At the crest a cool breeze blew and on the first day the surviving sepoys relished the break as much as I did. On subsequent days the escort found it more congenial to sit in the shade and guard me from afar. In this area land feuds are common; occasional shots were heard and the sepoys delighted in giving me a running commentary. So and so was due to shoot his uncle that day; another day it was someone else's turn.

The ancient Moghul kingdom of Swat lies in the highlands to the north and the capital, Saidu Sharif, had an old but comfortable hotel, fortunately within commuting distance of our investigation. The chalets had cool verandahs with wicker chairs, the temporary abode of biting bugs and though the food was normally mediocre our stay coincided with the expected visit of Pakistan's Head of State, General Ayub Khan. A minor conflict between Pakistan and India in the Rann of Kutch providentially erupted and the General had to cancel his visit. Consequently, heavy stocks of good food had to be eaten.

The Wali of Swat, Miangul Golshahzda Abdul-Wadud Badshah Sahib was a mild, gentle-looking man, a great Anglophile, though his father at first regarded Britain as the arch enemy. Partition and independence caused him to adjust his ideas and a great friendship was born. The last Wali was deposed shortly after our visit, when the kingdom was engulfed by the state of Pakistan.

Saidu Sharif lies in a fertile terraced valley reminiscent of Switzerland and on the irrigated slopes three crops a year are grown. In the cool evenings I took to meandering, sometimes leaping. One such leap landed me on the main road in front of the Wali who, with his escort, was taking the air. He regarded me placidly and invited me to take tea the next day. His drawing room was hung with tapestries as exquisite as his manners.

Pan American Airways once organised a tour of the North West Frontier, to include Swat. The Wali was deeply concerned for the safety within his territory of this coach load of blue rinse ladies. He deployed his entire army of some two dozen souls to stand sentinel along the road; as each individual was some two kilometres from his neighbour, the effectiveness against dacoits was problematic and the experimental tour was never repeated.

Upstream of Saidu Sharif the Swat river, spanned by ancient stone bridges, flows icy cold from the snows of the Karakoram range. Mahseer the size of mature salmon lurked motionless in the pools. Where there was no crossing, a wizened boatman in an ancient craft sat like Charon on the river Styx. Many of the people have red or fair hair and blue eyes and learned scholars ascribe these as characteristics of an ancient Dardic people. The more sceptical attribute these features to the army of Alexander the Great that marched through in 327BC, or more recently the Connaught Rangers. In addition there are semitic folk tenuously thought to be the lost tribe of Israel. Before the Islamic incursion of the 11th century the people were Buddhists and later Hindus. The stone tombs (stupas) of the Buddhists had steles (carved inscriptions), which sadly were disappearing to surface in the museums of Europe and the United States.

Our client, an elderly florid cement technologist called Horace Holman, set off to visit Garibhal, far off to the south of Swat, where he had set up a thriving cement factory. Horace kindly took me with him. The local landowner, Sir Sikander Hyal Khan, lived in some state in a fortified manor and here we lunched, his two daughters being released from purdah for the occasion. Though they regarded Horace as a benevolent uncle, they were not sure about me. Walking in the garden, they asked dear Uncle Horace what colour carnation they should pick and pin to his lapel. 'Red,' said he, 'to match my nose.' After some decorous mirth, they asked me the same question. 'White' said I, 'for purity.' They hunted until they found a muddy looking blossom, announcing with giggles that they thought an off coloured bloom would be more appropriate.

Alexander the Great marched his army through this area on his way south from Swat. Over the brow of a ridge he looked down on a delightful valley. 'Wah!' exclaimed he and the valley, called Wah to this day, is the site of the modern capital, Islamabad.

Crucial work in the Trucial States

The phone at Little Margate rarely rang during working hours but the event usually heralded a commission. Work was always thin on the ground and it was difficult not to respond too eagerly. So when a gruff voice asked if I could go to Abu Dhabi, which I had never heard of, my ploy as always was to say that I would check my diary. I added thoughtfully 'That's in Wales, isn't it?' and this occasioned a long silence. Then 'You're joking, of course.' 'Yes, of course, ha ha'. I wasn't joking but as soon as I realised that Abu Dhabi lay in the Trucial States agreed to go and thoroughly enjoyed the experience.

In those days the Trucial States, strung out along the Arabian Gulf, were little known to the outside world. Oil had only recently been discovered and for the inhabitants the impact of sudden wealth had not greatly affected the way of life. The origin of the title relates to a treaty between the British Government and the local rulers in 1892 to protect the sea route to India from pirates. The rulers were subsequently helped by British advisers but maintained their feudal status. Only a few decades before my visit a British representative had landed on a sand bar and was ferried across to Abu Dhabi village by an ancient gentleman. The envoy asked to be taken to visit the Emir, whereupon the old gentleman revealed that he was that very person.

Abu Dhabi had been ruled by Sheikh Shakhbut, a crusty conservative and the subject of many anecdotes. He deplored the sudden influx of oil money and in retrospect he may have been right. The money he stored in a great tin trunk under his bed until a British adviser suggested it would be safer in the bank. He loaded a million rials into sacks and was chauffeured to the bank, where his unexpected arrival took the staff by surprise. Cross-legged on the floor, he counted out the money and was given a chequebook. In the ensuing few weeks he wrote cheques sporadically, which his driver cashed at the bank. Not totally trusting the new system he later visited the bank and announced that he wished to count his money. After much coffee, the staff managed to assemble the balance and count it he did; then declared that he was several thousand short. The explanation that he had spent it did not satisfy him; he withdrew the balance and back into the tin trunk it went.

His majlis – a sort of weekly court of access for local elders and approved visitors to discuss their problems – had no water laid on and the Sheikh commanded that a borehole be drilled. There was much horror when the drill struck oil; how to break it to the Ruler? His rage knew no bounds. He jumped into a Land Rover and drove wildly round the site trying to destroy the evidence, muttering the equivalent of 'Bloody oil! All I want is water, water.'

His nephew, Shekh Zayed bin Calipha bin Nahyen, displaced him (hardly a coup, more a family arrangement) and this wise man steered the state through a long period of prosperity and development. In time the Trucial States became the United Arab Emirates with a benevolent family autocracy in sharp contrast to the oppressive rule of the Bahraini cousins further west.

Nowadays, the two leading and neighbouring states each has an international airport but when I arrived we landed on a sand airstrip and stood in the shade of the aircraft's wing while our baggage was checked. Having experienced the alcoholic desertification of Pakistan, where whiskey was like gold dust, I had thoughtfully brought a case of whiskey to Abu Dhabi. The welcoming party, in semi hysterics, took me forthwith to the Grey Mackenzie store where I signed in as an alcoholic, thereby giving me liberty to buy as much whisky as I wanted at 10 shillings a bottle.

The object of my visit was to find cement-making materials - limestone and clay - and was the first of a series of forays to the Trucial States as well as to Oman. For rich experience and high comedy this visit had no equal. Under the umbrella of the client, a major British consultancy, I travelled to the first target, in Buraimi oasis, in an elderly Land Rover at the hottest, most humid time of year - which in that area is very hot indeed. Southwards we lurched over sand dunes until through the haze we could see the mountains bordering Oman and Saudi Arabia.

From the security and comfort of the Ruler's guest house in Buraimi I explored the Jebel Hafid, a long anticlinal mountain running across into Saudi Arabia, and found abundant limestone. At first I could not find a clay bed until I chanced upon a blasted-out cliff, where the Trucial Oman Scouts had set up a practice bombing range. The Scouts were responsible for military security in all the Trucial States and comprised a very tough outfit trained and manned by British Army personnel. They maintained a fort in Al Ain nearby as a strong hint to the Saudis across the border nearby.

A grand event during my stay was a visit by the Bahraini 'cousins', wealthy oil sheikhs, who arrived in air-conditioned Cadillacs. A great bout of feasting broke out and as a courtesy I was invited to them all. Long tables groaned with chickens, sheep and baby camels roasted whole. Sheep's eyes there were but, not being the guest of honour, I was spared the ritual. So much food remained uneaten that I asked one of the genial cousins what happened to the residue. He told me to glance quickly round the canvas walls of the tent, and sure enough at each laced join were eyes of attendants, wives, children and so on anxiously making sure there would be food enough for them afterwards.

On the third day of their visit it was announced that the cousins were going hunting. Having seen no wild life, I asked for details. Hampers full of pigeons would be produced and each protagonist, armed with an automatic rifle, was in turn allocated a hamper to be opened on a signal. The winner was, of course, the cousin who peppered the most birds before they flew out of range. I deemed it expedient to be a long way away in the Jebel Hafid but none the less heard the frequent whine of spent bullets far overhead.

I journeyed down to the coast for a break, arriving on a Thursday, and went for a stroll on the beach in the relative cool of the evening. There I met the police chief and the head of the Abu Dhabi Defence Force who were strolling thoughtfully round a beached dhow. It turned out that this high-powered dhow had been caught smuggling between India and Abu Dhabi and confiscated. This flourishing trade consisted of carrying gold into India and trading it at an enormous profit for silver that they brought back. The organisers paid retainers to the Indian authorities and the Indian navy and still made a huge profit. I had been invited to buy shares in this trade but reckoned it was not my style.

So this dhow, fitted with twin marine diesel engines, was to take those who wished on a fishing trip the next day, Friday, while the devout were worshipping in the mosque. They co-opted the power station engineer to run the boat with the aid of the chief immigration officer. We set off, with a suitable store of lager and whisky for emergencies, relying on the fish we caught for food. The Ruler's brother-in-law, now a great power in the Gulf, brought his two small sons and he proved an expert scuba diver and a crack shot with a harpoon gun. We anchored against a sand bank and soon accumulated a horse mackerel and several large dorado, each accurately shot through the right eye. Laid out on the sand, they were covered with driftwood, ignited with the help of kerosene and soon under the soothing influence of the lager we were dining heartily.

Turning for home, we discovered that while we had made do with lager, the crew had discovered and made inroads into the whisky, to which they were unaccustomed. We strenuously loaded the unconscious bodies on to the deck, which towered a long way above us and after a struggle started the engine. The dhow weaved its merry way towards land on the falling tide, skirting and occasionally scraping over sand bars. Towards dusk, we inevitably lodged firmly and finally on a sand bank and could not struggle free. As the light faded, we could see the beach Club in the distance, with a flickering silvery screen showing the weekly film. It grew cold and we draped the two children in sailcloth. As the exceptional tide ebbed, the tilt on the deck increased until we were lodged in the scuppers against the rail. Shipwrecked!

Meanwhile back in town the worried children's mother went to see her brother, the Ruler. He mustered the entire shipping capacity of his realm and ultimately a Nordic wheeler-dealer hove along side in the Ruler's cabin cruiser and we were saved. As we pulled away from the disconsolate dhow the crew, involuntary and unconscious guardians, awoke and blearily called for help. My Arabic was by no means adequate to understand what the children's father told them but it sounded pretty crisp. It transpired that the tide that left the vessel stranded for three days was exceptionally low and prolonged and it was a while before the crew resumed their normal duties.

We were asleep in the Ruler's guest house long before the remnants of the co-opted rescue fleet returned to port and I expected a certain amount of backlash. But none came and a few days later I dared to attend the majlis. We all sat cross-legged while the Ruler read the newspaper and the beefy, roseate detachment of the Trucial Oman Scouts, on a routine visit, demolished large piles of food. Everyone ceremoniously drank coffee and all was sweetness and light.

Two years later the hunt for cement-making materials along the Trucial Coast continued. In Dubai, I conceived the notion of blending sand from two types of dune; the coastal dunes composed largely of shell fragments for the lime component, and the big continental dunes inland that contained aluminium silicate, albeit mixed with an unhealthy amount of silica. Samples taken using an auger were carefully bagged and labelled for kiln testing in Italy. Seeking iron oxide to supplement the mix, I heard of a source on the island of Tumbs, half-way across the Gulf to Iran. This scorching island was the source of splendidly coloured ochre, used in coloured pencils. We set off in the consultants' launch, well provisioned with a considerable retinue of expatriate attendants and their good ladies. In addition to crew we had a cook of mercurial temperament who muttered fiercely about the heat and inconvenience of sea travel.

Far ahead we discerned a cluster of terns diving for fry and immediately the atmosphere below deck brightened. We shaped a course for what proved to be a school of bonito hunting the fry and unreeled spinning lines to troll to and fro. The cook, in high glee, joined in enthusiastically. When battle subsided, with hands cut and chafed by the lines, we counted the catch - a veritable mound of fish. The cook lost no time in preparing delicious, mildly curried bonito steaks and for a while the launch steered itself.

We moored off the island and waded ashore in sandals. The sand was scorching hot and to prevent burns we moved rapidly, took our samples and soothed our roasting feet wading back. The way home stretched out forever; though we were comfortably replete with more curried fish, the heat sapped our joy. The cook lapsed into melancholy, grumbling audibly. Apparently he anticipated that by the time they could get the fish to market it would be rotten.

The client had arranged to have the ton of dune sand samples air freighted to Europe. This would be on a flight chartered to carry 40 tons of smuggled silver. At the airport, the diminutive Goan clerk found it difficult to comprehend why anyone would wish to send to Europe, along with 40 times that weight of silver, a ton of sand. Did they not, he wondered, have sand of their own.

The tip of the Arabian peninsula points to the Straits of Hormuz and here lies the northernmost of the Emirates, Ras al Khaima. It is a wild, mountainous strip of land with abundant deposits of limestone and here the search continued. As always, it was the hottest time of year and the small expatriate community spent the nights bobbing around waist deep in the sea; the water temperature was 30^0C but there was an illusion of coolness. My driver was a local man and after a scorching day in the mountains he would walk me through his shady garden, picking succulent dates for me to sample.

With the blessing of Sheikh Rashid, the Ruler, we set off on the first day's reconnaissance into the lawless valleys behind the coast. It rapidly became plain that there would be problems. A solitary man, with a rifle in one hand (while the other balanced a block of limestone on his head) blocked the track. He shuffled out of his sandals, put down the block of stone, strode forward to shake me by the hand and spoke to the driver: 'Tell this man that if he doesn't turn back I will shoot him.'

In vain I invoked the name of the Ruler.

'We do not know the Ruler.'

And that was that. Back in town I had audience of Sheikh Rashid who agreed that these folk did not recognise him as Ruler.

However, he undertook to mobilise his defence force to protect me. The next day the defence force mustered and we set forth. Ten men, heavily armed, jolted with me in the Land Rover to the limestone cliff and I set about sampling. The army sensibly climbed to a patch of shade at the top of the cliff and smoked pensively. As I sweated up the face, panting, chipping and bagging samples of stone, a fair-sized crowd gathered on the valley floor and between them and the army a very vocal volley of insults screamed to and fro above my head. This was preferable to an exchange of bullets but distracting.

Without a firm grasp of Arabic, I could only guess as to the content. Probably something like this:

'Come down here and we'll fill you in'

'Climb up here and we'll fill you in'.

In Buraimi I had strayed inadvertently into Oman and was peacefully deflected. A while later I twice visited Oman legally, through Muscat. The old Sultan Said bin Tamur had been replaced by his son, Qaboos bin Said. The new Sultan soon had to cope with the Dhofar war that had dragged on since the Sixties, masterminded by Chinese-backed rebels from Aden.

In 1970 I was told that I was a 'limestone hydrologist' and as such was invited to find water for White City in Dhofar. This high sounding city comprised a landing strip and a fuel store on the Jebel Samhan, which had been used by a flier called Chalky White. The SAS occupied this mountain top as a base and relied on supplies of arms, food and water flown in by light aircraft. The monsoon, which swept westwards across the Indian Ocean to the south of Oman, was by then almost a spent force of light rain and mist. This was a blessing for farmers but it prevented aircraft from reaching the airstrip. Water was essential for the SAS to operate and without a local supply they would have to evacuate the base. So a light rig had been flown in to drill for water in the limestone.

Enter the Limestone Hydrologist; what followed was pure comedy. In Muscat I entered the military domain. Under the wing of the aircraft that was to fly us south to Salalah we were all briefed by a British sergeant-major type. Salalah is a delightful town on the Dhofar coast and not far from the border with Aden. It was the base for the Sultan's Defence Force, with British officers variously clad in colourful uniforms. I mentally labelled them the Carnaby Street Regiment. The following day was a Friday and, in deference to Muslims, operations were normally suspended. Reporting for breakfast, I found the mess deserted but for the Chief Engineer, fulminating at a breach of etiquette. Apparently there was a battle in progress and this was simply not the done thing. 'On a Friday, dammit - on a Friday!' So we ate in one corner of a vast mahogany table surrounded by the regimental silver. This gave me time to study the air photographs, which were not encouraging. It seemed to me that the groundwater lay at great depth.

With a feeling of impending doom I made ready the next morning for the great work. An RAF officer drove me to the airstrip in an open-topped Land Rover with sand bags on the floor. The idea was that if we struck a mine the sand bags would spread the blast wave so that we would be blown cleanly out, with no roof to stop our progress. I was much affected by this thoughtfulness but felt a bout of melancholy creeping on.

The flight to the Jebel Samhan was in a sturdy, Canadian Beaver aircraft.

Briefing by the RAF was not conducive to a serene frame of mind. Issued with a venerable bolt-action rifle, I was enjoined to board the aircraft and on the way not to open fire until I was told to do so. The word 'until' impressed me greatly. No more reassuring was my seat, which was a case of ammunition. I had asked the pilot to circle over the site area so that I could take photographs of the terrain and the rig and he dubiously agreed. From the airstrip a furious flare was fired and on landing an equally furious warrior slated both me and the pilot for drawing the enemy fire. Who was I anyway, he demanded.

'A bloody geologist. That's all I need. Tchah!!'

Feeling suitably humbled, I was heavily escorted by some tough looking SAS types to a cave where the colonel sat at a camp table in deep thought. I received a courteous welcome but also the impression that the sooner I finished a reconnaissance and went back to Salalah the better for everyone.

Nigel the driller was summoned. As drillers go, he appeared frail and nervous, with a facial twitch, flinching upon sudden noise. He was neatly attired with a silk scarf tucked into a floral shirt; if these were his working clothes I wondered what his evening wear was. He escorted me jauntily to his rig. It was a pneumatic hammer rig of uncertain age and clearly too light to achieve the deep drilling needed to reach water. This may have been down to limitations on the weight that could be carried by air. The machine was shielded by a huge metal tripod clad with steel sheets. These were peppered with bullet scars and I began to realise the reason for Nigel's nervous twitch, though he confided that he felt safer out there on site than in the uncouth company of the SAS.

With a singular lack of appreciation of the hazardous nature of the terrain, I led Nigel down the slope to where I had a drilling site to peg. On the way we passed a machine gun nest manned by Baluchis and I began to feel a trifle thoughtful. Before long a heavy military presence came storming down the hill. Did I realise that we were outside the defence perimeter? It was time to hit back and they were informed this was the only site that had a prayer of being successful. It was conceded that they could increase the perimeter.

Without sadness I said farewell to the Colonel, regretting that urgent matters called me away, and was flown back to Salalah. Here the Mess was back to full strength and after a convivial evening with the Sultan's Brave Boys I had a slack day to explore this lovely corner in the far south of the Arabian land mass.

Taking into account the miniature rig Nigel operated it was no surprise when, two months on, I read a small item in *The Times* that the Jebel base had been temporarily evacuated.

A less lovely visit was to Jeddah in Saudi Arabia, on the inevitable cement materials hunt. After the free and easy way of living in the coastal states, working in Saudi was materially adequate but the atmosphere seemed repressive. However, the Saudis have a saying that in such a hot, infertile land Allah took pity and gave them oil.

Along the Red Sea coast there is much limestone composed largely of the detritus from dead coral reefs. Finding the clay component was to prove less simple. Patches of clay were reported to occur south of Jeddah in the Wadi Fatima, a dry sandy valley flat that extends to the Red Sea. For our reconnaissance a Land Cruiser with a local driver had been provided but it soon became apparent that the driver had scarcely been off a tarmac surface before. My companion was a young geologist in the capacity of a 'leg-man'. When our driver, with the confidence of ignorance, charged a soft dune and became stuck we looked for sand mats; and there were none; neither was there a shovel nor a jack. This is where the young leg-man proved his usefulness. We dug with bare hands until we were dehydrated and our water finished. We set out to walk towards the main road while the driver settled down philosophically to guard the vehicle. After an hour we found a Bedouin camp and staggered towards it. The men folk were away and the women, quite rightly, set the dogs on us. Thirst overcame our fear of canine teeth and we set course for a large water pot under the eaves of a big black shady tent. The women belaboured us with sticks and shouted imprecations that needed no translation. When at last they realised we were more interested in surviving than in them they let us be and much later the men returned from town in a truck. After unrolling the carpet, they offered the ritual mint tea and coffee, took us to the road and we thumbed a lift back to town.

The next foray was eastwards up the wadi and patches of clay began to appear. Wishing to mark our position on the plan, I asked the driver in which direction lay Mecca. 'Over there, about three kilometres,' said he. In those days, possibly even now, for an infidel to approach Mecca was liable to end in tears and I told the driver to turn back. He heartily assented and promptly turned tail.

Abstaining from alcohol is no problem if it is voluntary; but when it is enforced there arises universally an urge to sup the blushful hypocrene with, as the poet so rightly asserts, beaded bubbles winking at the brim. Hence there was a flourishing cottage industry in bootlegging. A booklet called 'The Blue Flame' was compiled by an American oil company. Perturbed by the incidence of rough toxic spirit made by expatriate workers, they set out the principles and practice of making pure ethyl alcohol and the pirated circulation approached world best- seller status. It involved fermenting sugar solution and distilling the resulting liquid, using a pressure cooker and a copper coil chilled by immersion in a continually flowing toilet cistern. The raw liquor is distilled three times, retaining the central portion each time. When a sample burns with a blue flame it is said to be safe to drink. Every major drug store in Jeddah had on its shelves an array of the various flavouring essences – Drambuie, crème de cacao, curacoa and so on.

The bootlegger, an expatriate engineer, took delivery of several sacks of cane sugar every week, and his roof space carried a row of plastic bins of fermenting juice. As a matter of curiosity the sugar supplier once asked, tongue in cheek, what he wanted with so much sugar, and he replied, equally tongue in cheek, that he had a very sweet tooth. His long-suffering wife operated the still, one run per day; they both had a highly nervous appearance. The siddiqi, as it was called, was traded by appointment outside the gate of the compound if it was uncut or by the front door if it was diluted to a level safe from accidental ignition.

Chapter 11. Burma, Liberia and Libya

*The President had been returned to power by the votes of 105
per cent of the entire population*

An alarming experience in Burma

At the beginning of the Biafra war in Nigeria, Brian Clark the regional Chief Water Engineer was stranded in Enugu. This town had, by the fortunes of war, become the capital of the breakaway self-styled state of Biafra. He was drinking a quiet beer in the Sports Club when a mortar shell landed on the nearest tennis court. It seemed to him that the federal Nigerian troops were uncomfortably close to the capital. So with Bob Scobie and a couple of friends, and some carefully hoarded petrol, he drove off eastwards to Cameroun, up the twisty narrow road to the Bamenda highlands then south to Douala. The party travelled by cargo boat to Lagos, the Nigerian federal capital. The first visit was to the British High Commission where there was a 'full and frank exchange of views' and after some adventures Brian reached Britain.

Water engineering in the UK bored Brian mightily and when a job in Burma came up off he went (though he admitted that the call of the east was not strong, for Africa gets into one's bones). The Burmese had entered a phase of self-inflicted isolation, which suited their gentle nature and religion but did nothing for the economy. Mature timber rotted in the jungle and the Bangladeshis were discouraged from coming in their canoes at harvest time to buy rice. The government, and much of the country, was in the hands of the relatively benevolent autocrat Ne Win and his less benevolent colonels. The books were balanced by the annual international jade auction when great raw lumps of jade were up for sale.

Since the departure of the British, public services had deteriorated. Brian's job at the head of a UN project was to rehabilitate water supplies. We had worked together in Nigeria and I was delighted when he asked me to go to Burma for a few months in 1967 to seek groundwater on the Arakan coast.

I was asked to bring with me two starting pistols that fired noisy blanks. On my arrival in Rangoon most of the UNDP presence in town came out to meet me, headed by Brian with two questions – did I have a good journey, and did I bring the pistols. Then to his rented bungalow in the northern suburbs where we sat down to a vast and superb curry lovingly constructed by my host, who had bought the ingredients in the waterside market that morning. In this corner of the world each nation has its own cuisine and in subsequent years I sampled curries from many of them. My previous experience of curry had been the Nigerian model, a glorified fruit salad heavy with peppers. But now my young and uncritical taste buds wallowed in the delicate flavours and the total absence of chillies.

And so to bed; but first the ceremonial rigging up of the burglar alarms. Brian had experienced miserable depredations by thieves. The worst was when he was drugged by opium fumes blown through his ventilator in the dark of the night. The best sleep ever and the worst outcome – but they left him his pillow. The home-made alarms were compounded of strings of empty tins hung on the bedroom doors, so poised that at the slightest tremor the whole issue crashed noisily down. With a pistol each under our pillows we looked forward to an untroubled sleep. But, alas! The curry got to work and deep in the night I woke and, forgetting where I was, set the burglar alarm crashing into play. Brian stormed out, in vivid pyjamas, firing his pistol wildly. And so to bed – again.

Breakfast was sombre and a hollow-eyed briefing in the UNDP office did little to raise the spirits. Transportation to Akyab Island was imminent and the entire team (Brian, a huge Hungarian of teutonic and military bearing and a small Serb with a large wife, of whom he was terrified) mustered to take me. Burma is a long, thin country and Akyab is a long, long way from Rangoon; clearly an attraction for desk-bound warriors. The domestic airline consisted of at least one DC3; the pilot had a distinctive style of taxiing; indeed Sterling Moss would have been hard put to keep up. In the air, we seemed to slow up a bit and could relax as we groaned and juddered along the interminable Arakan coast.

Akyab was recovering from a hurricane that had uprooted many coconut palms and wore a dejected air. The rest house, a delightful looking timber building on stilts, was lined with staff on full alert and the weight of Arakan hospitality descended upon us. The rationale for an inflatable air bed rapidly became apparent. Burmese beds are of spartan hardwood and Buddhists gain merit by sleeping on them.

Short ridges of sandstone dominate the scene and almost every ridge is occupied by a pagoda, a Buddhist place of worship. Between ridges are low sandy flats and on three sides is the sea. A causeway connects the island with the hinterland. Dacoits (bandits or patriots, depending on one's point of view) threatened from the beyond and it was considered unhealthy to stay out of town after dark. In the far off colonial days the British had constructed a reservoir fed by pipeline from the mainland. This mighty concrete tank leaked copiously and fragments of freshwater fauna sporadically drifted through delivery mains. When the naval commander allegedly found young oysters in his wash-basin it was judged to be auspicious to clean things up.

Before my colleagues left for Rangoon I was inducted into the rhythm of life: impressive and leisurely meals, siestas, and brief spurts of work. Akyab was a naval base and socialising with the officers was important. During extracurricular daylight hours there was plenty to see but not much to do. An expedition to fish from a canoe in the bay proved almost a disaster. The locally made cheroots were of uncertain composition and quality; tobacco may have been involved, but only to a minor degree. To relieve the tedium of inactivity I lit one of these infernal devices. In the excitement of the moment, when something (possibly a fish) tentatively nibbled my baited hook, I exhaled violently whereupon it erupted into flame before my eyes and incandescent fragments burned holes, painfully, in my polyester trousers.

In Burma it is rare to meet anyone who is not smoking a cheroot. It is said that as soon as a new-born baby starts breathing a cheroot is stuck into its mouth. The very best cheroots, made of tobacco, cost very little and I bought a drum of them to take home. To keep them in peak condition, it was best to keep them in contact with the fumes of 'country spirit' (local rum). Sadly, I did not appreciate that the rum should not be in direct contact with the tobacco but only the fumes. Thus the opening ceremony when I reached home was anticlimactic. A sort of porridge poured out but smelling wonderful. At a subsequent barbecue it scented the entire valley.

Walks were short, on account of alleged dacoitry. I took tea with 'the Englishman', an elderly gentleman born in Yorkshire but who spoke with an Arakan accent; we had little in common as he could not remember much of his native land and his interests were supremely local. I spent many jolly hours with an English-speaking naval officer but he had a speech impediment – of which he appeared to be oblivious - and I had great difficulty following the feast of reason and flow of soul. There were rare moments of rich humour, as when he gave a fairly serious demonstration in the accepted method of wrapping a betel nut in a lime leaf and working it into shape in his mouth. The copious deep red froth carried to his speech a distortion on the edge of incomprehension.

The American Catholic mission priest dedicated his time between good works and golf. It seemed an odd combination but the naval station commander explained the reason for having a golf enthusiast in town. His officers were all golf fanatics and modelled the game on that of the priest. As soon as the navy could beat him on handicap they would need to revoke the priest's residence permit. During the week the priest travelled on foot far inland to remote hill villages where no one else could penetrate and live to tell the tale, and Saturdays would see him back in town wearily plodding round the golf course.

Rare visits to Rangoon were necessary to obtain two forms of currency – Burmese kyats that superseded rupees after independence and whisky from the British Embassy. A visit to the bank took most of a morning and much patience, using a local guide to shuffle from teller to teller until at last one emerged with a great bag of bank notes stapled together in blocks. At Brian's hospitable bungalow a Eurasian girl cooked elegant Burmese lunches. These involved such unusual components as carp guts and mimosa leaves and were delicious. Dinner was predictably prawn curry dispensed by Brian. In Akyab, rice, fish, meat and fruit being cheap, I needed little money so my daily living allowance piled up.

For a fair sized town such as Akyab a thick layer of fresh groundwater was needed and without much optimism we set about assessing the sand flats. The Ministry had provided two English speaking Burmese assistants and a vehicle. These stalwart lads from Rangoon contrasted strongly with the dark, slightly built Arakanese. Immaculately dressed in lungis – heavy wrap-around kilts - overlaid by blazers with bold brass buttons, both had received overseas training in Australian universities and were keen further to improve their minds. They undoubtedly smoothed my path, physically by brushing away goat droppings from the turf should I show signs of preparing to sit down (which was often) and soothing the Arakanese by explaining my odd ways. The team was topped up by the dilettante son of a Chinese entrepreneur who moved gently along with us, presumably to fill in the idle hours between meals. He was if anything more elegantly attired, with a proud array of coloured propelling pencils and notebooks to record my many wise utterances.

I had been enjoined to look around for underground water. The pagoda-bound sandstone ridges were off limits and were in any event unlikely to hold enough water. That left the sandy flats just above sea level, normally saturated with brackish water. At first the problem seemed insoluble but geophysical traverses produced a surprise. The fresh water appeared to extend right down to the buried sandstone. It dawned on me that the mighty tank was leaking enough fresh water into the ground to push the sea water back, creating a broad mound of fresh groundwater that depressed the saline water. Oh joy, oh rapture! Inadvertently, the relaxed Burmese had accidentally created conditions to bring filtered underground water to their very doorstep.

To prove the resource a test borehole was needed; this is when the fun started. Brian was able to locate and dispatch a light drilling rig with a driller who spoke no English but quite good German. Technical and restaurant terminology was easy but for any other topic I needed an interpreter. He had a drilling bit of only one size so when he asked what diameter hole was wanted I was puzzled. It became clear ultimately that the drill pipe lengths were far from straight, and these pipes were old friends. They wriggled as they rotated down the hole and (as a shepherd knows his sheep) the driller could assemble a combination of pipes to produce the diameter of hole needed.

We were working in no-man's land; by night the 'dacoits' moved in so that all equipment had to be withdrawn at dusk. To drill a hole, line it with screen and casing, test the yield and move out in 12 hours was not easy but this man managed it.

Visitors to the rest house were few. The most interesting were a Russian marine biologist and his minder. The minder was chunky, self-assured and wore a blue serge suit whatever the weather. The biologist was small, self-effacing, homesick and emotional. The evening following their arrival I was practising on my flute when there came a diffident knock on the door. It was the minder. Said he 'May I sit here and listen to your music. It is so beautiful that I weep.' And weep copiously he did while I struggled on with scales, arpeggios, trills and shakes of a most unbeautiful timbre. Then he spoke again. 'Have you some of that most excellent Scottish whisky? It will make me happy.' So I dished out a tooth mug of Scotch (as a British citizen working for UNDP I had access to the Embassy's shop in Rangoon.) And shaking his great head in time with the music he wept again, obviously deliriously happy. After drinking toast after toast to 'international collaboration', he rose to leave. First, though, he announced that he had abundant supplies of tinned crab and much bread. So I was to visit his quarters with my whisky and eat his crab meat. And to remember to bring my music.

The port had a thriving fishing industry. Every morning early the biologist went down to the fish market and bought freshly landed fish that he dissected and later sold the filleted bits back to the market at a price lower than he paid; thus acquiring a reputation locally for eccentricity.

In the evenings I watched the crews leave in their canoes. They would throw a sack of rice and a few trussed chickens into the dry ends of their canoe and disappear for two nights and a day. I asked how the men went about killing the chickens without infringing their Buddhist tenets. Of course they did not kill them; they simply immersed them in sea water for a few minutes and the creatures simply stopped breathing. In the same way the fish were never killed; they just stopped breathing when they were hauled in.

The reluctance of non-seafaring Burmese Buddhists to kill living things had its downside. In the market one day I watched a rabid dog, lurching round in great circles. The people left it alone and simply kept the children out of its path and after a while it lay down and died.

The work was finished a little before Easter. A final hair-raising ride on the DC3 back to Rangoon, in time for the Maundy Thursday service in the Catholic cathedral, where as a 'distinguished stranger' I had my feet washed. A meeting with the Minister in charge of water, Colonel So Tin, an anglophile with a heart condition who loved roses, led to an invitation to go fishing – though we knew not where. Very early next morning we were collected in a Land Rover and driven for a long time up into the hills in the dark, with Halley's comet blazing in the sky, and there we were at the fishing grounds. These were stew ponds where carp were fattened for the Rangoon markets. Protocol demanded that we fish these innocent creatures out but it was slaughter. Dozens of them were caught and tethered below water in a gruesome string. After about an hour the survivors realised that something nasty was going on and they sulked; whereupon a very old gentleman brought out a large bag, rang a big brass bell and cast great handfuls of rice husk into the ponds – thus the game started all over again.

To keep in touch with Rangoon 300 miles away, the routine was to walk down to the telephone exchange where there was a radio telephone of sorts. The Rangoon exchange was undermanned and the local operator would sit cross-legged on a charpoy chanting over and over again: 'Rrangon, Rrangon, Rrangon….' Folk in Akyab with a radio (there were a few) and plenty of time (there was) would tune in to the frequency for prolonged entertainment. After incautiously eating under-cooked oysters, I contracted dysentery and managed to send a message through Brian in Rangoon beseeching the nurse at the British Embassy to send some medication. Walking back through the town I was besieged by well-wishers expressing sympathy and practical advice.

Life amid Liberia's 'Honorables', 1968

In those days Liberia was run by the descendants of freed slaves and government was run in the style of the United States. Each minister was an 'Honourable' and the official residence of President Tubman was The Mansion. I joined a small team from the World Health Organisation charged with sorting out rural water supply for the state. A wing of *the* hotel in Monrovia, the Ducor Palace Hotel, was made over to UN staff, and our happy little band lived there at a modest rental. Bureaucracy decreed that there was much spare time and the swimming pool had shady areas for relaxation.

We were a team of three, our leader a Hungarian engineer. In 1956 he had fled to freedom, at first to Britain where he spent some months working for the BBC as a programmed all-in wrestler. Then to Canada where he perfected his English and acquired a Canadian wife whom he termed the Princess. To add to our joy, we were joined by a sanitary engineer from Wichitaw, Kansas, who never worked out what he was doing there.

A delightful Belgian doctor, Albert Adam, was the oldest inhabitant. He had been appointed to furnish and commission the J.F. Kennedy memorial hospital and as months passed while no equipment, beds, furnishings or staff arrived, Albert orchestrated our idle lives. He held court in a suite of rooms and with old world charm prescribed and dispensed cocktails using scales and measuring glasses. In the belief that his room was bugged, we would at intervals state loudly that President Tubman was a fine chap. As this worthy had been returned to power by the votes of 105 per cent of the entire population I doubt if he was much worried. Later events proved that he should have been.

The centenary celebration of the rubber industry was held while we were there, sponsored by Firestone. For some reason, Lord Thompson of Fleet was invited. We knew him to be reclusive. A still figure in a high-backed wicker chair by the swimming pool was reverently avoided but, egged on by Dr. Albert, I felt emboldened to invite him to one of our little drinks parties. He blinked and accepted. This sombre presence had a steadying effect on our jollity but he accepted a cocktail of startling colour and brightened up sufficiently to say -

'You know who I am of course?'

'Yes my lord' said Albert.

The guest set down his glass before replying. 'My lord! What is this nonsense? I am a diamond buyer from Amsterdam.' However, he did thaw to the extent of confiding that he sat by the pool because he enjoyed watching a Turkish lady, an authentic blonde who swam for hours on end.

The Hungarian wrestler organised flying lessons for his Princess, though exceptionally we used the aircraft to fly to the four corners of Liberia to check water supplies. In those days there were few navigational aids and the only forest landmarks were airstrips beside workings for alluvial diamonds. Our pilot's courageous attempt to reach a remote station (Sanokole) in the north was full of event. Unknowingly, he strayed over the border and approached a large airfield where huge Russian transport planes were liberally scattered and the flag of Guinea flew proudly. A large crowd on the ground shook their collective fists and some more positive signs of resentment erupted, whereupon the pilot prudently turned southwards, back into Liberia and when he reached the Atlantic coast turned east until Monrovia and Roberts Field came into view. Flying a few hundred feet above the ocean, we could look down on canoes carrying barracuda to Monrovia. These huge silvery fish were almost as long as the canoes they lay in.

As 'Honorables' all Government ministers enjoyed great status. The Minister for Mines, the Honorable Barclay, hosted a reception at the iron mine up in the mountains and the US Geological Survey were kind enough to take me along. In the dusk we sat in wicker chairs in a great lamp-lit circle.
The Honourable Barclay, a mountainous man whose chair was slightly raised in accordance with his status, drank champagne in considerable quantity from a silver tankard. We lesser mortals drank beer. He discoursed eloquently, each statement punctuated by a vigorous thump of

his stout walking stick on the protesting floorboards. We were solemnly introduced in turn to the great man who in the process discovered that I was English. This excited him greatly and he summoned a steward: 'Give the Englishman champagne.' This seemed a good idea to me and thereafter the steward was commanded (with a thump) to 'Give the Englishman more champagne.' Thump. I waxed under the influence and swelled perceptibly. Pride before a fall: in the middle of a statement, which seemed to me at the time to be profoundly wise, my appreciative audience heard from me an unexpected and vibrant belch. A horror stricken silence, then: 'Give the Englishman NO more champagne.'

Libya: Gunther's little secret

Following the wane of Italian power in north Africa, Idris al-Mahdi es-Senussi, originally the Emir of Cyrenaicia, became King Idris I of Libya in 1951. A population of Italian settlers greatly assisted the wave of economic prosperity that ensued. From being an inspirational and highly influential leader, recognised and admired by the desert tribes, King Idris I lost popularity. Old and sick, he handed over to his nephew. The opportunity was immediately seized in 1969 by the military, who took control. The coup was headed by a young Colonel Gadaffi who immediately imposed a strict interpretation of Islamic law that struck at the heart of the many Italian colonists.

Of all this I knew nothing when I arrived shortly after the coup. The restaurants of Tripoli still served superb Italian food but mineral water in place of chianti invoked a far from cheerful atmosphere. The joyful ambience of Italian diners was replaced by utterly gloomy countenances and drooping absence of conversation.

A German-staffed cement factory along the coast in Homs was running short of limestone and it was up to me to find some more. My mentor was a thoughtful-looking self-styled philosopher who took me on a courtesy visit to the Geological Survey. The nominal Director was a sombre heavily built Italian who sat in silent, stony-faced isolation at an elevated desk looking out on a vast open plan office. The philosopher ignored the poor man and took me to a young Libyan enthusiast who masked his utter ignorance of the local geology by treating me to an expansive view of the future under the junta.

And so to Homs to set the ball rolling by meeting the manager and chief chemist. The embarrassed manager had the tricky task of explaining that Gunther, the chief chemist, was not available having locked himself in the laboratory. He struggled, then mentally shrugged and explained that Gunther very much enjoyed his glass (or three) of schnapps. On leave when the coup erupted, he schemed to arrive in Tripoli prepared. He had prepared his mind for the coming ordeal by lining his stomach with ardent spirits and his pockets with full flasks. Walking unsteadily from the aircraft, he stumbled and fell. The customs men were well disposed but could not ignore the crash of splintering glass and the rich aroma of schnapps and he was gently relieved of every bottle.

By the time his taxi reached Homs in a state of sober agitation he was able to view the future with foreboding. His first action was to order a sack of dates, for scientific purposes. Without further ado he locked himself in the lab, announcing that critical research was about to take place. Emerging only for meals, he built a fermentation chamber and a still. I was present for the first tasting of date spirit. It was remarkably good and his colleagues backed his further research to the hilt. His accommodation in a block of flats was opposite that of the chief of police, outside of whose door each morning a bottle of spirit was left, to be briskly spirited away. Thus was equilibrium maintained.

With the chief engineer and his two colleagues, all fuelled with good cheer, I embarked on what was to be an interesting journey to the quarry. The Volkswagen 'beetle' seemed very full and I noted with alarm that they all wore white helmets. I was strongly encouraged to sit in the front passenger seat and soon discovered why. The chief drove with great impetus and lubricated courage and conversation was minimal.
Homs, or al Hums, is the Arabic name for Leptis Magna, one of three well-preserved relics of the Roman days, complete with arena. It was a joy to walk the streets and recognise features familiar to a 20th century town dweller. Exceptional were the central heating systems, possibly

more energy efficient than those of our time. Kitchen sinks, though carved out of limestone, were depressingly identical in design to those of my early days. All the labels in English were plastered over, and replaced by Arabic script.

The contents of the museum were unremarkable but for two contrasting statues. One was very masculine, of a Roman soldier in rough textured sandstone but bearing remarkable detail of uniform. The bare legs showed veins and the muscles were in tension. This was clearly the work of a Roman. The other was of a very feminine goddess, in polished marble, and must surely have been carved by a Greek.

Homs sported one run-down hotel that in the palmy days of the kingdom had been a thriving centre catering for culture-hungry visitors. The food was mediocre though the coffee, in three varieties, was interesting. The best was Turkish, a hangover from the days of the Ottoman Empire, with good full flavour and the texture of thick soup guaranteed to obliterate the memory of the set menu. The next in rank was 'French' - instant coffee mixed in the kitchen and presented in a battered silver jug. Finally came 'American', a tin of coffee and a china mug of hot water.

A permanent resident and valuable source of information on what she termed 'the Leptis', was Miss Preston, a retired Scottish lady. Formerly a house matron at Harrow, she remembered as a scholar Prince - later King - Hussain of Jordan, the subject of affectionate, almost motherly anecdotes.

Helping me was a young geologist, John Mark Pike, who observed that the drowned limestone pavement along the sea shore abounded in spiny sea urchins. In swimming shorts and armed with borrowed table spoons we prised them out of crevices to vary the menu. We were sternly admonished by a local vigilante - not for harvesting sea urchins but for appearing in public indecently clad.

Waves of conquest through the ages – Carthaginians, Romans, Turks, Italians, British – had left their mark and field work was enlivened by the discovery of deep trench fortifications probably dug by Turks of the Ottoman empire. A whitewashed Roman villa stood, apparently undamaged, far from anywhere. This area must have been an archaeologist's paradise.

The flat-topped hills abounded in beds of limestone and marl but high-grade limestone was also needed. Every hill had at one time been capped with the highest grade stone but most had been quarried away by the Romans to build 'the Leptis'. Along the working face of one abandoned quarry were wooden wedges driven into joints, ready to be expanded by soaking. Given the dry air, it is conceivable that these were surviving Roman relics.

My report to the client pointed out there was abundant high-grade limestone already extracted and available but it comprised the structure of the Roman city. By consolation there was enough second-rate material to fill their purpose.

I left with some regret, being booked to fly by Aeroflot to Kano in Nigeria. Unwisely, I persuaded the driver to take a short cut from Homs across the desert to the airport, a long, dusty and thirsty journey. There was no drinking water at the airport and the aircraft was four hours late arriving. The Russian crew disembarked, immaculately clad in powder blue uniforms in powerful contrast to my dust-stained working clothes. But buoyed with thoughts of a long cold drink on the aircraft I eagerly boarded. There was only one other passenger, a Nigerian girl on her way home having resigned her scholarship at a university in the Soviet Union because of 'racial prejudice'.

When the elderly aircraft reached cruising height and began the groaning journey southwards I rang the bell for the stewardess. This lady was by no means handsome, or even comely. She bulged out of her uniform, the bristles on her legs attempting with some success to escape the confines of her stockings. She opened her mouth only to speak, which was just as well as stainless steel dominated her dentures: a living image of Colonel Kreb of James Bond fame. A polite request for a drink met with 'No! You drink only when you eat.' The dialogue thereafter was hardly edifying but in the fullness of time there arrived a plastic tray carrying peppered chicken and a small glass of 'Ukrainian white wine.' With a heavy residual thirst I asked for a second glass of wine.

'When you drink you eat'.

So I caused consternation by asking for another plate of peppered chicken and choked it down to win my reward.

For four hours we droned over the Sahara and I read many times a cheerful bulletin describing the benefits of life on a collective farm in Uzbekistan; and dreamed of water.

The Guinness Deep

In 1969 the Guinness brewery on the outskirts of Lagos faced a shortage of water. The shallow boreholes on which they depended were drawing on an aquifer progressively overused and abused by others. The shallowest aquifer drew in water from a stream where lorries washed down and in due course became richly laced with engine oil. It was common practice for a driller to place the filter screen against several sand aquifer layers so that water could enter the borehole from a shallow, polluted sand and seep into a deeper, clean sand. This cross-contamination ruined the whole shallow groundwater system. I was called in to advise and rapidly learned a lot about brewing. (It takes about four tonnes of water to make a tonne of Guinness.) Guinness from the Ikeja brewery is like no other in the world. The first 'run' of Guinness was accidentally made sweeter than the standard 'Liffey water' model. It was an immediate success, suiting the Nigerian palate. In drinking circles dominated by Nigerian alpha males, the dark colour of porter is associated with 'power', so that a black, sweet drink is doubly blessed. By contrast, when in a French tavern one orders a 'blonde under pressure', a pale lager appears and definitely not a stressed-out straw-haired lady.
I had long nursed a theory that a deeper, older aquifer lay under Ikeja, about 700 metres down, and said so. The chief engineer asked the odds of success and I gave him three to one on. So he sanctioned the considerable expense – this is an unusually great depth for water. Supervising the

drilling of a deep borehole in new terrain is stressful and as the drill churned deeper and deeper my nerves were in tatters. When the driller called for an urgent meeting I feared catastrophe but - eureka! He announced that the circulating drilling mud was steaming and bubbling. I told him the good news that we were in an aquifer and the less welcome news that the water was hot – the mud was conducting the heat away. The deeper the aquifer the hotter the water. In Ikeja what is called the 'geothermal gradient' is abnormally high due to the insulating effect of a thick soft shale that is like a blanket on top of the aquifer.

A thousand years ago a borehole was drilled in Artois in northern France from which flowed water under pressure. This first recorded flowing hole gave rise to the name artesian. The Guinness brewery has an artesian flow of hot water at 160°F. The brewery is on the flight path of incoming aircraft and a new landmark, a vast plume of steam, became known as 'Guinness Spa'.

The 'Guinness Deep' was at the time the deepest water borehole in west Africa and surely qualified for inclusion in the Guinness Book of Records.

Chapter 12 The Seventies

Food at the Garden of Eden Hotel was indescribably bad. Outside stood a wizened relic of a tree with a notice in English and Arabic: 'This is THE tree of knowledge'. This may be true but in the time of Adam and Eve at least the fruit was fresh.

Baghdad

In 1973 I was fortunately invited to work with a friendly consultancy. They had the job of sorting out the rural water supply organisation throughout Iraq. The project was needed as there was little if any structural plan. Our team had no problems on the technical side nor with our client, the World Health Organisation, who retained specialists to visit us and make sure we were highly motivated and relishing our work. We were indeed fortunate in having delightful souls to share our moments of enlightenment and grief. On the other hand we were enjoined to work harmoniously with the ministry team of Iraqis who were keenly conscious of their position and great tact was needed to maintain their co-operation.

This was long before the days of computers but typewriters, manual and antique, were provided for those with dexterity enough to use them. In the best consultants' tradition we generated vast reams of paper. After weeks of research and much deep thought I had produced a summary of groundwater occurrence throughout Iraq. Being young and naïve, I left the document on my desk over the weekend. The following Monday the whole thing was published verbatim in the national press, presented as the work of a government geologist unknown to me.

To alleviate office tedium we invented small ceremonies. At mid-morning, when the keen edge of our initiative was in danger of becoming dulled, our little team foregathered for the tea ceremony. The tea was horrible, the powdered milk was of the old lumpy variety, the cups were thick and grey white. But the conversation rose high above the mundane. The Japanese verse form, a triolet called a haiku, had been in the news and we vied among ourselves to throw off the most elegant, the most thoroughly and secretly rehearsed, the most completely spontaneous product. Our object was to condense in three short and witty lines a pithy commentary on our environmental limitations as we perceived them. In this we succeeded, in the process mystifying our Iraqi counterparts. Our management expert, Alan, created a haiku so allegorical, so full of poetic thought, that no-one had any idea what it meant. However, when invited to explain the plot he had to admit he had snatched phrases out of his subconscious mind and had no idea either.

Alan was a cheerful extrovert whose humour broke through despite a painful spinal condition. After he suffered a bad night he entertained us immensely by describing his night's agony. I believe the Germans call it schadenfreude but it cheered us when our ministerial colleagues were being particularly difficult. The corset he wore to render his life tolerable resembled a chunk of mediaeval armour and to wear it must have been as agonising as the back condition. For comfort it was sometimes worn outside his shirt, giving him the appearance of a pregnant armadillo. Alan was also a classicist with a bent for ancient Greek verse. However, his chief claim to fame was that his wife was the only lady toastmaster in the profession, with an incisive personality and a carrying voice. As this was in the early days of the Guinness Book of Records we could not verify the accuracy of this claim. Alan's domestic equilibrium must have been maintained by the armour protecting him from domestic threat without and the lumbar pain within.

Our team of rugged individualists was co-ordinated by a bluff Yorkshireman, who endured much in the process of maintaining harmony and diligence in the ranks while providing rational explanations for our more bizarre activities to the resident representative for the WHO. The only serious hiccup was occasioned by the appointment of a short-term legal expert to formulate water legislation. Much difficulty was encountered in finding someone suitable. Ultimately a retired high court judge from one of the ex-colonies was found and shipped in. Undeterred by his considerable age, he attempted unwelcome amorous advances to the secretarial staff. Our small hotel had a cramped and creaking lift that one morning unaccountably jammed between two floors. Ultimately it re-started and arrived at the ground floor, disgorging a furious and flustered young lady followed by the judge who, in high good humour, declaimed: 'Upon my soul, I declare I almost pinched her bottom.' After a fortnight of concentrated effort the judge announced he had formulated the penalties for non-payment of water charges, which penalties proved so draconian that the judge was invited to cut short his stay.

'Lord Robeen' at the court of the Graf von und zu Schwellisee

Hugo, a sturdy Swiss hydrogeologist, entered my life in 1973 as my opposite number from WHO. Life in Baghdad was comfortable and outside office hours there was time to look at life in the whole; we toured widely. Both born under the sign of Pisces, travel came naturally to us. We were able to visit the Marsh Arabs in the south; and not far away to the north, where the Euphrates and Tigris rivers join, the alleged location of the Garden of Eden. Near Baghdad are the ruined arch of Ctesiphon and the sites of Nineveh and Babylon. We visited the mountains and springs of southern Kurdistan and even further to the borders of Turkey and Russia and peeped across into Iran to watch tanks exercising on the dusty plain.

Hugo is a traveller of legendary proportions. With a detailed knowledge of airline routes, he would persuade gullible tourist agents to convert his issued ticket into one that was remarkably flexible. He once travelled back to Geneva from the Middle East via Anchorage, Alaska. For each adventure he chose a different ticket agency but one by one they rumbled him and he ran short of available shops. So he 'went legitimate' and unearthed strange and very ingenious deals. For a time in Brazil he was the Professor of Geology at Bahia. When his contract ended his savings in the soft local currency could not be taken home; so he bought a rubber plantation and enjoyed subsequent visits to Brazil to see his estate. He would buy a flexible ticket that gave him unlimited air travel within Brazil. Wisely, he timed his jaunts to the interior to coincide with mealtimes – lunch on the way out, dinner on the way back.

Hugo's ancestors came from a valley beyond Arosa in the Graubunden canton of Switzerland and he inherited an ancient farm high in the mountains. Dendrochronology showed that the logs for the walls were harvested in 1740. In the spring and summer the wild flowers in his pastures are a blaze of colour. In winter the snow lies deep and a piste passes his porch. The younger skiers used to try to leap over his roof, not always succeeding. In spring, as the ice melts, wild flowers appear in profusion: crocuses, then gentians, anemones, cowslips ('schlusselblume' – key flowers), harebells, azaleas, geraniums, violas and many more. One can stretch a season into a day by walking uphill (colder climate and later flowering) or downhill (earlier). The fauna, too, are delightful: crested tits, alpine choughs, snow buntings, red squirrels, marmots, ibex and chamois.

By some process I never understood he became the Graf von und zu Schwellisee, a medieval dukedom with an alleged ruined castle west of his home. It looked to me like a pile of rocks; but then, castles are just that only neater. In July 2006, Hugo held his annual court, which in former times involved a Swiss form of droit de seigneur – a component mercifully lapsed as Hugo is of modest physique. I was invited, though my function was not clear till I arrived, when it was revealed that I was to make a speech on behalf of 'the Queen of England'.

I worked long and hard to create a suitable Vice Regal address, which Hugo's long-suffering wife rendered into Swiss German. My dress was sober, a restrained stock and jacket of ancient cut. Hugo made a magnificent oration. His Grafin (an elegant blonde lady) then introduced 'Lord Robeen of Cornwall.' My speech, translated a sentence at a time, was received with undue rapture, possibly due to the influence of glasses of rugged Austrian red wine tapped from a barrel and widely circulated.

The substance was that the Queen of England was heavily occupied with affairs of state and with keeping her family in order (applause). Had she been able to attend she would have commended the Graftschaft on the gemlike quality of its subjects (more applause) that with a little polishing (laughter) would shine through the ages. And so on. An ovation followed and we tucked into the roast pork and spilled over into a keen wine appreciation coterie. Even the Lutheran faction relaxed. A sturdy citizen purred away with a camera and by chance I asked him later if a video would be made; 'nein nein' said he, 'the whole ceremony has gone out live on Swiss television.' I hear the Tower of London is quite comfortable nowadays.

The following morning Hugo and I strolled, languidly, down the slopes to our normal morning rendezvous at the Kaiser coffee house to find that I had achieved celebrity status overnight.

Hogmanay and Burns night in Baghdad

The social calendar in an expatriate's year is punctuated by tribal rituals which, enhanced by isolation, represent energised and often hazardous versions of the home-grown variety. For instance, a pig roast in a Muslim state needs to be executed with discretion while rugby played on an iron-hard pitch regularly attracts casualties.

Of all the northern tribes, the Scots feel most keenly the need to emphasise their identity in extravagant dress and gesture. For the Englishman a dinner jacket is the ultimate expression of national feeling. But the festivals of Hogmanay and Burns Night awaken, in the heart of every soul possessed of a dram of Scottish blood, the urge to resurrect from tin trunks the appropriate regalia. Kilt, plaid, a fierce sporran, hairy socks lined with a knobbly dirk to lacerate any surviving varicose veins, all redolent of camphor. December nights in Baghdad are cool but even so a dinner jacket or a gown is more comfortable, certainly more anonymous.

The institution of 'The Club' is one of the blessings exported by the British to remote parts and copied in dilute form by the French and Lebanese. The club is the automatic venue for expatriate functions of any magnitude. In Baghdad the New British Club filled the role. In The Bar (the sanctum sanctorum) on feral evenings male scions of empire sat more or less erect on uncomfortable stools, facing row upon row of tarnished trophies, club notices and bottles.

The Annual General Meeting of the New British Club was a solemn affair, presided over by an Iraqi judge.

My colleague Alan dragged me from my sick bed in the library of the New British Club to attend Burns night downstairs. It began gently enough with an issue of Athol Brose. This is a delightful blend of whisky, the water of life, with oatmeal, honey and cream. Alan assured me that a moderate quantity of Athol Brose would subdue the feverish bark that periodically and unpredictably escaped my fevered lungs. It did. After repeated prescriptions, the reason for the very small size of the glasses holding this exquisite nectar became apparent. Local anaesthesia was giving place to a more general numbness when the word went round that the haggis had arrived (flown in by courtesy of BOAC) and was shortly to be ceremonially processed in with full tribal honours.

We lined the broad hall beside the bar, the ladies forming the front rank, resplendent in tartans or pastel gowns. The gentlemen loomed in the shadows behind, clutching thimbles of nectar. I was somewhat overshadowed by a lady of Junoesque stature shrouded in coffee-coloured muslin following, I imagine, the principle that what you cannot hide you emphasise. However by craning my neck I could witness the procession.

In the lead marched two pipers hired from the Iraqi military pipe band. A mighty silver dish on which quivered a small haggis came next, borne aloft by the Acting Chieftain, the second secretary of the British Embassy, in his full splendour. The pipers droned to a halt. As their cheeks shrank back to normal one could detect an expression of wonder and disgust, tempered no doubt by the knowledge that they were being paid nine dinars each. The Acting Chieftain harangued the unfortunate haggis at length in a foreign tongue before ritually plunging into it his skean dhu.

Quite overcome by the magnitude of the occasion I took a deep breath. Catastrophically, this coincided with the urge to cough. Try as I might to contain it, a great vaporised jet of Athol Brose, lodged temporarily in my mouth, swirled from within and enveloped the outer layers of the large lady's chiffon. As I lurched forward, handkerchief at the ready, to apologise, Alan held me back, and whispering urgently 'Can't you see? it's the same colour as the muslin!' Thus was calamity avoided.

The Magic Carpet

The small hotel had its limitations but the food was plentiful and cheap, featuring large helpings of meat. The menu differentiated 'beef chop', 'sheep chop' and 'crumb chop', though we experienced some difficulty in distinguishing them on the plate. The waiter had been an orderly in the NCOs' mess when the British Army was in Baghdad. He spoke limited English with a strong cockney accent. His greeting was, invariably: "Salaam alaikum, 'ullo." The bedrooms were cramped and the beds unsuited to one suffering from lumbago. When a large, book-lined bedroom in the New British Club became free I was happy to move in and a priority was to acquire a floor covering. An early visit to the carpet bazaar was fruitful. Hostilities on the border with Iran had led to the expulsion of many unfortunate Iranians who had to leave behind most of their chattels, including many Baluchi rugs.

How, I hear you ask, does an elegant hand-made rug enter the priority list of the spartan traveller? Fellow sufferers from back pain will not ask, as they appreciate very well the virtues of a firm floor softened by a sleeping mat. By day the preoccupations of office work thrust pain into the background.

I have mentioned already that my colleague Alan suffered in the same way but more acutely. It was fated that we should have been booked to travel home on the same flight. Strapped to our baggage were our respective rugs, and at the customs desk these became an object of keen scrutiny. It appeared that we had no licence to export valuable antique rugs. Deeply affected by a spinal twinge, occasioned by a seizure in two adjacent tectonic plates in his corsetry, Alan was so patently in agony that even stony-hearted officialdom was moved to express concern. It was an 'outside day' and the workings of the steel plates caused some fascination. I was able to explain our infirmities and added for good measure that we carried with us our sleeping mats. Not only was our baggage chalked and cleared but the customs officials commanded Swissair to produce wheel chairs and we were processed to the aircraft in comfort and dignity.

Landing in Athens for fuel, we were gratified and impressed to discover that two wheelchairs with attendants awaited us at the foot of the gangway. Our progress through the drizzle towards the transit lounge was interrupted by the appearance in our path of a very large green, **iridescent** frog. It subsequently became known that this monster, escaped from a cargo aircraft, was an Argentinian tree frog. At the time, however, the dramatic potential of this phenomenon was too great to ignore. Imperiously bidding our minders to stop, we peered down through our blankets at the frog and the frog peered up at us.

'Aristophanes?' I whispered.

'Aristophanes indeed,' rejoined the urbane classicist and fixing the frog with stern eyes declaimed: 'Co-ax! Co-ax.'

The frog was either a very good actor or genuinely did not understand ancient Greek, for it responded not.

'This,' announced Alan, 'is not an Athenian frog,' and forthwith commanded our attendants to proceed.

The flight terminated at Zurich, where we asked peevishly the whereabouts of our wheel chairs. From the frosty response we gathered that we had been rumbled. A sick transit indeed.

By the waters of Babylon

The water of the Tigris is about as potable as Thames water in Victorian days before the great clean up. The city fathers of Baghdad ingeniously set up a dual supply, one set of pipes carrying cheap second class water from the river for irrigating and car washing, the other - more expensive - for domestic use.

Our work was concerned with much smaller village supplies, though nonetheless spectacular. Most rural water supplies are from springs and boreholes fed from local aquifers, with one important exception. Some 3,000 years ago the Persians invented the qanat system of collecting and transporting water from the hills down to the villages of the plain. In Iraq these devices are known as kehariz. The water collects in a tunnel draining a shallow aquifer in the hills and an extension of this tunnel forms a subterranean canal of great length. The water flows down the gradient of about one in a thousand for great distances. Every so often a shaft connects with the surface, originally so that the construction workers could see where they were going and could breathe and left for maintenance and ventilation. At the exit the water gushes out uncontrolled and supplies the community and gardens of fruit trees – citrus and dates. From an aircraft, the ventilation holes look like a vast mole run disappearing into the distance.

In Kurdistan the springs emerging from cavernous limestones are vast, pure and sparkling. (By contrast a very smelly hot spring associated with sulphurous oil residues at Hammam Ali near the Tigris is frequented for with its alleged curative properties by folk spectacular skin complaints.) Our excursion to Kurdistan was certainly one of the more interesting. From the Mesopotamian plain the road carried us northwards up to Erbil and an obligatory stop at the Rest House for an expensive tea. Erbil is the gateway to the highlands of Kurdistan. There is a Kiplingesque rest house there where I took afternoon tea. The waiter was a very superior person with a suit of tails, wing collar and white gloves. His manner was detached, almost distant, and he unbent only when I was rising to leave, sufficiently to tell me that perhaps I did not know that Agatha Christie stayed there while her husband was on the diplomatic staff in Baghdad and wrote one of her mysteries. I wonder which one.

Then onwards into the heart of Kurdistan and Ruwanduz. It was at this latter location that we encountered one of the surviving 'Meccano' bridges devised and built by our family friend Archie Hamilton, whom I knew as a 12-year-old and described in an earlier chapter.

Another time we travelled south to the confluence of the Tigris and

Euphrates rivers where we stayed at a dreadful place called the Garden of Eden Hotel. The food was indescribably bad and one of our party – none other than Hugo Buser - succumbed to food poisoning. Outside the hotel was a weary wizened relic of a tree, surrounded by a railing, with a notice in English and Arabic: 'This is THE tree of knowledge'. This may be true but in the time of Adam and Eve at least the fruit was fresh.

Leaving Hugo sedated but green and groaning, we set off to the edge of the Hor al Hammar where the marsh Arabs lived on rafts of reeds. The explorer Wilfred Thesiger lived with them for a year and gained their trust but from the way a group of them ran towards us brandishing knives I received a clear impression we were not welcome.

Arshak the genius of Baghdad

A hint to the traveller leaving for Baghdad: check that your certificate of smallpox vaccination is not about to expire. Quite disturbing to hear from a colleague that the incidence of viral hepatitis from infected vaccine was currently running at 40 per cent. The safest, hence the most expensive, clinic was chosen and at the appointed time a well-starched nurse took charge. From a tobacco tin, rust mottled and with vague unwholesome stains, a moderately clean needle was shaken out and given a brisk rub on the nurse's immaculate apron. The point scratched across and across the dribble of vaccine meandering down my upper arm and my soul was possessed of gruesome forebodings. This was merely the prelude to the serious business of certification. An interminable questionnaire was produced in Arabic with English sub-titles. This proved to be a precis of my personal history and aspirations and with the application of a little creativity took only half an hour to complete. Then, inevitably: 'You have the photos?'

I trudged off to the recommended photographer while the process was put on hold. An imposing shop front, a framed wedding group swathed in maroon velvet and the simple sign: 'Arshak, Photographer'.

'You are clearly a photographer of repute.' My ranging shot drew fire.

'A photographer indeed, of great repute; but much more than this, I am Arshak the Genius.'

Mr. Arshak expanded visibly to fill the little studio. 'My inventions have attracted the admiration of many.' Beneath beetling brows his eyes flashed and his impatient fingers sketched in the air.

He gestured me to a gilded studio throne where I lolled, feeling faintly decadent and sipping coffee while he expatiated on the applications of his genius. These, I learned, related mainly to aeronautics. Airport runways with roller coaster slopes at each end to assist take-off and landing. A silent aircraft cabin, the engine pods high above the fuselage, almost out of earshot. And so on. And for each, a framed acknowledgement from the patent office in London: 'Your application has been filed . . . .'

Hours later the business of taking my photograph was anticlimactic. The velvet drapes were produced and I was adjusted on the throne in heroic pose. Shrouded behind a mahogany box of great antiquity, Arshak the Genius operated the shutter. I left him in recession but calling the next day to collect the photographs I found he had regained his stature. Enjoined to secrecy, I heard about an invention freshly evolved from his overnight cranial activity, a concept so radical and imaginative that the world would scarcely be ready for it.

Thirty years on, the world is still not ready and I assume the invention is still under a cloak of secrecy.

Iran

The overpoweringly soporific effect of reading full accounts of my two professional visits to Iran would defeat the purpose of this narrative. So here are the bits I want to remember and perhaps some of the bits I wish I could forget. During long, dusty bumpy unforgettable journeys across this vast country I had excessive leisure to ponder the maxim that it is better to arrive than to travel uncomfortably.
First impressions of Iran, on my arrival at the airport in Teheran, were

confusing. My clients were represented by a delightful Englishman from the upper deck of Rio Tinto Zinc, a devout Catholic who was muttering something disconcerting about beads. The matter, which overshadowed the welcome, related to the fact that a charity repeatedly sent to him large consignments of home-made rosaries, held up in the customs department which demanded a heavy duty. If he did not pay up, the freight department demanded demurrage. He had repeatedly entreated the charity not to send any more, as the recipient organisation simply could not afford to pay up.

He cheered up when he saw that his car was still in the parking bay as it was commonplace for gangs to drive them away. He then recovered from the boot the hub caps and windscreen wipers (failure to take this precaution meant sending down to the souk next morning to buy them back).

The weekend was spent in enjoying the client's hospitality, visiting the snowy slopes outside the city and appreciating liberal quantities of caviar, the recognised source of which was a certain Colonel Caviar at the American Embassy. But it was piercingly cold and I looked forward to the flight south to Isfahan.

This delightful ancient Safavid capital was dominated by exquisite tiled domed mosques and an Elizabethan atmosphere. The caravanserai museum exuded an atmosphere akin to that of the Tudor court, with large ceramic vessels depicting gallant mounted knights. Apart from the weather, only marginally less cold than Teheran, a more pleasant place to dally could scarcely exist but ultimately our caravan was assembled. The road from Isfahan to the Great Central Desert was, like the curate's egg, good in parts. The poet who extolled the sweetness of riding forth to take the golden road to Samarkand clearly had not experienced the reality of a mid-winter journey even more uncomfortable than ours. Accompanied by two Geordie drillers, muffled against the cold in a short-wheelbase Land Rover, I was accorded the seat of honour beside the driver. This vehicle, designed by sadists for masochists, sported above the rudimentary instrument panel a stout steel bar to be gripped fiercely during eventful moments, of which there were many. Those in the back seat resorted to prayer. The floor, in close communion with the engine, effectively roasted our feet while the rest of the body froze.

In Bafq, a bleak settlement whose charm escaped me, stood a rest house known as a 'Point Four'. We had entered an area that on climate maps officially had zero rainfall throughout the year. Outside the rest house stood a Standard Vanguard saloon car while inside three intrepid British travellers were playing solo whist. The first words I heard were, 'Do you play bridge?' With lowered resistance and a desire to maintain harmony in this far-flung corner of the universe, I admitted that I did and the evening passed agreeably.

These folk, it transpired, were on their way towards the mysterious east and, in this supremely arid area, their progress was blocked by floods. When two weeks later we returned from the desert site the three stranded travellers without a word interrupted their game of solo to resume our bridge session.

In the Great Central Desert was a Rio Tinto Zinc mine run by a genial Australian. We arrived crunching on a bed of snow, which in a matter of days turned to a layer of ice draped over the gravel and soon evaporated showing a very dry surface below. On the far side of a vast shallow valley were dolomite cliffs, which the Australian assured me were syngenetic. This gave me great comfort and in my report this was the longest word, though it is only a posh way of saying that they were formed at the same time as the rock that enclosed them.

The atmosphere surrounding the strange assortment of European staff that gathered for meals in the mess was tenuously cordial due to the efforts of the syngenetic Australian, though periodically fragmented by the antics of his unhappy wife.

My brief was to find water of acceptable quality. In this I made minimal progress. Fluid intake in the mess was a free choice between brackish water from the mine and bottled dry ginger ale diluted with rum. By contrast the food, prepared by a Zoroastrian in clay ovens in the open, was exquisite.

The memorable event was a traverse on foot across the valley toward the smiling cliffs, tacking erratically between huge boulders and huddled in an overcoat. After four hours it seemed the cliffs were as distant and their smile had turned frosty so I returned in the waning daylight. The rest of the investigation was so unmemorable that I cannot recollect how it went.

The return journey was marked by irksome delays but in Isfahan I shed much of the weariness. Having missed the weekly flight to Teheran, I wandered again round the splendid mosques to revive my soul. The physical ennui was resolved in a Turkish style hairdresser's with hot scented towels, an elaborate haircut, a nasal swab dominated by eau de cologne and a prolonged shoulder massage. The total cost was 10 (old) pence.

Finally there was a 12-hour coach journey northwards through a long night, with stops at caravanserais with shishkebabs and hubble-bubble pipes. The piped music in the coach was an enchantment to other ears but not to mine. Following an interminable wailing recital a miracle: Beethoven! But a storm of indignation caused the driver hastily to switch to another wailing source.

A journey some years later was enlivened by two companions. Let me introduce them. On my right Tony Crossley, a Yorkshireman of modest physique, long since departed this earth, who is doubtless sitting on his chosen cloud of tobacco smoke discussing cement technology with the nearest saint. Always immaculately dressed, with a whole magazine of cuff links, and a lover of good claret and opera of the interminable sort, he was a trifle delicate for the harsh reality of traversing the wild Persian land.

On my left a burly Farsi (Zoroastrian), Dr. Rahim Neer, head of mineral resources in some Iranian ministry. Dr. Neer had enjoyed 12 years in Hamburg obtaining a high degree in some esoteric branch of mineral technology as well as a German wife. He was fluent in German and reasonably understandable in English. Though like Tony devoted to music, he was tone deaf and some misunderstandings were inescapable.

Our mission was to locate limestone deposits in Baluchistan, possibly the dustiest place on earth, where tectonic plates restlessly rub together and earthquakes are common. The Arabian tectonic plate is moving away at several centimetres a year and adjustments are inevitable. As one looks back from Chah Bahar on the Persian Gulf, the jagged slabs of mountain resembled a sliced loaf tilted over. Early in our journey south, three abreast in the cab of a vintage Land Rover, Tony was showing signs of tension. It may have been due to nervous exhaustion, attributable to the doctor's dashing driving style; or possibly to the vocal gems rendered by him in a droning monotone. It was a relief to stop and stretch our legs under the lee of a slumbering (but smoking) volcano to look at an alleged outcrop of limestone. Scattered over the land lay large bombs of volcanic ejecta that I assumed were ancient until I noticed that one boulder lay half on top of a crushed sapling. Dr. Neer was reassuring; there would be several minutes' warning of an eruption and he had considerately kept the engine running.

Chah Bahar has little to commend it apart from the seafood, which was divine. The Gulf coast is uncomfortably hot and humid in the summer, the air conditioners seldom worked and the mosquitoes enjoyed robust health. Life was made tolerable by the discovery that Tony and I shared an appreciation of Dave Allen jokes. One in particular aroused him to prolonged mirth, concerning a bird fancier, drunk in a bar, boasting of having crossed an eagle with a budgerigar. The result, he announced, was "a buggle, sixsh feet long (hic), with yellow feathers on its chest. It perches on a tree and bellows 'TWEET!' "

After a restless night we set out to climb a mountain called 'the twins', two peaks each capped by yellow tabular limestone. Dr. Neer explained that 'twins' is a transliteration from Sanskrit 'do brohdar' (two brothers). We also learned that he had organised camels to carry us up from the road. Beauty is in the eye of the beholder and these ships of the desert are distinctly an acquired taste: their deafening digestive acoustics come from deep within their being, their temper is uncertain and they made it obvious from the outset that they disliked climbing mountains. We chose to walk. The camel boy mounted and followed us, hauling the string of burping beasts with one hand. We found, when parched and weary at the peak, that the boy had used his free hand to dismantle the water cooler, had thrown away the ice cubes and unwittingly leaked the precious fluid.

The disgruntled party trudged down toward a hollow containing a green, scummy pond. The camels sniffed the air and raced off ahead and by the time we arrived were rolling in the muddy water. Fully clad, we found a corner remote from the frolic and lay down to soak. Tony was less cautious and slurped down a pint or two of what was by this time a semi-solid fully flavoured green soup.

Oozing and weary, we rode down the lower slopes. The accepted style is to lurch fore and aft in rhythm with the animal's plod. This kama sutra-like ploy was not for me and I sat sideways-on; this I commend to those who are unfortunate enough to rise to the command of a camel.

Next day Tony came down to breakfast immaculately dressed from the neck down with a kipper tie, fresh cuff links and onwards to gleaming black shoes. The effect was marred by the dull green hue of his face and internal rumblings reminiscent of those of our camels. For the entire length of the long, dusty drive north, with frequent comfort stops, he silently endured the singing of the ebullient Dr. Neer. A minor crisis arose when we were commanded to join in the chorus of a lengthy number which, try as we might, we were unable to identify. It turned out to be a chorus from My Fair Lady in German but our group effort was diminished by our inability to discern which verse was which.

On we drove through the hot, stiflingly humid scented poppy fields until we reached Iranshahr, the capital of Baluchistan. Touched with uncharacteristic compassion, our leader marched us into the Gendarmerie Club, a comfortable haunt of the privileged. We panted under fans, in leather lounge chairs, while Dr. Neer commanded food. 'Doctor Temple Ghazell, you will have six frriedeggs. Mister Crossley, four frriedeggs. And I will eat two frriedeggs.' Tony managed to haggle his portion down to two eggs but when the great dish of greasy, limp eggs arrived he went into a fairly solid decline. He choked down one egg and in desperation asked me in a whisper if I would eat the other. Being by then supersaturated I had only to glance at his face to agree; it had turned from dull green to a terminal grey. We almost managed the transfer but were caught in the act.

Calamity! 'Doctor Temple Ghazell, to take the egg of Mr. Crossley! You had only to ask! Garcon, four more frriedeggs for Doctor Temple Ghazell and two more for Mr. Crossley.'

Half an hour later, in a valiant effort to achieve internal equilibrium, I strode to and fro restlessly across the vast lounge, breathing deeply and arrived finally in front of a screened-off alcove. Curiosity aroused, I pulled away the curtain to reveal behind a glass panel a huge fierce-looking yellow bird. In excitement I stumbled back to Tony with the news. 'Tony, I've found a buggle!' 'Nonsense (hiccup), nonsense, there's no such thing. (Urrp)' But confronted with this creature he had to agree and immediately felt better. All would have been well but for the need to explain to Dr. Neer when he asked, 'Bliss, vot iss a buggle?'

We temporised at length with what appeared to be a reasonable explanation but the doctor was clearly troubled in mind. Hours later, slithering in the half dark through gravel along a particularly chunky road, he sought further and better particulars. Not only did we fail but the mental strain was such that, still arguing, he temporarily lost control of the wheel and we left the road entirely. The remainder of our long journey north passed in silence and in our final parting I detected a wary respect.

The Shah was deposed in 1979 and the peaceful co-existence of Farsi, Islamic and Christian communities crumbled. I suspect there was not much room for men such as Dr. Rahim Neer in the new order of things.

Chapter 13. A coup, a petite mademoiselle and a liberated parrot

'Did that burrd say what I thought that burrd said?'

The birth and youth of Water Surveys

By 1974 my freelance work had grown to an untidy volume and I decided to form a Nigerian company. Tony 'Hot-line' Hatfield, a friend and colleague, encouraged this notion and we set up a meeting in a Soho club. Tony enjoyed life in London. A guildsman of the Worshipful Company of Armourers and Braziers, and a potential Lord Mayor, his life was tragically ended by cancer. In his day, he was delightful company and apart from being a stay and support to the Players Theatre under the Charing Cross arches, and tasting wine in the City vaults, he spent long and happy evenings at the Tatty Bogle club. This subterranean watering hole lay round the corner from Carnaby Street in Soho and here our paths met whenever I passed through London. An intriguing feature of the Tatty Bogle was a stag's head with a cup hook on its nose. A curtain ring on the end of a long cord hung in front of it and long hours were spent in releasing the ring at the end of its swing so that it latched on to the hook.

One quiet evening was born, on a beer mat, the infant Water Surveys (Nigeria) Limited. Undisturbed but for the sonorous snoring of a bibulous Australian at the other end of the bar, we chose each word with care. 'Now for a logo.' said Hotline. 'You must have a logo and (nodding in the direction of the unconscious Aussie) – he's your man'. And so it proved. Gently woken, he asked a string of questions and, with a supply of beer mats, came up with a logo that stood up to the years ahead.

In those days my office was on the outskirts of humid Lagos, on the coast, where rainfall could be measured in feet rather than inches. In the earlier colonial days houses were built with broad, shady verandahs and the night breezes provided natural air conditioning. In the Fifties mediocre British architects produced in Nigeria a rash of housing more suited to northern Europe and air conditioning was a must for a good night's sleep. With independence came power to the politicians but not enough electric power. With multiple illegal connections to inadequate distribution networks and lack of maintenance to power stations, power cuts were frequent and prolonged. Drainage ditches, starved of attention, abounded in mosquito larvae and malaria flourished.

Almost a thousand miles of Nigeria spread northwards and away out there towards the desert edge lie the northern states. In the long dry season nights are cold and the days pleasantly cool. So, on a map of Nigeria I put crosses on all areas where we had worked. The 'centre of gravity' of these marks was in Bauchi, a small town overlooked by time and tide. Traditionally a source of slaves for the raiding fulani, it lies between the mighty emirate of Borno to the north east and the Jos plateau to the west.

With the help of friends I found a house in the Government Residential Area. An impoverished local government surveyor could not afford to complete building work so in return for a rent-free period I took it over. We put the finishing touches to it in sympathy with the happy-go-lucky style we inherited; there were few right angles. To enliven the stark white of the inside walls we created innovative murals. Selected married couples were invited to a party and the ladies were invited to stand in sequence between the kerosene pressure lamp and the walls; the silhouettes created were outlined with charcoal and artistically embellished with multicoloured paint

This was the beginning of a pleasant and fruitful decade. In contrast to the feverish bustle of Lagos, moving around the Government Residential Area was idyllic. Ten yards from the house we built a cool office in the hausa style, of circular mud walled buildings, thatched and linked. The trees we planted attracted many colourful bird species. The next house we built was beside a military grave where Major Price, of a Welsh border regiment, was laid to rest in 1916. His slate memorial was the focus of many carefree parties; we could truthfully aver that drinks were on the major.

Soon after we opened the office the quiet backwater of Bauchi was transformed when it became a new Federal State, hived off from the vast unwieldy North East State.

In those days a tolerant form of Islam prevailed. The northern half of the State was Muslim but the tribes in the Benue valley to the south were Christian. A practical consequence was that in those villages pigs led a good life, running free like the chickens, and the pork was delicious. At the end of a long week of field work one of the returning vehicles sometimes carried, in addition to mounds of geophysical kit, a hairy, odoriferous protesting pig. By Saturday morning the mighty beast would be on a spit turned gently by a somnolent office messenger temporarily promoted to the post of 'turnspit (acting)'. Under a shady tree, the roasting process became a spectator sport and advice was never lacking on the finer points of procedure offered by our panel of weekend thinkers. The turnspit was adjured to keep the charcoal bed from flaming by damping it down periodically. Not with water but with lager beer for added flavour. For obvious reasons the turnspit was a Muslim. If he thought it odd that from each freshly opened bottle of cold lager a libation should be poured he was too courteous to discuss this odd custom.

After eight hours, when the technical committee had been augmented by the first few guests, the mighty beast would be carried in state to a great wooden bench, and the black crust peeled off to reveal an expanse of steaming meat, so tender that it almost fell off the knife.

Islam was so relaxed and tolerant in those days that we could throw these parties without giving offence, though we tested the limits once when there was a longer than usual power failure and to keep the slaughtered pig from rotting we had to find temporary refrigeration somewhere. We drove fruitlessly, with the pig's head dangling over the tailboard of the pickup, from one darkened house to another in search of a friend with a generator. On one sharp corner we swung so sharply that the pig rolled alarmingly, its head lolling and leering to the dismay of some elderly citizens, one of whom was so upset that he fell off his bicycle.

To travel hopefully in Nigeria

On a Friday 13th (a lucky day for some) in 1976 I was working in our local office in Maiduguri. Early in the morning our landlord, Alhaji Ali Kotoko, called in for a routine chat. An entrepreneur of small stature but large influence, Ali was from a fishing tribe on the Logone river but his eyes were on higher things. He regularly visited London to indulge one of his hobbies, the collecting of swords. Maiduguri, the capital of the Borno empire of the Kanuri, lies south of Lake Chad and is influenced by the cultures of three major tribes, the dominant Kanuri, Arabs and Hausa. The Borno dynasty descended from Rabah, a leader in the army defeated at Omdurman, who led his rabble westwards to Lake Chad. They brought with them their chain mail that clad men and their horses and a tradition of sword flourishing.

Following the routine civilities Ali broke the news quite casually. The Nigerian head of state had been murdered and a coup was in full swing. 'Better not travel to Lagos till things quieten down.' Ali was a 'big alhaji', a 'heavy man' who could lift the phone and command a connection to anyone anywhere, even in the middle of a coup. He called later in the day to say, equally casually, 'It's finished, coup failed'. Murtula Mohammed was a popular head of state. His death in a hail of bullets provoked such outrage that the coup attempt never stood a chance.

Though the coup was finished, paralysis was only just getting under way and all internal flights were cancelled. An older and wiser man would have sat tight for a few days. However, I was obsessed with the need, as I saw it, to attend a meeting two days on down in Lagos to discuss with the chief of the Nigerian Army Engineers the wellfield supplying the Maiduguri cantonment.

Against the counsel of good friends I accepted a lift to Jos aboard a Land Rover of a certain age. Five hours' travel along a deserted road we drove, into a silent town to the Hill Station hotel. A relaxed sort of curfew had been set up. So far north, far from the centre of things, one coup was much like another and no one was seriously concerned. Equally, no one much wanted to travel south and an evening reconnaissance drew blank after blank.

The restaurant was deserted but for a rotund Frenchman and his petite amie, a handsome lady, also French but a deal younger than he was. They were delighted to share their grief with me. A romantic weekend to look back on but a possibly hazardous journey back to Lagos lay ahead. And – pouf! – 'e 'ad 'ired a car, but – pouf! – she did not care for 'is driving and as for passing the road blocks. . . . . and of course she did not want to stay in Jos, she would be missed in Lagos . . . . and so on. My offer to share the costs and the driving was rapturously received.

Early next day we set off down the winding road among the granite hills of the Jos Plateau to the Kaduna Plain; no road blocks on the way and not a soul to be seen. Then through Sabon Birnin Gware, the fairly new capital of the Gware tribe, and southwards between long granite ridges to Kontagora, seat of the wicked Emir of Kotangora in days long gone. And still no sign of life. Indeed we enjoyed the absence of aggressive mammy wagons as we travelled across a long stretch of sandy, waterless bush, emptied long ago by the raiding parties of the wicked Emir. In 1954 I had sited water boreholes but tsetse fly and sleeping sickness had outlived the Emir and the people had not come back. At Mokwa on the edge of Nupeland the first road block was cursory and I drove on cheerfully while in the back the Frenchman comforted his petit chat.

At Jebba the Niger river was spanned by the only bridge for hundreds of miles. Hearts sank when in the dusk we saw far ahead a long, long line of stationary traffic. After a trudge to the head of the queue I located an army patrol commanded by an uncompromising officer barring all movement south. By his facial scars the officer was recognisably a Kanuri from Borno, good-hearted and prepared to let us pass when he found that my objective concerned water in Maiduguri.

As it grew dusk we optimistically planned to reach Ilorin and stay over at the pleasant state hotel. Alas the roadblock patrol outside Ilorin was from the local cantonment, commanded by a relative of the popular military governor of Ilorin – and that governor had been shot by the coup plotters. The patrol captain was in no mood to let anyone pass. Equally, petit chat was in no mood to spend the night in the mosquito-ridden swamp that surrounded us. With the enthusiastic help of her patron she wriggled some loose car cushions under her clothes and waddled off to the head of the queue to explain to the officer that she was enceinte and preferred to give birth in the hotel not far ahead. She returned very soon thereafter; apparently the officer was not sympatique, not a family man and *definitely* not a gentleman. There was more to it than that and she was reluctant to discuss the matter but she had retained her dignity and the car cushions. By hinting that petit chat had her patron's comfortable paunch to languish on, I commandeered a car cushion and I was able to enrich my knowledge of gallic epithets until petit chat eventually nodded off in her patron's arms. So until dawn, huddled in the car, we endured the ravenous mosquitoes.

At dawn we were waved through and after a good hotel breakfast set off for Lagos where we parted company. It was clear that for petit chat the end of the romance coincided with the end of the journey. A subdued patron left me no address and did not – as promised - send me a bill for my share of the car hire; maybe he wanted to forget the whole thing.

And to arrive

Murtala Mohammed murdered in a failed coup, a popular leader and an honest man who might have dragged Nigeria up out of the mud. The hunt was on for the killer, the frontier posts and airports were closed and a dusk to dawn curfew was strictly maintained.

So there we were, three resident expatriates, a systems engineer, a geologist and a driller, chained by the curfew in a great barn of a house, bored with each other's company. The owner was overdue to return from leave and his parrot, inevitably named Polly, reminded us incessantly that he (or she) was pretty. After a few long evenings tempers became frayed and trivial arguments arose, against a background of inanities from Polly.

Salvation came unexpectedly when an erudite dispute erupted over the precise wording of one line of one verse of a ballad of great antiquity that chronicled the adventures of a spirited lady, one Eskimo Nell. A positive spirit of inquiry bubbled up and a few long evenings later the manuscript of a critical edition of this opus was completed. Marginal comments, rubrics and footnotes abounded and a great wave of pre-publication euphoria swept over us.

But like a sore tooth, the background problem of Polly nagged on. We were tempted to shroud the poor creature under a cloth but sought a kinder option. After much thought a positive action plan congealed. Quite simply this bird's vocabulary must be enlarged, in a style more in keeping with the Long John Silver image we planned for it. The systems engineer embarked on repetitive discourse to which the bird listened with great patience but reverted to the default mode during each break for refreshment. As a last resort a loop of recording tape was assembled and left running by Polly's cage during daylight working hours.

It worked! My word how it worked. After two days the engineer breezed in, turned off the tape and was immediately enjoined by Polly to leave forthwith. Or words to that effect. Biblical scholars are referred to Genesis Ch.1 verse 28. I came on the scene a little later when the engineer, in a state of glazed shock, was attempting with total lack of success to de-program this brainwashed bird. Liberated from inhibitions, Polly gave of his or her best, hushed only by resort to artificial darkness.

Still, life must go on we mused and time, the Great Healer, was invoked. Until one day the airport opened and with it the moment of truth. What, we feverishly asked each other, is Billy going to say! Billy being the gentle, fond and long absent owner. Consternation was followed by industry as we took turns, deputising for a broken tape recorder, putting great and positive effort into reinstating the harmless phrases that had so annoyed us. Alas, to no avail. A totally emancipated Polly chanted, often to an empty house.

Though it would have been prudent to be absent on urgent business when Billy returned, an unwholesome curiosity prevailed on us. Billy, a cheerful Scot, was greeted with a cold lager and held in prolonged conversation until, inevitably:

'Where's Polly?'

'Oh, she's fine.'

'I dinna see her.'

'She's under the stairs, resting.'

'What's the cloth doing over her cage?'

'Well, she has an eye condition, and we felt . . . . '

'Havers!' And off came the cloth.

'**** ****!'

'Did that burrd say what I thought that burrd said?'

Then explanations, which fell rather flat. What had seemed a good idea at the time now seemed a trifle daft. There was a long silence while Billy sipped his beer and reflected on a troublesome possibility. Then, in mournful tones: 'What's Alice going to say?'

Alice was due to join her man two weeks later and Bill spent long, reproachful hours striving to tidy up Polly's conversation. But Polly had tasted liberation, and would have none of it. The day approached and Billy lapsed into a strange state, muttering his speech of welcome. He reluctantly accepted our offer of support so that Alice – a lovely though strong-minded lady – was agreeably surprised at the size and loquacity of her reception. But inevitably the moment came:

'Billy, where's Polly?'

'Well, you see . . . . she's, well she's under the stairs.'

After some shuffling: 'What's that cloth doing over her cage?'

'Well, it's the strong light, Alice...'

'Ridiculous!' And off came the cloth.

'**** *****!'

A long, long silence. Then: 'Billy, did that burrd say what I thought that burrd said?'

It was many weeks before strong emotions subsided and diplomatic relations could be resumed. As for Polly she aged but not gracefully and, full of years, passed away. In her little corner of pet's paradise she (or he) is no doubt entertaining new arrivals with his (or her) wit and wisdom. And forgotten on some dusty shelf – possibly in the Bodleian - lies a neglected masterpiece.

Chapter 14. Chief of all leopards and mighty leader

The true beauty of our predicament dawned when the pilot, skimming the trees, asked for directions to Lisala . . . . 'I'm a stranger here myself' does not easily translate

Zaire 1976

Tsessebe Mobutu had a dream. In his dream water flowed from the ground and by happy coincidence irrigated his kitchen garden. Troubled in his mind he called together his wise men and soothsayers and commanded them to retire to divine the meaning of this dream. The wise men and soothsayers had achieved their status by wisdom and prudence and in selecting the most politically sooth to say. So it was, therefore, that after casting the bones and murmuring secretly among themselves they returned to their mighty leader and made obeisance. Then the oldest and wisest soothsayer spoke: 'Mighty leader, chief of leopards and leader of the Zaire empire, it must be that your kitchen garden will flourish but only if copious water flows upon it. An omnivorously nourished mighty leader may thus lead our nation on to even greater glory.'

In high good humour the mighty leader bade them keep their own counsel and sent them away; then summoned forth one Citizen Mwanyenge, the Minister for Agriculture and of all growing things, and gave tongue. 'Citizen Mwanyenge, Minister for Agriculture, graduate of a seat of learning in a far land, it has been revealed to me that copious water must be made to flow upon my potager. See thou to it.'

In those days it was the custom, indeed it was prudent, to obey the wishes of Tsessebe Mobutu, chief of all leopards and mighty leader of the empire. So Citizen Mwanyenge pondered in his heart and browsed his archive. He summoned his Chef de Protocol, a medium sized, affable Belgian and charged him to find one Hazell and cause him to be brought from a far land, with his black juju box.

So it was that I was invited to visit Gbado Lite, Mobutu's birthplace, where lay his summer palace. I was not greatly charmed by the prospect of trekking to a remote village 1200 kilometres from the capital and perilously near the border with the Central African Republic. If Zaire were the Heart of Darkness, Central African Republic would be the shadow of that heart. Not long before a British journalist rash enough to write critically of the leader of that land was thrown into a dungeon. So I tried to discourage the invitation, stipulating half my fee and a first class return ticket were to be up front. When an economy class ticket arrived I returned it with a regretful note and thought no more about it. Within weeks arrived a first class ticket. So I made my will (again) and left for Kinshasa. What followed was comedy so rich as to be barely digestible.

All went well as far as Paris, where the connecting flight had been cancelled. I arrived in Kinshasa on the next available flight late on the eve of a public holiday, unheralded and unannounced, and went to ground in the Hotel Regina. The next day, having located the deserted Ministry of Agriculture, the Chef de Protocol with his assistant and deputy assistant, with much hand wringing, arrived to say how desolated they were; that a suite in the Intercontinental Hotel had been held for me. And so we set forth to claim it. At Reception a deeply regretful manager was desolated to inform us that because of my non-arrival, the suite had been taken.

Then said the Chef de Protocol: 'I wish immediately to telephone Citizen Mwanyenge.'

'Not Citizen Mwanyenge! Patience, I entreat.'

And it transpired that the bridal suite would shortly be free if I would care to take it. 'Very shortly, no doubt' said the Chef, and within 10 minutes a rather flustered, dishevelled bride and groom were led away.

A glass of champagne later, we repaired to the office of Citizen Mwanyenge, a charming man. He was Minister because after independence he was the only black man with an agricultural degree. How, I mused, could so urbane a gentleman strike terror into the hearts of so many. The Minister decreed that next day, my fatigue ameliorated by rest, the Chef would fly with me to Gbadolite. An early start, said he, before the storms and very early next morning we drove to the airport where a Hercules transport was being loaded with bags of cement.

For two hours we stood on the tarmac diverted only by the comings and goings of highly decorated military men in individualistic uniforms. Each greeted us gravely, furtively eyed the aircraft and scuttled away. Long after it was clear that no more cement could be forced into the cargo bay nothing much happened until a jeep bustled up and an elegant Egyptian pilot, smoking a cigarette in a long holder, strolled to the Hercules, kicked one of the tyres, barked 'Remove one ton of cement', and drove off. An hour later, he reappeared, called to the navigator demanding a weather report.

'Dull and dry, excellency.'

'Attend to your radar scanner. Is there not a mighty storm coming?'

'No, excellency.'

We all climbed aboard and taxied to the take-off point, when a solitary drop of rain landed on the windscreen.

'As I predicted - a mighty storm. Gentleman, we leave tomorrow.'

So, back into town. At the Intercontinental, the Manager was desolated, but . . . ! The Chef had only started to say: 'Your telephone . . . when the Manager discovered that there was after all a suite available.

Another day, and with no sign of rain we all set off, sluggishly because we were overloaded - the Chef and I with the previous evening's champagne, and the aircraft with cement. But after hours of droning first along the Zaire river, so wide that the banks were out of sight, then over drab green forest, we crossed the Zaire river at Lisala and soon touched down at Gbado Lite.

There are in fact two settlements: the village where Mobutu was born and – at a discrete distance - a pre-fabricated township made up of bits flown in from Europe. It includes a cathedral, many rows of houses, a gendarmerie and a very smart hotel. The hotel had been visited by General de Gaulle, no less, and was appointed accordingly. The Chef and his entourage escorted me to my suite and retired to their rooms to assuage our fatigue with rest. It became clear the Chef and entourage were in no hurry to return to Kinshasa and at dinner the reason was revealed. As I recall, we started with caviar, quails' eggs, then an escalope with salad, a sorbet . . .and so on. And the wines were quite superb.

Next day our little party visited the Palace. The walls were punctuated with life-sized silver leopards; the gardens were superb; and the potager would not have been out of place in the grounds of a Loire chateau.

One can become accustomed to enforced luxury and any lingering perceived need for haste soon evaporated. No stone was left unturned during the brief periods between meals and deep thought dominated the evenings. Ultimately, borehole sites were pegged among the asparagus beds of the potager, and a message was sent to Citizen Mwanyenge in Kinshasa that the field work was finished.

A day or so later, on a Saturday, a light aircraft arrived. The Belgian pilot was quite desolated at my preparations to leave that day. It was much too late and he was fatigued. Besides, he had his reputation as a gourmet to maintain. So there we languished, wistfully sipping champagne (as the poet sang) until his stamina was sufficiently recruited. Sunday brought a cloud base at about 200 metres and the pilot thought long and hard before taking off. He would need to land to refuel at Lisala 24 kilometres away on the Zaire river. But the true beauty of our predicament dawned when the pilot, skimming the trees to keep in sight of the ground, asked for directions to Lisala. His direction-finding gadgetry was playing up and he hoped my local knowledge would come into play. A fairly terse exchange of views followed. 'I'm a stranger here myself,' does not easily translate. Fortunately I carried a geological map showing a strongly lineated gneiss belt and we navigated southwards by structure and lithology.

We landed at Lisala airstrip with tanks almost empty under clearing skies. A sleepy controller, moderately desolated, told us that the fuel tanker came weekly, on Fridays. Another 24 kilometres further south an oil palm research station had a few drums stored. And he resumed his slumbers. We took off gingerly and economically and headed for the smoke of the factory chimney, landing with dry tanks, and parked by a corrugated iron shed, some fuel drums and an excitable Belgian aviator performing a little dance of welcome. This worthy had been stranded for a week with engine trouble; not only did he need a lift to Kinshasa but he knew the way!

But first, to Sunday lunch. We trailed through the oil palms to the research manager's timber house, tree-shaded and verandahed. In the kitchen an imminent palm oil stew seethed and bubbled. Those familiar with 'palm oil chop' appreciate that one does not treat the occasion lightly. In west and central Africa this international cultural event has long held cult status. As on the deep plates the red gold of the sauce laps against the receding islands of meat, yam, occra and the score or so 'side dishes', conversation falters, then dies. Much later the survivors, rumbling gently, subside into long chairs for deep meditation.

Ultimately and glowing with goodwill our little party, with replenished fuel tanks, sped southwards. Our new navigator, clutching his faulty carburettor, woke intermittently to keep us on track. In the dusk we reached Kinshasa to an anxious committee of protocol. At the Intercontinental Hotel the manager, by now well alert to the priorities, needed no prompting; there was only a brief checking-in delay while some unfortunate was evicted.

Debriefing at the Ministry was relaxed and chatty; only a hint of desolation when I revealed my plan to travel that day back to the rigours of Europe. At the airport that evening the entire protocol contingent escorted me to the check-in, somewhat late. The news that the Brussels flight was closed and ready to board invoked a procedure that had become familiar. The station officer was summoned and was desolated; after some time the telephone routine was invoked, desolation gave place to resignation, more paper work filed until with full escort I was marched to the flight. In first class splendour I was insulated from some ill-bred comments made back in the steerage compartment (though only after we had left Zaire airspace); unreasonable, one felt; after all, the aircraft had been delayed for little more than an hour.

In Brussels the aircraft was led to a remote corner, near what proved to be quarantine huts. Unknown to us all, we were the first aircraft to arrive from Zaire following the eruption of the Great Green Monkey Disease Scare, linked to lassa fever and later to the ebola virus. A team of sinister looking masked medics in (appropriately) green gowns boarded, and individually we had our temperatures taken and filled in forms of great complexity. Ultimately we were released and I sought a transfer to London.

At Heathrow a chalked notice at the disembarkation point asked that any passengers recently arrived from Zaire should report to the Port Health Office. Having trailed through immigration and customs, with time to spare before the next bus and being young and naïve, I asked the way to the Port Health Office. Near the departure lounge it lay and, unchallenged, I hefted my suitcase back through customs and immigration to the departure lounge. In those spacious days security was minimal. The sole presence in the Port Health Office was a nurse with strong Joyce Grenfell tendencies, who gushed that I was the first person to visit for days. A form was filled in, I assured the lady that I was not consciously suffering from Green Monkey Disease, and with expressions of mutual regard we parted.

And so to the bosom of my family.

Some tranquil days later came an irate telephone call. 'County Health, Truro, here. You arrived from Zaire; you reported to the Port Health Office. I have now to come and check your temperature every blasted day for a fortnight.' Luckily, during his maiden visit we found that we had African friends in common; my tentative olive branch was that I visit my local doctor every morning for a temperature check, he would then report to Truro the onset of any alarming symptoms. A subsequent deal with my doctor was that I take my own temperature and report to him, together with any of those said symptoms.

'Treasure Island' concludes thus: 'Neither oxen nor wain ropes would drag me back . . . . ' Well, Zaire was at that time more Lewis Carroll than Stevenson, and I would go willingly.

Turkana Basin

Lying at the north end of Kenya, Lake Turkana is long - about 200km - and narrow. The drainage basin extends to the north for about another 100km in Ethiopia. In common with much of the east African rift, the basin is littered with volcanoes and unstable fault lines.

In 1977 when the relationship between governments of Ethiopia and Kenya was frosty, someone hit upon a scheme to keep them talking to each other. A study of the Turkana basin, which occupies parts of both countries would, they reasoned, provide a harmonious basis for co-operation. Earlier epochs had been covered by Professor Leakey; the contemporary scene would now be revealed and vast plans submitted. The Turkana people must be among the toughest humans on earth, surviving where life is very tough indeed. Quite how a well-meaning collection of experts could improve on their lifestyle was not clear.

So I joined a high-powered team enjoined to study and report on every aspect of life in that remote corner and to put things right. A cattle man, a tourism expert, three bird specialists (including an academic expert on swans), a water finder, an agronomist, a fisheries expert and so on. Between us, we knew it all.

We started off in Kenya where the government departments were less than thrilled. We were not the first team of experts to visit Kenya. A safari firm was engaged to drive us around in three vehicles – two Land Rovers and a Suzuki jeep, laden with bundles of camping gear. There were no problems as far as Marsabit. Then the first of many punctures revealed that no puncture outfits were provided and that the spare wheels were in a sorry state. We limped to the Chalbi desert and beneath thorn trees on the edge of the desert flatland we munched packed lunches in cardboard boxes supplied by the Marsabit safari lodge. A hundred yards away a small nervous family group watched in wonder. We tidied up to leave and I gathered the cardboard cartons and wedged them into a tree for these shy warriors to salvage. The swan expert took me severely to task; all rubbish must be burnt. And burnt the boxes were, while the locals folk drifted away in disgust.

This bit of flat desert has little vegetation. The rare rain showers fall on the slopes to the east, the groundwater migrates down the slope through a basalt dyke, on its way leaching soda from cavities filled with a mixture of white crystalline salts. So when it reaches the flat sands it is concentrated by evaporation to a ghastly groundwater heavy with soda. Well water used by the local folk was barely drinkable. At first sight the solution seemed appeared to be simple. Sink boreholes uphill of the dyke before the young groundwater becomes vitiated and pipe it down to standpipes on the flat. But the consequences would be that the nomadic cattle folk would settle by the taps, the cattle would eat all the sparse vegetation and would die - not of thirst but of starvation - in the midst of plenty of water. The pastoral community would thus become dependent on charity to survive. This is a prime example of the perils of interfering with a precarious equilibrium in a marginal environment.

The next stop was to visit a mission settlement run by an Italian priest with the help of nuns. Here was good groundwater and wind pumps to lift it; and a settled community in the situation we had discussed some hours earlier. Their livestock were all gone and the people depended on handouts from mission charities. The children asked for pens and writing paper and a supply of these would probably have done as much good as all our ultimate project recommendations. The overworked priest gave up two hours of his working day to answer our many questions. When conversation faltered the team leader sidled up to me and said 'You ask him.'

'Ask him what?'

'If he can lend us a puncture outfit.'

'Why me?'

'Well, you're a Catholic.'

There's logic for you! So I nervously put the question. The priest took a long, deep breath. 'You people!' he spat out. 'You have come to solve the problems of these tough, resourceful people and you can't mend your own tyres!'

We reached the southern end of the lake, where the bird experts had a wonderful time, and we visited various projects, commercial and charitable. The next stage was to visit Ethiopia but due to a conflict – I forget who was fighting whom – we could not continue northwards but had to return to Nairobi and fly to Addis Ababa. So, south again, this time through the territory of the Samburu tribe. Their hairstyle is striking: mud is plastered like a skull cap and lasts, I was informed, for many weeks without topping up. Rather like the nest of a song thrush. Another endearing personal ornament that the Turkana also sported were coloured leather wristbands that could be popped open to reveal a row of razor blades in case some enemy needed discouraging with a swift swipe.

We were by this time on a safari route, so took tea on a café veranda in North Horr and watched the local folk at work. In the dry river bed they made a living by panning for crystals – garnet, tourmaline, beryl, corundum – and selling them to tourists such as us. By this time I was travelling with the fisheries expert in the little Suzuki jeep while the rest of the team rolled along more ponderously in the chauffeur-driven Land Rovers. Our scientific observations on ostriches were extra to our planned programme. We were able to pace them across open country and proved that they could sustain a speed of 45 miles an hour, after which the Suzuki became wary of hidden tree stumps.

From Nairobi we flew to Addis Ababa and repeated the routine of going round government offices; this time with a difference. We were welcomed and enjoyed useful dialogue with our opposite numbers. In due course our little convoy set off south. Echoes of the war hung around with food shortages in Addis. Because of a continuing ban on shooting no one carried a gun and in the open country wild creatures abounded. Those tiny antelope called dik dik, about the size of large rabbits, did not run away but stood lazily to watch our spluttering convoy pass.

The Omo river follows the rift valley, where the crust is thin; and glassy, steaming volcanic mounds abound. Hot springs feed the lakes at Arba Minch and in the warm water huge Nile perch multiplied. Here the local tribesmen are fierce; youths who wished to marry were obliged by custom to mutilate strangers and nail the trophies to their door as proof of manhood. Until this was explained to us we puzzled over why hunched-up travellers scampered furtively, at considerable speed, across this territory. An impressive bird peculiar to this area is the thick-billed raven, a huge pied creature that croaked deafeningly.

On southwards down an empty road (fuel was rationed and we had special treatment) to visit a village overlooking the rift. Unlike the big rift valleys further south and west, the Omo river valley is narrow, barely a kilometre wide. It was an idle time of year; the harvest was in and every able-bodied male lounged in the shade. In a big pile, rough surfaced spherical lumps about five inches in diameter and suspended from palm fronds lay gathering dust. They were too heavy to be elephant dung and my counterpart struggled to tell me what they were. They smell good if you burn them. Light dawned – this was raw incense. In peaceful times it was collected regularly from the desert acacia, taken to Addis Ababa market and exported. For a few coins I bought a few kilos and, 30 years on, I still add a few shavings to my bonfires, bringing fragrance to our valley.

My final useful contribution to the expedition now came up. We had reached a proposed dam site, almost where the valley widened near Lake Turkana. On the other side where the western abutment of the dam was planned, a raw cliff several metres high, ran along the contour and parallel to our road. Was this a new road? I asked. No, this was the trace of a recent earth movement and the valley floor had dropped on that side. This is a common feature in the rift, where after many millions of years the earth movements have still not petered out. So it was necessary to point out tactfully to my counterpart that it was not a good idea to build a dam where the ground was liable to move up and down. Yet, in the year of grace 2010 plans were again afoot to build the dam.

Our fuel tanks were running low and with no fuel supplies ahead we prudently turned back. At the first fuel station we would have to wait long for the attendant to appear. Frantic activity such as ours they were not accustomed to. This was an excellent opportunity to commission my new watch. An elaborate affair, it was bought at a reasonable price from a street peddler in Lagos who then proposed to sell me the operating instructions. Pride forbade me to pay up. Four different knobs could be pushed, each several different times, and ultimately this wonderful instrument would act as an early-day personal organiser. Eight highly intelligent experts, perforce immobilised, wrestled for four hours with this conundrum and made no headway whatever. Whether a Turkana warrior could have done better I never discovered.

Benin Republic, 1978

In the Seventies the Republic of Benin was nominally a Marxist state and at the approaches to the capital Cotonou banners strung across the road read (in French) 'We are true servants of the republic'. I asked the taxi driver if he was a true servant of the republic. His mirth so overcame him that (thankfully) he had to slow down. 'Jamais de la vie!' he cried, joyfully punctuating each word by a blast on his horn. Benin is a long, thin state bordered by Nigeria to the east and Togo to the west. Cotonou is a delightful little town and overlooking the harbour a little hotel had a shaded veranda. In the evening a refreshing breeze blew from the sea and the lager tasted good. A Russian naval vessel docked whose captain stepped ashore and strode magnificently into the town; a humble rating followed carrying the captain's briefcase. At precisely six o'clock the national anthem was relayed through loudspeakers and we all stood while the national flag was hauled down. By a little market square labelled 'les halles' an open-air restaurant served delightful fish dishes. A bouillabaisse I had there was extremely cheap and extremely good.

Kath and I were on our way to Pobe, a little to the north near the Nigerian border. There, Tony Preston was supervising some drilling for a cement factory. I had met Tony in London where he was 'between jobs' at the end of a contract in South Africa. He had reached the final of the Daily Mirror darts competition and was in a nervous, expectant mood. He agreed to take what could be a temporary fill-in job with the possibility that if I needed another man in Nigeria he would come across when the drilling was finished.

Outside the oil industry at that time good drillers in Britain were scarce - usually mechanics who had shown an interest in making holes in the ground. There was no formal training and apprenticeships were unknown. If a driller was needed the employer sent down to the Labour Exchange. It was therefore a revelation to meet in Pobe a Danish 'drillmaster' who held his job with pride, a member of an elite class of trained drillers in Denmark. He began each day with a generous swig from a flask of aquavit, reserving his Carlsberg intake for the evenings. And he drilled excellent holes.

Tony had been primed to obtain a new passport before leaving Britain as his existing one had Republic of South Africa stamp on it - then anathema to states in West Africa. He came to Benin with a party of Danes who enjoyed VIP status as non-colonial powers but for some reason, maybe Yorkshire thrift, Tony used his old passport on entry.

When the job was done and it was time to leave Tony drove down blithely to Cotonou to have an exit visa from the Salle de Police stamped on his new passport. Inevitably, it was discovered that his entry stamp was in his old passport which also had an RSA stamp in it. Gallic style logic kicked in. It was heavily illegal to enter Benin on a passport with an RSA stamp in it. So as for official purposes he had not entered Benin, he could not leave it. Dejectedly, he walked over to the Bureau des Mines where the chief geologist undertook to go over and 'fix' it. He came back grey with terror. There had been a big blitz from on high and heads could roll. So back went Tony to ask the police chief what to do. It is simple, said he. Pobe is 12 kilometres from the border, within walking distance. 'So, naturally, one walks.' He walked out of Benin along a smugglers' path to Ilaro on the Nigerian side then took a taxi to Lagos. He lacked an entry stamp on his fine new passport, but we had a retained 'Mister Fixit' who made a little financial transaction in the immigration office and the problem was solved. Tony boarded a long distance bus for the 700-mile journey to Bauchi and found his way to my office. 'No problems?' I asked. 'Nothing serious' he replied. When later I had the full story it was obvious that I must sign him up. He became a good friend and colleague and, more than 30 years later, he still is and flies the company flag in Botswana.

Somalia 1978

A visit to southern Somalia was meant to focus on a field programme in Baidoa, on the Juba River, to look at raw materials for cement making. In the event it comprised an extended stay in the capital, Mogadishu, and a brief venture into the interior. The Italians had ruled the territory so firmly that the stronger rival clans had no chance to fight over control of the weaker. When the Italians left an uneasy peace prevailed, with a stagnant economy and a remarkably inefficient bureaucratic government centralised in Mogadishu.

On arrival it soon became plain that it was going to take an age to obtain the necessary permissions to travel - and that my hotel, the only one habitable, was in a shaky state of repair.

The Croce del Sud (aka the Southern Cross or to weary travellers the sweaty crotch) had about 100 shabby marble clad rooms on three floors built round a once-magnificent swimming pool. My air conditioner did not work but the obliging desk man lent me all the master keys so that if I found one operational AC in the building I could move in. Needless to say there was none. It was high summer and the theory that mosquitoes did not exist more than 20 metres above ground level proved invalid. The scummy swimming pool boasted such a rich fish population that I saw an osprey diving in for food.

However, enforced idleness during the day was filled pleasantly enough by the comfort of the Anglo American beach club. This was a large wooden structure open to the breeze from the sea, with comfortable chairs and facilities for bridge and chess. The beach led down to limestone reefs with long pools for bathing safe from sharks. A small restaurant served fresh fish and seafood. Fresh it certainly was, carried in when ordered from holding cages in one of the pools. A favourite lunch was lobster or crayfish followed by Somali style flatfish, smeared with a mild curry sauce. Following a routine daily visit to a Ministry, to receive a routine regret for the delay in issuing a permit, I slid easily into a gentle life of leisure.

I received frequent invitations to spend evenings in the British Embassy compound, where the staff welcomed a fresh face. The ambassador and I met in his office for a briefing. He was the very model of an ambassador and contrived to wear his khaki tunic, complete with cloth buttons and what are known as 'admin' shorts and socks, with great style and authority. Pleasant though life was in Mogadishu, there came the day when I could embark, in a vintage Land Rover with a vintage driver. The first leg to Baidoa was inland on a tarred road but the next stage was a rough sandy track south-westwards and entailed several halts for the driver to rest and chew qat. This mild narcotic leaf, imported from Yemen in large quantities, inhibits sleep but leads to garrulous, interminable and inconsequential chat with anyone within earshot.

So when a herd of camels blocked the track around half an hour of discussion ensued to enable the herdsman to clarify his mind as to what needed to be done to clear a way for the Land Rover. Doubtless some conversation was exchanged with the camels but this passed over my head, camels being tall creatures. However, the herdsman gave me a large gourd of camel milk - to drink on the spot as he wanted his gourd back. Somalia has had a bad press recently but in the countryside, far from political and commercial pressures, people are friendly and decent and this works almost anywhere in the world.

Ultimately we reached Baardheere on the Juba river. This small town boasted a comfortable lodging house with an excellent lamb stew on permanent offer. A reconnaissance showed that cement-making components existed but a drilling programme was needed. Another requirement was a sample of river water, as a cement plant needs process water with not too many nasties in it. A sample of water was solemnly bottled and sealed and we set off for Mogadishu. This was a deal easier and faster than the outward journey as the veteran driver had a veteran wife to go home to and his supply of qat was exhausted (as was he).

Back in base, I looked for the water sample. The driver cheerfully admitted that since he was thirsty he had drunk it.

The drilling investigation was carried out most competently by my colleagues and the saga of the subsequent drilling program as relayed to me was colourful. I had seen the Chinese drilling rig. Clearly designed by Chairman Mao on a bad day, it had an abundance of built-in limitations. The drilling crew, being government employees, were in no hurry. Having spent long nights chewing qat, they were barely conscious during working hours, achieving on average one metre of drilling each day. Our supervising geologist was lucky not to be in his tent when a runaway tractor, parked on level ground the night before, flattened the tent and all within it.

Rehabilitation in Uganda, 1979

When Idi Amin was chased by vengeful Tanzanian troops out of Uganda I was invited to join a team to follow the devastated route of his retreat and plan the restoration of water supplies to the principal towns. My input was professionally unremarkable in this land of abundant rainfall but I enjoyed meeting the hospitable people of Uganda.

Goods were beginning to return to the shops, though there was no wrapping paper and all items were wrapped in bags made of paper from government files. A bag of sugar could be a report carrying the stamp: *'CONFIDENTIAL! Restricted circulation.'* The glass entrance doors of the only functioning hotel in Kampala were peppered with bullet holes and accommodation was basic.

As a fleeting visitor to Uganda, I had enough time only to gather superficial impressions. The people I found to be courteous, articulate and intelligent - some of them highly intelligent. In some developing countries discussion with fellow professionals was somewhat one-sided. At the Geological Survey in Kampala a proposition was invariably the target of immediate, perspicacious and well-informed debate. Inevitably the deposed dictator Idi Amin was a topic of discussion. One citizen averred that in some ways he preferred Amin because, though brutal, he was predictable whereas Milton Obote, his successor, was not!

Food was short, except for bananas and coffee. I rapidly learned about the many, many different varieties of banana, and matoke is one of the few Ugandan words I remember – savoury for roasting or frying, sweet, very sweet, small, long, angular, yellow, red – and my visit was just long enough to sample them all.

In West Africa, I was accustomed to buying a kola nut from a market stall to chew as I trudged along. Floating high on physostigimine and caffeine one's weariness vanished and the miles grew shorter, though the sweet-sour taste was acquired slowly. In Uganda a few roasted coffee beans wrapped in a leaf cost hardly anything. One bean tucked into the cheek and sucked produced an hour-long high and an exquisite flavour.

In Mbale by the Kenya border on the lower slopes of Mount Elgin was a large coffee co-operative sorting station where I was told I could not buy the product. Instead I was given a conducted tour of the premises and saw a bewildering variety of size, type and quality. In the director's office at the conclusion I was told that, though they could not sell me coffee, they could give me some. Amid expressions of goodwill I came away with several kilos of top grade beans – and an appreciation of the kindness of ordinary Ugandans.

At Jinja on Lake Victoria my brother Tony had many years before grown strawberries while in charge of construction of the mighty Owen Falls hydroelectric scheme. Here we crossed the infant Nile some 3,500 kilometres from the delta at the other end and I wondered idly if a strawberry, suitably wrapped, might bob its way through lakes and rapids to the Mediterranean Sea. Probably not.

At Entebbe an Israeli aircraft had earlier been hijacked under Amin's orders and the passengers confined to the airport building. The Israelis had launched a successful raid to rescue the passengers. When I flew in the disabled aircraft was still there in a far corner of the airport. We had been forewarned that we should pretend not to see it, as national pride had been mortally hurt by the Israeli rescue.

The civil service still functioned and I found the Geological Survey staff to be knowledgeable and helpful, qualities somewhat lacking in some less developed African countries. Ugandans enjoy a considerable intellectual capacity balanced by inherited tribal feuds with much blood letting.

Malarial mosquitoes were rife but I had taken a device supposed to emit the high-pitched whine of male mosquitoes. The theory was that female mosquitoes were lured away towards this source, which was placed well away from our work place. In practice the opposite happened; our previously mosquito-free office was invaded by females fleeing from what they felt were the unwelcome attentions of predatory males.

India

Around 1980 I was surprised one day to hear that I was the United Nations expert on hydromuscovite; surprised mainly because I had never heard of this mineral. A learned Russian had revealed that this mineral occurred in India and funds were available to find out. A flight from New Delhi to Lucknow was enlivened by a view of the Himalayas far to the north. The Geological Survey of Uttar Pradesh were there in force to welcome this high-powered expert and after much discussion preparation for an expedition to the south of that state began.

There was ample time to visit the location of the famous siege of Lucknow in the Indian mutiny. The museum displayed a three-dimensional model of the embattled British troops and civilians, as well as depicting the mutineers' positions. Since independence the only change to the display was to change the labels 'mutineers' positions' to read 'Indian positions'. This showed great restraint.

A long journey by road to the south of the state seemed longer on account of the wandering cattle and the many buffaloes pulling carts; in this tolerant part of the world these beasts are given right of way. Frequent stops were made at tea houses and Hindu shrines but in the end we reached a well constructed camp and I was allotted a British army-style bell tent complete with camp furniture and an orderly whose morning greetings were 'Tea Sahib' and 'More tea Sahib.' My congenial Indian colleagues called him 'Mister Morti.'

In due time I was taken to a pattern of deep prospecting trenches reminiscent of the Western Front in the Great War and introduced to hydromuscovite and its first cousin pyrophyllite. Of the latter I knew only what I had read in the text books and it seemed to me that the two looked remarkably similar. One is greenish brown and the other is reddish brown and the bands merged into each other. The two minerals formed vertical stripes, with cobbles of diaspore. Diaspore is a gemstone and to my mind attractive but locally thrown away. Pyrophyllite is allegedly used in the manufacture of furnace linings and hydromuscovite is much the same only more so. When the time came for me to leave India I was presented with two beautifully made dishes, one of each material. With a twinkle in his eye, the chief geologist told me that clearly I knew which was which but to this day I can only guess.

After hours of chiselling channel samples in the trenches, meals were taken in the camp in the shade of a large tree. They were agreeable, adequate and remarkably cheap. When I offered to pay my share I was told that the amount of money needed was inconsiderable. Curries were brought in from the village, neutralised by a rather bland beer while chapatis were prepared before our eyes.

One day I was intrigued to hear a regular chime coming from down the road; into view lumbered an elephant, unattended and swinging a bell from his trunk. No one appeared disturbed or interested in this phenomenon. What did disturb our routine however was the disappearance of a surveyor. It transpired that he had wandered one day beyond the village, was captured by a gang and led before a famous lady dacoit. A sort of Robin Hood figure, on retirement she was ultimately pardoned. The surveyor was well treated and later released unharmed to return to base. Doubtless some delicate negotiations had been carried out beforehand.

Chapter 15. The groundwater decade of the Eighties

*A Nigerian proverb says 'Things fall apart.' This encapsulates
the improvidence that permeates black Africa*

For most of this decade, the spotlight was on Nigeria, where our good
relationship with the World Bank in Nigeria led to our involvement
in some major projects. Our lives were further enriched by unplanned
excitement resulting from two coups d'etat.

Water for villages in Bauchi State

Four years after we set up our office in Bauchi the Groundwater Decade
erupted. Paddy Fleming, a brilliant agronomist, was at the helm of
the Bauchi State Agricultural Programme, the first major World Bank
agricultural effort in Nigeria. He foresaw that the most cost-effective
strand of the programme would be improving water supplies to villages
and to farmers.

Before the 'Groundwater Decade', so designated by UNICEF, village
people drew their water from the village well. One of the great unsung
achievements of the British colonial regime was the design and
development of a standard, robust, hygienic dug well. This began in
Nigeria in the Thirties when a water engineer called Cochrane was
charged with the task. After much trial and error he evolved a design
that proved so successful it acquired a name – a 'cochrane' - and most
colonial British and French West Africa territories adopted it.

The village well became the social centre of village life. Water spilled
from goatskin buckets nourishing shade trees and under them rough logs
became polished by the nether zones of robed ancient gossips. Until
Nigeria's independence the government department responsible for rural
water supply received enough funds to maintain these wells. A Nigerian
proverb says 'Things fall apart.' This encapsulates the improvidence
that permeates black Africa. In the past people saw no need to plan and
provide. The climate was sufficiently benign to permit growing of cereals,

root crops, fruit and so on and serious famine was rare. With urbanisation in the 20th century, the economic structure changed but old habits did not. So through lack of maintenance and of a red-nosed supervisor the village wells, one by one, silted up and parapets collapsed. Village folk reverted to using unsanitary waterholes.

Drilled wells for village water

The advent of the groundwater decade was timely. A delightful Dutchman. sent on a mission by the World Bank, decided that repairing dug wells was not the 'way forward' and that mass produced drilled wells were needed. Bauchi State was to be the pilot project and 2,000 boreholes would be constructed in the space of three years. There was insufficient capacity for this within Nigeria so international tenders were put out for the drilling.

We were agreeably surprised to win the borehole contract in competition with the largest international consultants, each with more than 1,000 personnel at its disposal compared to my 20. Our overheads were low, we carried no vast burden of directors and specialist advisors, we had much local knowledge and the work was on our doorstep. But the deciding factor was that the expatriate programme manager was an honest man. This contract was among the last to be free of corruption and this decade signalled the end of an era.

So under the shadow of a giant Japanese drilling company, we embarked and set sail. The operation was technically highly successful, though due to my other-worldly attitude to business matters we made little profit.

Most people in northern Nigeria live in villages of around 1000 souls, so that a modest sized borehole for each settlement is adequate. Where groundwater is plentiful and a borehole anywhere would yield enough water, a brief visit to put in a peg was theoretically adequate. However, such is the nature of small hierarchical communities that it was necessary to put on a charade involving at least one black box with electrodes and brightly coloured cables. Then, with great ceremony and local participation, a peg would be hammered in and, surrounded by local dignitaries, photographed. The peg, for technical reasons of course, would be just outside the chief's compound and everyone was happy.

The snag was that about three quarters of the villages are underlain by crystalline rocks. There is usually enough groundwater to support small communities but it lies in fractures cunningly concealed beneath the soil. Finding these involves the use of geophysics together with a deal of common sense. This meant operating several crews working flat out. Using the standard resistivity method would be too slow and I opted for the previously little used electromagnetic technique. The establishment was sceptical and ponderously critical – it was not in the text books - but it proved highly successful and the World Bank programmes that followed in other northern states followed suit.

Small-scale irrigation

Apart from the village water supplies, we were fortunate in becoming part of an exciting groundwater irrigation project, also in Bauchi State. This was designed for use by individual family farms, the brainchild of David Wendover, a visionary agronomist working for the World Bank. We were able to work with him and sort out what went on below ground and the best way of raising the water to spread it on the land.

A strip of terrain about 500 kilometres wide between 12 and 15 degrees north of the equator is the semi-arid Sahel, extending across Africa for more than 2000 kilometres. There is an annual contest between the wet tropical winds from the south and the dry Saharan winds. For a couple of months each year the wet winds saturate the land along the southern margin. In West Africa the water runs off northwards in the seasonal rivers towards broad ancient valley flats called fadama in semi-arid land. The alluvium is covered by fertile silt dumped from desert dust. The river water coming in replenishes the body of groundwater in the alluvium.

By jetting down shallow boreholes in good silty land, farmers could irrigate their family plots. They lifted the water by using their own little petrol pumps (petrol was cheap), which they took home on bicycles every evening. The wide valleys were made green with beans, peppers, capsicum, lettuces, onions, tomatoes and carrots.

Under each farm was enough groundwater for a dry season crop and each wet season this was replenished. If the farmer poured too much water on the crops the excess quietly drained back into the ground. This system, completely waste-free and very cheap, was born in Bauchi State and became widely used in northern Nigeria where 'home grown' petrol was cheap enough. Over the border to the north, in Niger republic, smuggled petrol was still cheap enough to be viable – a charming example of what the World Bank termed the 'dual economy'.

The World Bank masterminded many projects in west Africa; some sank without trace, some had moderate success. The 'single farmer irrigation' schemes had an outstanding and enduring impact.

Coups d'etat

Each decade from 1960 to 1990 was enlivened by at least one coup d'etat. Practice made perfect so that by the Eighties the blood and thunder that attended earlier efforts had abated and the coups of that decade were relatively tame affairs, which focussed less on high idealism than on power and money. For us they were a combination of inconvenience and slightly hair-raising but amusing adventure.

The coup of 1983 broke early on New Year's Eve just as we arrived back from Christmas in Britain. By chance we heard on the radio in Kano a crackly broadcast announcing the great news that General Buhari was taking over. Relying on organisational delays, we resolved to leave by road forthwith to reach Bauchi, 200 miles away before the road blocks went up.

On the way we branched off to a dam construction site to scoop up Gordon and Elaine, Scottish friends, who had not heard the news. New Year's Eve was to have been a vigorous Caledonian triumph and they had been invited to inject the true tribal spirit into the event. We reached Bauchi by driving the last few kilometres along sandy detours to learn that a curfew was imminent and gatherings after dark were sternly prohibited. So, weary from the long journey, we dined formally: the Scots resplendent in kilts and plaids, Gordon with a deadly dagger in his sock. Then sat and looked at each other, sipping restoratives to keep awake until midnight when we staggered to our feet, sang *Auld Lang Syne* and tottered off to bed.

On New Year's Day the rebellious spirit was strong in the expatriate community. We assembled in full dress on the tennis court of the agricultural project club where, under the blazing sun, we flung Highland flings and stripped the willow. Interdispersed with this tribal dancing we refreshed our souls with cold drinks and sang vigorous songs of a patriotic nature while an improvised barbecue reached fruition. Heavily armed military patrols passed by occasionally but, either alarmed or puzzled - we were not sure which, they wisely ignored us. Gordon, with his flaming red hair and dagger that he brandished when protocol demanded, may have been the deciding factor. This, though postponed, was the most enjoyable New Year's Eve in living memory.

The next coup, in 1985, was heralded by martial music on the radio laced with announcements and dire warnings. Of these the most frivolous was a ban on playing 'cards and games of chance'. We decided to go ahead with our planned bridge match, with a planned exit strategy, and because of its furtive nature thoroughly enjoyed it.

A slightly more threatening announcement was that anyone possessing an unlicensed firearm would be sentenced to 21 years' hard labour. This bothered me not at all until a friend called Bill Bell came round to tell me that he was looking after 'my' firearm on behalf of Dutch Gibson. Dutch was under the impression that I had offered to buy it. Bill made very plain to me that I should come to collect it forthwith. So I did, though alarmed to find that the .22 rifle came complete with ammunition and a micro factory for making bullets. In a highly nervous state, I tucked this collection under the bench seat of my pick-up and drove home. Maybe

I had made insufficient allowance for the indolence of the military but I deemed the roof space of the house to be an inadequate hiding place.

An ad hoc committee conceived the idea that the rifle should be dismantled and bedded into a concrete block. In record time I built shuttering, mixed concrete and wrapped the gun in an oily cloth. Bill had written an ode, which he tucked into the package for future generations to read. In the midst of pouring the concrete friends unexpectedly called. They were less than satisfied with my assertion that my obsessive hobby was to make concrete blocks on my verandah on a Sunday morning – or indeed on any morning.

The next project was to invent a way to mark the block so that in future days the gun could be retrieved. It seemed to me that the principle 'what you can't hide you emphasise' was appropriate so I converted the block into the pillar of a bird bath, adorned with the letters 'NSPB 1983' (Nigerian Society for the Protection of Birds). I capped it with a concrete dish in the shape of a Mexican sombrero, painted black, and the ensemble I installed in a rock garden behind the kitchen. The bullet factory at first presented a problem, but I shoved it all in a large earthenware pot, filled the interstices with dry sand, and sealed it. With more artful terracotta work I decorated the body with wings and a head to resemble a cross between an angel and a penguin. This I stationed tastefully beside the bird bath. In time friends became accustomed to the result of my artistic activity but for some reason the birds never did. This may have been due to the menacing Mexican black hat.

Over a year later a driver arrived with a note from Dutch Gibson asking for his armoury; it was a sad parting for me, and puzzling for the driver.

The Caledonian Ball

This was held annually in the Eighties on the Jos plateau 80 miles away and groups from all over the north attended. Bauchi was considered to be a rather backward centre and we had only two Scots of any dancing ability. We were determined to shine and in the weeks before the event practised to the edge of exhaustion. In the chilly November evenings we danced on a tennis court dazzlingly lit, attracting all the insects in creation. Out and away the best dancers were the sari-clad Indian ladies who made the most vigorous dances appear to be serene and graceful. At the other end of the spectrum of ability the Indian men held sway. Manoeuvres such as 'peeling off' saw them spinning out of control into the outer darkness and a temporary halt was needed to reassemble them. The event was hosted by the Caledonian Society of Jos, which found overnight accommodation for us all, mainly at the headquarters of church missions. The early Christian missionaries preferred Jos for two reasons. One was that the local tribes were 'pagans', isolated and protected by the forests and rocky terrain from the fulani jihad and Islamic revival of the 19th century. The other reason was that the climate at 1,200 metres above sea level was agreeable to pale skinned expatriates. The missionaries spread the faith and provided these intelligent people with western education.

On one occasion our team was allocated visitors' chalets belonging to a rather strictly temperate denomination. We were enjoined neither to smoke nor drink on the premises. Knowing some of our team this made me nervous from the beginning.

We gathered in the vast hall of the Bukuru club. For these events British Caledonian Airways flew in a complimentary load of haggis and a splendid piper with full Highland regalia. All the esoteric rituals were faithfully observed presided over by the Chieftain with the improbable name of Smith.

Some danced the night away; we of riper years peeled off at midnight and slept soundly until dawn. Feeling uneasy as to the fate of the young bloods, I rose early in the dawn of the Sabbath. The first task was to pick up a considerable number of cigarette butts around the chalets. Just in time, for the good missionaries were emerging to go forth and multiply their flocks, clad in black with gloves and with prayer books at the ready.

It was singularly unfortunate that a car should roll in at that moment and disgorge my hydrogeologists and their wives, highly relaxed and executing improvised reels. The meeting between them and the holy ladies is imprinted for ever on my mind.

Children pumping from a borehole

Children at a well

How to hide a rifle from the authorities'
prying eys, turn it into a concrete bird bath!

Chapter 16. Missions, programmes and projects

'The bitch is on heat again . . . Not the wife, I mean the labrador'

For several years I enjoyed the experience of joining teams of 'Experts' who went on 'Missions' to Nigeria and planned wonderful things intended to carve out the destiny of developing states. These were carried out under the aegis of the big international agencies - World Health Organisation, World Bank, FAO, UNDP, IFAD and so on. All these endeavours were carried out with irreproachable aims and it is possible that some of the more practical schemes proposed played some part in shaping the development of these nations.

At the sharp end of a mission, conditions were at best uneven though our official hosts, with limited resources, ever strove to smooth our path.

One such mission was in Northern Katsina, during a time of unrest, and the tension was palpable. Our purpose was to put together a model for integrated village development, combining the various components of progressive activity. We stayed in the Military Governor's Guest House, guarded by two soldiers, a Christian from the south and a Muslim northerner. Each deeply distrusted the other; the northerner's English was imperfect but I was not allowed to chat with him in his own tongue.

Our team leader, a Basque, was a first class diplomat who contrived to keep the peace, and not only with our hosts. Leaders had the task of controlling, cajoling and smoothing over the many differences of opinion intrinsic to highly individualistic team members without discouragement.

Our agronomist was a sturdy Yorkshireman who – like all of us – felt isolated, being unable to get in touch with the outside world. He fretted that his wife would not be able to cope with his farm and his dogs. He managed to be taken, with an escort, to the Posts and Telegraph building, and called his wife. He returned, silent and troubled in spirit, and after a long silence with a sigh announced "The bitch is on heat again." Sensing the ghastly silence, he stuttered "Not the wife, I mean the labrador."

All went fairly well until the local wind-up meeting, chaired by the State Military Governor. To start with, each team member expatiated on his or her vision of water supply, sanitation, agriculture and so on. We waxed on at some length, each of us saying his or her piece. Our hosts listened attentively and if they disagreed were too courteous or diffident speak. My party piece was enlivened by a huge air photograph of a typical village about 30 inches square. This seemed a good idea at the time but caused considerable grief at the end of the mission.

The tough nut to crack was to seek acceptance of our ideas as to how the improvements could best be implemented. In Katsina society was highly stratified, the top layer being scions of aristocratic lineage. We recommended the 'go in sideways' approach at grass roots level, dealing with chosen men and women who represented their fields of activity; by contrast, working from the top down, the training methods would be so diluted as to be ineffectual.

This led to the next explosion. An immaculately clad army major, with a Sam Browne belt and highly polished boots that he flicked with a silver knobbed swagger stick, stood to attention and barked, "It doesn't work. I sent in a sergeant with a platoon to a village and they wouldn't co-operate."

Anxious to cull the views of all interested parties, the Governor then called for the opinions of other agency representatives, civil, military and so on. A big agency man went in to bat first, and said his piece all in one sentence: "Any project we have carried out around here has ended in unmitigated disaster." Following a stunned silence, the Governor made diplomatic and soothing noises and the meeting lumbered on, tapered off as lunch time approached and limped to a muttering close.

A great contrast was a meeting earlier with an otherworldly Emir. Daura is an ancient emirate in the eastern part of the State, the remnant of a kingdom reaching back 1,500 years. It was not surprising, therefore, that the Emir, an anglophile with the courteous manners of another age, should have found somewhat daunting an arranged meeting with our bustling and intrusive team.

We left Katsina having exchanged sentiments of mutual regard with our hosts. Then the interminable journey to Kano along a dusty single track road, with narrow bridges, among piles of baggage crowned by my great rolled up photograph. Before us lay the last great hurdle.

Kano International Airport, which served all of northern Nigeria, had a grim reputation for relieving travellers of their excess cash. Our special

FAO passports were of some help, but an eagle eyed, elegantly suited civilian at the check in desk spotted my shiny map roll, and took a dislike to it. My explanation, which seemed reasonable to me, failed to make him happy; he announced that I was under arrest and I was to accompany him to his office, which bore an impressive label. He pondered long and earnestly over the flattened-out photo and was not cheered by the fact that it was of an area near Jibiya. Did I realise, he asked, that this was close to the Niger Republic border and sported an air force base? It took 20 minutes of close reasoning to convince him that I was a simple seeker after truth, en route for a debriefing meeting with high officials in Rome, the eternal city. After searching his mind and indulging in deep thought he told me I could go, and wished me a safe journey.

Marching along the long corridor towards the emigration controls, I encountered a second official, suited almost as elegantly as my arresting officer. His restless eye homed in on my great map roll and he demanded an explanation for such a strange export. So I gave him the same explanation, though it received the embroidery it deserved, making much of the sensitivity of the area which adjoined, as I explained, an air force base. In no time at all I was arrested, turned round, and marched back to what was obviously the office of his chief. It was time to enjoy the situation, and I was not disappointed. Did this fellow realise, his chief demanded, that he was fully satisfied that 'this gentleman' was on his way, legitimately, to a summit meeting in Rome. The crestfallen underling was to escort me to the passport control forthwith and to pilot me through.

It remained only to pass the final hurdle at the security check where a relatively minor controller eagerly awaited his monetary award. Following years of frustration this was a great moment. I opened out the photo and explained, fully and freely, that not only was this shot near the location of an air base but that it was also on the Niger border. I was immediately arrested as a preliminary to a bargaining session. When I insisted on escorting him downstairs to his superior's office doubt flickered in his eyes. Half way down the stairway, he whispered, confidentially 'Perhaps we can come to some arrangement.'

I had to explain that I was quite hard of hearing, and enjoyed hearing him repeat, more loudly, the same question. And then fortissimo: 'PERHAPS WE CAN......' Then, with an angry shrug, he muttered 'You can go', and scuttled away.

In the departure lounge the relief of the team was palpable, and I was welcomed like a stray lamb returned to the fold. Mainly since their loose change had been extorted, and I was able to buy drinks all round.

The high spot of any Mission was undoubtedly the debriefing session in Rome, where some agencies very sensibly located their headquarters. All the spade work had already been carried out and, with a battalion of resident experts for discussion and constructive criticism, it was a pleasure to polish up a report.

The FAO building is a concrete lump of no great beauty but by way of compensation is near the Terme di Caracas. From the restaurant on the roof, where we refreshed our brains with coffee at very regular intervals, the view of Capitol Hill is magnificent, although the chariot racing season had ended. The daily living allowance was liberal and we spent most evenings dining comfortably out of doors in this elegant part of a civilised city. The mornings were equally agreeable; after coffee and hot rolls we would stroll to work with the commuter stream. No one was in a hurry, smiles everywhere, and the women were elegantly dressed and pleasing to the eye.

Never a dull moment

I know of no country on this earth where driving is more exciting than in Nigeria with the possible exception of Iran. During a rather boring meeting held high up in a glass and concrete office block in the centre of Tehran, our deliberations were interrupted by a veritable battle of sound more worthy of our attention than the agenda item. Far below, a taxi had collided with an ambulance and the proponents were advancing their separate points of view. Two burly drivers, stripped to the waist, were trading punches. A large crowd bawled indiscriminate encouragement. To the fore, the partisan passengers from the taxi were egging their man on. The unfortunate occupant of the ambulance was neither to be heard nor seen; he probably had other things on his mind.

However, Lagos taxi drivers stand in a class of their own. Emerging from the international airport there, it is necessary to carry one's own bag, holding it very firmly indeed. Failure to do so commits one's mortal body to a taxi with a driver swifter and more muscular than his rivals.

An earnest and God-fearing man once asked me did I ever feel overwhelmingly close to God. Truth triumphed over tact and I responded that this occurred whenever I was in a taxi bound for Lagos, when with white knuckles I was muttering fervent prayers through clenched teeth. The dear man was mortally though mistakenly wounded by what he perceived as my frivolity.

Long distance taxis, sleek ten seater Peugeot models, were marginally safer provided one bought two seats (for comfort) and as near as possible to the rear (for safety).

Passengers who could not afford taxis 'went public'. Cheap but not cheerful were the 'Mammy Wagons'; the luxury versions of these were five tonne lorries fitted with rows and rows of wooden benches packed so closely that the occupants could not fall out. The economy class of traveller rode on goods lorries, perched with their baggage high on the windy peaks of bales and crates, and they could fall off. Fascia boards proclaimed proverbs, often in the mother tongue, though the most entertaining were in English. They are pithy, philosophical, witty and embody a faith in God and a fatalistic realism.

'No telephone to heaven'

'One with God is majority.'

And one cry from the heart: on a lorry that had tried to drive onto the Calabar ferry, missed and plunged into the river, the fascia just above water level read: *'God help us!'*

With the commuter era came minibuses; at stopping points competition was fierce and vocal, an echo of traffic conditions in London a hundred years before, when the 'barkers' were called 'cads', and the appellation stuck. Long haul buses, big, brash, brutal and Brazilian, flourished for a while but by the millennium were undercut by private air travel.

Drivers of all these public transport vehicles were young; inevitably, as either they did not live long or they repented and changed their profession. They were looked upon with scorn as being the dregs of society. A popular ballad had the repetitive chorus:

'I don't care if you marry moto dreva

I don't care if you marry tassi dreva.'

A famous feature of Lagos was a driving school that sold coffins as a sideline. This is private enterprise high on statistics but low on taste.

Trunk roads in northern Nigeria are under-used and a joy on which to travel long distances, in a chauffeured car and cans of spare fuel. Road blocks set up in periods of lawlessness and manned by soldiers or police are negotiated with caution. It is a tribute to European passengers, especially elderly ones, that they are regarded with respect by the average Nigerian. This is partly because they are so rare as to have become a protected species and partly the folk memory of the incorruptibility of colonial officers.

The toll required from Nigerian drivers is exacted with courtesy and a deal of restraint. However, towards the end of the month, before pay day, the guardians of the highway with children to feed feel the economic pinch and the rules change slightly. Passengers in a hurry tend to thrust a sheaf of bank notes into an eager pair of hands; this sets a bad example and is thus frowned on by the leisurely, less affluent end of the market.

No-one refers to this benevolent funding as highway robbery; this epithet is reserved for the real thing. In their golden age, armed gangs dressed in military or police uniform manned their own, highly mobile road blocks. The risk of being robbed of everything was so great that one major highway was for some months devoid of traffic after nightfall.

In the cities there used to be a band of saffron-uniformed urban warriors called traffic wardens, or less formally as 'yellow fever'. Expert at creating minor traffic offences they played their part in preventing travel from becoming dull.

All participants in the business of keeping the traffic moving were restrained by a simple precept. Expounded at its most intellectual level, a parasite that is too successful wipes out its host and source of sustenance, and so withers away. More mundanely, as our transatlantic cousins say, 'always give the sucker his car fare home'. The practitioners of this form of benevolence regard their work as spreading more fairly the wealth of the nation.

Chapter 17. The Nineties

*The younger, more athletic priest arose, genuflected, and bowled the
cat vigorously the full length of the corridor. Greatly excited, the cat
slithered back to base ready for more
and this sequence was repeated until the bowler was exhausted
– though the cat plainly wanted to continue.*

The Adventure of Baroness Trumpington

The distinguished Baroness was in the news not long ago when in the
Upper Chamber she raised two polite fingers to Lord King over the matter
of her extreme seniority. She displayed the same light hearted approach
to life when, around 1990, as Minister for Ag and Fish, by personality
and charm she won over her Nigerian hosts at an agricultural conference
at Abuja, the capital city. The event was organised by the British Council
in the palatial Hilton hotel.

The plenary sessions maintained a varying level of excitement, but she
attended them all, weathering imperturbably even the less than gripping
presentations. Throughout them all, smiling and quietly smoking, she
maintained a facade of good natured intelligence. It is difficult to become
over-enthused about the role of vetiver grasses and similar challenging
topics,

At the evening receptions the various breweries made available their
finest products and extolled their enterprise in boosting local maize
production. Indeed Nigerian lagers have as much charm as European
brews and more character than many.

At the first reception the Baroness really made her mark. She toured
unattended the swilling, swirling throng, interacting freely with
everyone, from the great and good to the anonymous and humdrum. I
had just arrived and was chatting with an Old Etonian freelance when
this impressive lady hove to and asked him what he did. Unabashed he
responded: 'Wheeling and dealing mainly'.

Turning to me she put the same question. I hadn't the foggiest idea who she was but admitted that I was a relic of colonialism. I then asked her who she was. In high good humour she told me - and I was hooked.

Afterwards, the British High Commission Rolls Royce, complete with ensign, wafted her gently to Kano where the British Airways flight, coming in from Lagos, would speed her in comfort to London. Alas, the resident BA engineer had malaria and could not carry out the statutory flight check; until a substitute arrived from London the aircraft was stuck on the ground.

To the rescue came the British Council, their representative hurrying to organise temporary accommodation at very short notice. After a false start he struck gold when Moira, from the British High Commission, volunteered the use of the family guest suite in a quiet suburb.

This is when the fun started. Her husband, Derek, a sturdy son of Newcastle on Tyne, was welding steel rods on their verandah, dressed in shorts and gym shoes, unaware of the imminent excitement. Slumbering affectionately at his side was Snoopy, a huge guard dog with magnificent fangs.

The High Commission cortege on final approach reached the quiet, tree lined road in the Government Residential Area. It comprised, from front to rear, a police escort on a motor bike, the stately Rolls Royce and bringing up the rear - in a more modest vehicle and with dread in her heart - Moira.

The steel doors to the high-walled compound were flung open and to the prolonged music of a siren the cortege drove towards the verandah. Snoopy, scenting an easy meal, erupted with slavering jaws. The police escort abandoned his charge, swerved and, wailing merrily, set off around the small plant-lined bathing pool. A high speed chase ensued until the escort misjudged a sharp turn and plunged into the water. Here at least was safety, though the siren was not waterproof and the wah-wah declined into a groaning gurgle, then finally and mercifully ceased.

The Baroness, from her grandstand vantage point, enjoyed the show immensely, but clearly yearned for an interlude of peace thereafter. She settled in the guest suite, behind closed doors, until a day or two later her aircraft arrived.

Rwanda 1994

The Rwanda massacres in May 1994 led to a mass exodus of survivors west across the borders into Zaire and east into Tanzania. The oldest died of exhaustion; ditches were full of the desiccated corpses of these poor people, anonymous yet strangely serene and dignified in their long white robes. The rest coalesced into camps of 250,000 people. On the north shore of Lake Kivu the town of Goma had been a holiday resort for the great and good, including President Mobutu (the Leopard King) who had a summer mansion. The slumbering peace of this playground was shattered when half a million refugees tramped through.

Half of them trudged northwards to Kivumba under the looming menace of a live volcano. They all needed fuel, food and water. Cutting wood from the forests for fuel was at first easy but around the camp the deforested perimeter grew ever larger. To the south a pretty little tree-lined cemetery on the outskirts of Goma was razed; to the west the slopes of the volcano were cleared. The big charities, under the aegis of the United Nations High Commission for Refugees, brought in sacks of maize and a shuttle of flat-bed trucks with saddle tanks of water groaned up the road from the lake.

Under the shadow of the smouldering Nyiragongo volcano, a quarter of a million people settled in Kivumba camp. (The volcano slopes were, for obvious reasons, uninhabited.) Up on the main road they queued for their ration of maize (mealies). A short distance back towards the camp they were stopped by Rwandan paramilitaries who forcibly extorted a percentage of the maize. At the heart of the vast plastic-sheeted encampment a market had sprung up and the food section was run by the same paramilitaries, who sold the maize back to the refugees. So, in Mafia style, the food circulated.

Water trickled in but a local supply was needed. This is where I, literally, came in, having previously in armchair comfort put together a wise but highly theoretical report for Oxfam.

The international airport near Ramsgate in Kent is a departure point for cargo aircraft. Oxfam had chartered an ancient Boeing 707 cargo carrier. I arrived with my luggage and bedroll and joined a little group drinking tea and munching cold greasy chips from paper bags in the aircrew rest area. I was reminded of a line from Saki: 'nibbling with the nervous intensity of deer feeding in the open.' The munchers were Simon Bates, an extrovert disc jockey from Radio London (Simon was to gather material for highly effective tear-jerking appeals) with his minder, a pretty press officer from Oxfam. Then a 'logistician', also from Oxfam; a nervous dispatcher who assembled passengers and cargo; the air crew, from West Africa and Somalia. And me.

A peaceful journey to Nairobi, I thought. And Oxfam would brief me gently before sending me on to Zaire, I thought. But it was soon clear that we were bound for Goma, on the Rwanda border. Equally clear that I should phone Kath but should give East Africa as my destination.

We boarded after the cargo of plastic water pipe was stowed and made ourselves comfortable in a little cabin behind the flight deck. Our first stop was to be Athens for refuelling. The dispatcher invited me to sit in the jump seat for the landing. He enjoined me that if I saw anything unusual I was not to comment and – sure enough – the first unusual thing was a light glowing yellow over a label reading 'Starboard outer engine: pressure low.' After landing, the dispatcher raised an interrogative eyebrow and I nodded. The observant Simon was keen to know what was amiss. 'Oh, nothing much,' said the dispatcher with a twitch. So when we were again ready for take off, after a delay occasioned by the need to flush away tonnes of kerosene spilled on the apron, Simon resolutely climbed forward, having been enjoined to say nothing. As we reached cruising altitude he came back, wild-eyed: 'Did you see it? Did you see it?' We shushed him and disposed ourselves for sleep. I crawled aft with my bedding roll and slept fitfully on the water pipes.

At the Goma airstrip a detachment of the Irish army was playing football. They called time and unloaded our cargo; this by the simple expedient of unlatching the side of the cargo hold, whereupon a cascade of plastic pipe tumbled out. Among it somewhere was my bedding roll; I was glad to see the last of it.

A first reconnaissance around the camp revealed that the guesses I had made in my armchair study were accurate. The shiny lava from the latest flow was cracked and in those cracks sturdy bushes had sprouted. There is no surface drainage, though every year more than a metre of rain descends. So porous is the surface that the rain immediately drains down through the cracks in the lava into a bed of volcanic ash. Below that layer is another lava flow and so on – cracked lava – volcanic ash – cracked lava – for hundreds of metres. All the water seeps southwards down to Lake Kivu where earnest Oxfam volunteers pumped it into tanks and sent it back again.

UNHCR had at its disposal a large drilling rig and a Swedish driller who on a good day could operate most efficiently. On a bad day (he had a heart condition) his crew propped him up at the controls, where he was visibly unhappy. He drilled through the top basalt flow and hit water in the ash bed below. This is when the technical problems started. We wanted to drill down to a healthy depth but the ash was unstable and collapsed into the hole as fast as the drill 'sucked' it out.

One misty day I hired us a small helicopter from Medecin Sans Frontiers (MSF) and with a water engineer on board had a good look at the terrain, hoping to locate a major fracture in the surface of the flow. At the end of our allotted half hour we asked the pilot to set us down beside the Red Cross compound. This was a mistake as, unknown to us, a helicopter from the French air force had been showering the camp with political leaflets the day before. Thereafter the resentful refugees associated any helicopter with trouble. We alighted nonchalantly and waved the helicopter goodbye and immediately a great stampede of hostile humanity rushed towards us waving cudgels and uttering fierce and warlike cries. We sprinted very nimbly over the fence into the Red Cross camp with little space between our rear elevations and some extremely sharp spears and cudgels.
One problem that the Red Cross and MSF had to address was an epidemic of dysentery. The constant shuffling of foraging parties seeking firewood created a dust haze that we all had to breath and like most of my colleagues I succumbed.

In a hotel beside the lake I shared a room with Simon the disc jockey. One of us snored reverberatingly and it was not me. The hotel was run-down but we did have an en-suite bathroom. With my innards churning I made frequent forays to the bathroom in the long sonorous night hours. To simplify this transit I wedged the bathroom door open with a wastepaper basket. On one particularly rapid transit I forgot the basket which wrapped itself round my ankle, whereupon I skidded across the bathroom and slammed into the bath at great speed. Thereafter with each deep breath my ribs stabbed with agonising pain. Laughter was agony. How kind people were, asking me how I had cracked my ribs. And they promised not to laugh when I explained. Despite earnest reassurances they guffawed. Such mirth is infectious and strive though I might I had to join in.

At night, a lumiere show was provided by the flickering rose colour of the molten pool of lava in the Nyiragongo volcano reflected from the clouds. A feeling of impending doom was never far from our thoughts; the UNHCR organised a visit by two vulcanologists from the US Geological Survey. Their visit was brief indeed, arriving by helicopter, with a short buzz in the same helicopter around the cauldron and they were ready to depart the same day. The UNHCR chief managed to buttonhole them for a statement. The volcano could blow at any time; the lava was thin and highly mobile, it could race down the mountain at 60 kph. They would send a report - and Goodbye! Some months later the lava did flow not into the camp but south-eastwards into Goma, where it neatly filled the streets with a rectangular network of cooling rock. More durable than tarmac but all the ground floor rooms became basements.

Simon the DJ was busily gathering material for his radio appeal and a regular session interview became a feature of the day. His tape recorder logged all our hopes and fears, with a big build up of drama when water glugged up the borehole and a sigh when the hole collapsed. Came the day when Simon announced his work was done and he was off to London. 'By the way,' he said, 'your interview goes out on Saturday.' I was horrified; it was possible that Kath might hear it and as I had been economical with the truth on departure, she thought I was 'somewhere in

East Africa.' Simon thought this a great joke, but promised to hold back until I had squared my yardarm with the Management.

My next stop was to be Tanzania and a few days later I met a group at the airstrip to join a flight to Nairobi. A sergeant major type dispatched us in groups to join outgoing empty cargo aircraft. In due course a Hercules of the Canadian air force lumbered in and our group was briefed by a stern Canadian officer: 'Get this and get this good. You take your gear up the ramp and stow it. You strap in to the seats and stay there. No smoking. Questions?' I piped up nervously, 'Is there a toilet?' 'Mister, you use the toilet at your peril.' Strapped up, I dragged my case up the ramp and for four hours while the aircraft droned up to Nairobi meditated on the joys of travel.

At the Oxfam office in Nairobi I was received with great kindness and permitted to phone home. 'Where have you been? You said East Africa; I was worried sick.' The following few minutes were a trifle fraught and I held the phone a little away until things quietened down then murmured 'Do you know about Simon Bates of Radio London? Well, he was with me and you should listen to his broadcasts. It was perfectly safe.' This defused a highly explosive situation and we were able to converse amicably. The news that the next stop was Tanzania went without fuss.

A light aircraft piloted by a religious volunteer flew me westwards, on a wing and a prayer along the southern edge of Lake Victoria to Ngara in north-west Tanzania. The pilot dropped me at the end of a dusty airstrip and took off for base. It is a long walk into town, my suitcase was heavy and my rib cage ached. Continuing a meditation interrupted by translating from one side of Rwanda to the other, I was ultimately awakened by the roar and clatter of a Land Rover arriving to pick up someone else. The Oxfam house, when I reached it, was bursting at the seams with volunteers and I was allotted a bed-roll on the floor of a bell tent, the last of a row, down-wind from the pit latrines.

An hour away by Land Rover, down a spine-jolting track, a refugee camp sprawled by a spring-fed reservoir. A road construction firm called

Benaco built the reservoir and unknowingly gave the camp its name.

Many small springs and seepages emerged from fractured quartzites. These trickles, channelled into improvised ponds and pumped into bowsers, supplemented the supply from the reservoir. With the help of Mark, a groundwater colleague who followed me to Ngara, we set up a geophysical survey to locate decent fractures in the quartzites. Our geophysical crew was selected from the cream of the refugees. The foreman was a displaced professor of mathematics from Kigali; destitute like the rest, spectacles held together by sticking plaster, this decent man stood straight and with dignity. We communicated in French, the common denominator language.

Much help was given to the refugees. Water by Oxfam and by the 'Tanganyika Christian Refugee Fellowship'. Roads by a Russian army detachment who lived in luxurious air-conditioned tents brought from Afghanistan. The ensemble included an air conditioned sauna and a cinema. As they spoke no French they could not communicate with their labour force and for them my arrival with just passable French was providential.

By contrast, the ultimate losers in the great game of international politics were the local Tanzanian communities. These innocent folk had their villages raided, their cattle stolen and wooden cattle pounds torn down and taken for firewood. As the villagers were not refugees there was no provision by UNHCR for their welfare. Tant pis!

Mark and I decided the journey every day down to the valley and back exhausted all our energy and left none for the task in hand. We were invited by the Refugee Fellowship to pitch a tent between their tents and the Russians'. First, however, a visit to a New Zealander who ran a medical centre at Ngara, for a professional opinion as to my strapped-up rib cage. Lips were definitely pursed and eyebrows reached great heights and I was enjoined to avoid sudden movement. Then came the inevitable question, and a promise not to laugh, and the inevitable consequence.

Oxfam gave us a great send-off, lent us a brand new tent and envied the gastronomic delight ahead in the mess room at the Christian camp. The reality was short of the dream; whereas the Oxfam cook boiled chicken and cabbage mercilessly, together in one pot, the Christians boiled the cabbage and roasted the fowl.

Erecting the tent was a great event. I sat on a log and read the instructions line by line while Mark strove among the folds of canvas. In a tree, a bird sang a singularly sweet song that I recognised. For many years in West Africa I had heard this air but the elusive creature had never come out of hiding. It was a joy, then, when this bird flew down to sit on another log and could be identified. Most ugly birds have sweet songs as a compensation. The yellow throated long-claw is no exception.

Mark emerged from the tent where he had been installing the inner chamber and we were able to enjoy the final paragraph of the instruction leaflet, while the yellow throated long-claw flew back into the tree and sang again. 'Your Cumberland tent should be erected in your garden before you go on holiday and exposed to showers. This enables the fibres to expand and become fully watertight. If you are unable to do this, you may notice, in your first few nights in camp, a fine mist within the tent. This is perfectly normal.'

So we slept in a fine mist and dined on roast chicken and cabbage and it was something of a relief when a message came in from Oxfam: would I go across to the Burundi border south of Goma to look at a potential problem? As the crow flies, from Ngara in Tanzania across Rwanda and Burundi to Goma is only 100 miles but getting there involved a long roundabout journey via Nairobi, Kigali and Goma; then by air south over Lake Kivu. A brief stop at Kigali airport provided a moment of hilarity. The perimeter bristled with US Airforce C130 (Hercules) transport aircraft and a US pilot explained to me some of the finer points of their capabilities. With a mighty roar, a huge Russian Antonov transport came in to land. I remarked innocently that this must be the largest transport in operation. The American reacted strongly: maybe, said he, but compared with the Hercules the Antonov was unreliable. The conversation faltered but I had a picture of these huge creatures falling out of the sky when their engines failed.

The stage from Goma to Bukavu was a short flip by a three-engine Islander. Beside me sat an aid worker whose face was familiar. We studied each other surreptitiously for some time then this abbreviated dialogue broke out:

'West Africa?' - 'Yes. West Africa.'

'Nigeria?' -'Yes. Nigeria'

'Kaduna?' - 'Yes. Kaduna.'

'Rugby Club ?' - 'Yes. Rugby Club'

'Drinking Section?' - 'Yes. Drinking section.'

Beaming recognition and nostalgic anecdotes between two sedentary sportsmen.

The shores of Lake Tanganyika around Uvira had the planning aspect of D-Day beaches and likely landing places among inhospitable swamps were located for a late stage invasion of refugees. The feared influx did not happen so that this early planning for water supplies, in the event, was not needed.

Returning to England, it was pleasing to discover that interviews by Simon for Radio London had reached some friendly ears. Less pleasing to discover that I had been caught speeding at 37 miles an hour early on a Sunday morning and dealt with in the full severity of the law. The taxman was also cross with me, prompting this little biblical essay.

In those days did the children of Hutu flee the wrath of Tutsi of Rwanda and did enter into the land of Goma. And the people of Goma welcomed them not yet rather cast them out unto the fiery slopes of Kivumba. And on the stones did they sit and mourn. Then cried out the people of Hutu for water and for food to fill their bellies. And did the lords of Oxenford hear their cry?

Ground view of refugee camp, Rwanda

Aerial view of refugee camp, Rwanda

There dwelt in the far land of Cornubia a man of rocks who lived in peace and rendered his taxes. And his name was Robin of the lineage of Hazell. Then did the lords of Oxenford say unto the man of rocks, Go forth to the land of Kivumba where the people cry out and in the land seek water for their souls and bodies. And did the man of rocks say then unto the lords of Oxenford, Yea will I go unto the land of Kivumba where the people cry out. And he called for his scrip and his satchel and his staff. And he bade his staff assess his taxes until he should return.

Then did he venture in the mists of the heavens unto the land of Goma. And did the people who did dwell in the land of Goma say unto him, Wherefore comest thou unto this land? And did he make reply, I go unto the fiery slopes of Kivumba where the people do cry out and there will I seek water for the people. Then did the people of Goma curl their lips in scorn. Knowest thou not, oh man of rocks, that under the shadow of Kivumba there is only fire and molten earth? Go if go thou must but dismal will be thy end.

In the shadow of Kivumba did the man of rocks gather tribespeople from northern lands and together did they roam for many hours amidst the people who cried out give us to drink. And it came to pass that after many hours did the man of rocks espy a certain stone and did say unto the northern tribesmen, Smite this stone. And after that they had smitten the stone for long hours they said unto the man of rocks, There is no water yet the people cry out. Go to, said the man of rocks, and smite yet again. And they smote yet again. And it came to pass that from the rock came forth water.

Then did the man of rocks go back to the people of Goma and then did the people of Goma say, Yea we did ever aver that in the shadow of Kivumba there is water. But did the lords of Oxenford say well done thou good and faithful searcher. Return to thy land in peace and pay thy taxes. So did he travel through the mists of the heavens unto his land of Cornubia and set down his scrip and his satchel and did call for his staff. And did his staff say yea verily have we assessed thy taxes and yet do the lords of our land demand yet more. Then was the man of rocks wrathful and vowed that water from the stone could he bring forth but, from the stone, blood he could not bring forth.

Clerical capers in Zambia

Outside the main consultants' office in Lusaka stood a pick-up truck, appropriately black, with bullet holes through the driver's door. The unfortunate driver had been carted away and the blood was being washed off the seat. The passenger, a German engineer, was shaken but unharmed. He had somehow steered the truck away to safety with the dead driver's foot wedged on the accelerator. This happened on the Zaire border near the copper-belt where armed brigands from Zaire, high on drugs, occasionally lurked.

I planned to traverse this stretch of road the next day in convoy with an Italian water engineer and was a trifle nervous. The rule was to travel in convoy and not to stop. In the middle of this danger zone one of my tyres blew. Skidding on to the verge, I flashed my lights for Juliano to stop; he did not see the signal and vanished blithely into the dusty distance. It was quiet, there was no one about to help; a very religious moment. The spare tyre was heavy, the jack was recalcitrant and it seemed an age before I was ready to set off, though it was probably only around 20 minutes. Just then, back came Juliano, in beaming good humour.

'Robeena, whatta keepa you?' A frank exchange of views followed.

The north-west corner of Zambia near the Angola border is home to backward and intensely superstitious tribes. Local government officials make little impact on the lifestyle of these people, though Christian missions have some influence. In the course of my work in this area I got to know some of the Catholic missions and developed an admiration for their tenacity and hardihood.

In Mufumbwe I stayed with Eric, a Polish priest. He provided the accommodation and I chipped in the beer and food – fish, mainly tilapia, locally called bream and sweet potatoes. We shared the cooking and the conversation. One Sunday I was for some reason unable to attend Mass and as a result Eric took some flak from his flock. Over some very bony fish for Sunday lunch I was firmly instructed to be on deck the following morning. The evening followed its usual course of lager and discourse but a fish bone wedged in my throat became intrusive and the discomfort and worry made sleep impossible. The nearest medical help was a long way off. So I was uncharacteristically early for Mass. After receiving the host, I was stung on the lip – not by an insect but by the dislodged fishbone. Our discourse at breakfast was inevitably about miracles.

In Kabumba, further west, a larger mission enjoyed the luxury of two priests – the younger one to tour outlying parishes. Dinner was a sumptuous affair, with Windhoek beer smuggled in from Namibia (and that's another story). A large and glossy cat held court and was highly regarded by the clergy; a diet of fish, oil and vitamins gave it a splendidly glossy coat and it purred deafeningly. Along from the living and dining room a long corridor, with doors at intervals, led to many tiny bedrooms each with a hard bed, and mosquito net and a wash basin. Two features intrigued me – so many rooms and the very high polish on the corridor floor. Even after many cans of beer the explanation that a very long corridor was necessary so that bedrooms could be built seemed to me inadequate. As to the high polish, I was to wait for the after-dinner entertainment when all would be made plain.

So, contentedly full of food and drink we adjourned to the west end of the corridor with the cat in hot pursuit and sagged into cane chairs. The younger, more athletic priest arose, genuflected, and bowled the cat vigorously the full length of the corridor where a cushion had been placed as a long stop. Greatly excited, the cat slithered back to base ready for more and this sequence was repeated until the bowler was exhausted – though the cat plainly wanted to continue. I did not like to ask whether the bishop, far away in Solwezi, ever knew why he had provided funds to lengthen the corridor.

The honey from this area is exceptionally good. The hives – rolled matting in the trees – were harvested by the traditional method of unrolling the mat and scraping out about half of the honey. Anne Roddick of Body Shop fame contracted with the local co-operative to buy a quota of this honey and the locals for a while prospered - until the producers, in search of greater profit, doubled the selling price. This killed the whole endeavour.

On the west bank of the Zambezi is a school staffed by American monks and reached by a foot bridge – a cut-price version of the recent wobbly bridge over the Thames. Before the bridge was built, when the river was high, it was necessary to travel downstream about 500 miles to reach the first crossing point at Livingstone. A resourceful brother resolved to build a suspension bridge. With strong faith but no engineering experience, he journeyed to the copper mines far to the east and begged condemned cables from the dump. There was nothing wrong with them – mining regulations ruled that cables must be replaced at fixed intervals. His first attempt was too low so he built another. When I visited crossing was a swinging, vertiginous experience; competing with many local folk going to market added to the fun. With produce piled on their heads they strode fearlessly from slat to slat and scorned to hold on to the struts.

While the bridge was yet young, and with the New Year approaching, Brother George volunteered to journey to Zambezi township to buy beer. Brother George was vast, built like a Dalek and almost two metres from tonsure to trainers. Returning after dark, he strode firmly on to the bridge holding aloft a case of beer. The extra weight was too much for one of the wooden slats, which fractured and he slid rapidly downhill. Though wedged for a while between adjoining slats, he ultimately lost his frictional hold and splashed into the water below, miraculously missing rocky reefs. His cries attracted help; he was hauled into a canoe and – after wringing him out and checking that he was not badly damaged – his fellow monks packed him off to a doctor in Zambezi. An earnest search for the beer followed immediately and it was found lodged in the bridge structure. So they got on with the party and toasted 'an absent friend.'

Not far away in Chavuma, within Kalashnikov range of Angola, fundamentalist Christians from the United States maintain a mission. One very wet day they were good-hearted enough to invite me to a hot drink (something grey and anonymous) and home-made muffins. As an afterthought, and in startling contrast, they produced a bowl heaped high with Ferrero Rocher, an exotic brand of confectionery in appearance rather like Faberge eggs. Apparently the Italian manufacturers had over-produced and rather than flood the market they shipped a container load to their pet mission in Central Africa.

Africa South of the Equator

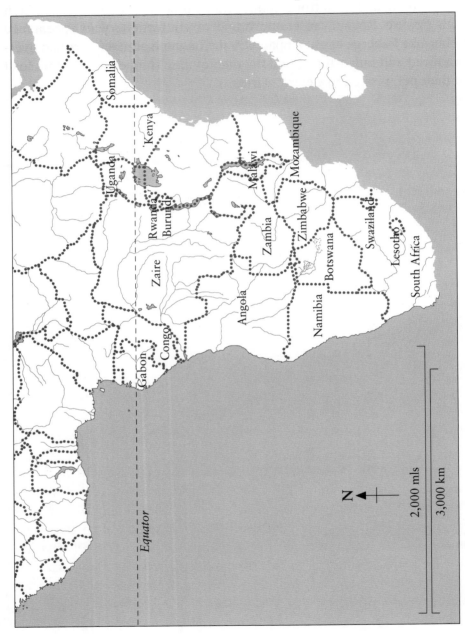

Chapter 18. The Millennium

Though the villagers owned nothing they were cheerful and optimistic - great qualities throughout black Africa and in shameful contrast to many of the grim-faced complaining folk in Britain.

Birds and the great Kalahari migration

It was still almost dark when the birds began to stir. A pair of drongos tumbled around the morule tree and a little later a solitary dove brooded. Slouched in a camp chair within the snug folds of a blanket my soul expanded, aided considerably by an early mug of redbush tea brewed on the braai over the embers of the dying fire. The aesthetic side ascended as it pondered how to describe the remarkably subtle colours of the dove. Memory dredged up from sensitive authors, words like sepia, umber and biscuit, hovered between chocolate digestive and old wafer and finally settled for dove coloured. Just in time, for a vulgar crested barbet blundered in like a clown, heading straight for the paw paw skins left for it. As the sun glowed over the ridge the serious birds arrived. A black-headed oriole and then the flutter of the resident kalahari robin, flitting its tail and fluting its clear triplet song. A pair of francolin minced across the clearing to the birdbath; their short steps reminded one of Burmese maidens in laungis though there any resemblance ended. Fancy cuddling a bush fowl! The male circled while his good lady drank and pecked at rice grains in the water before flopping down for a good old soak.

In the early sun the Waterberg sandstone slopes glowed around us. Again imagination failed to define the colour, a component of 'old rose' with other tints but definitely not dove. Boulders of this delightful and very ancient rock I had piled up, cemented in and topped out with an almost equally ancient wheel hub, the rust patches blending quite delightfully, and a birdbath was born. I nursed a blue hammered thumb and awaited developments. The good and great of the Gaborone bird-watching fraternity had warned me that it would be weeks before the birds came near it. We all knew this but I had neglected to inform the birds; they turned up long before the thumb stopped throbbing.

Normally at a mid-winter Saturday dawn we would have been thumping along an abominable sand track into our Gaborone base office to field the radio schedule of distant geologists' reports. Deep in Ngamiland on the Namibian border a young and tough field team would be breaking the ice on the water bucket while the leader fumbled with frozen fingers at the microphone. Back here, within sky glow of Gaborone, though the temperature hovered above zero mature adults experienced no guilt feelings.

But this was the day of the Great Kalahari Rally. Adventurous souls who during the working week navigated padded desks arrived from afar – Namibia, South Africa, Zimbabwe – to join the local adventurers and enjoy the agony of the ruts, potholes and deep sand ridges along the tracks that led into the desert. At seven in the morning the road was firmly closed and within half an hour the peace was shattered by the first wave of goggled desperados.

A noisy cackle of babblers had arrived. Of their nature they were impervious to the lesser roar of the motorised cavalry but other more fastidious birds huffed off. Only the 'go away' lowries rode out the storm in the thorn trees and some rather cross pied crows. (Cross indeed – the scene was set for them long ago by the four and twenty blackbirds.) A pair of rare sub-Saharan blue helicopters (helicopterus newsreelitus) wheeled and quested high above.

The revving and spluttering of the heavies – 'the 4 X 4s' - revived memories of a Peter Ustinov sketch describing with appropriate sound effects a farcical and fabricated rally that ran the gauntlet of the Duke of Edinburgh, proud and naval on a stationary grandstand. On the whole I preferred the Ustinov version but the real thing was entertaining enough. The thought of great comfort was that, not only were these brave men softening up the track for the lighter armour, they were – we hoped – also flattening the more spine-jarring humps which we dreary grey commuters endured daily for our country's good.

After a thoughtful breakfast, with meditation on the diverse tastes of our fellow men, I strolled down to the arena in time to witness an extraordinary sight. What appeared to be four-wheeler mechanised lawn mowers, with the cutting blades removed, were romping through the dust, their jockeys standing up and lunging in ecstasy on their stirrups. They carried no riding crops - it would have been imprudent; masochism enough without that. The two-wheeled tail-enders were less exciting, though two hours of stirred-up dust from the pioneers had left their mark; below anxious goggles, stern countenances were veiled with grime. Tonight they outspan in a lager far to the west; tomorrow the survivors return. Sick transit . . . .

The Limpopo flood of 2001

The windscreen wipers battled with the mud spraying over our truck; we slithered from one side of a greasy track to the other, hanging on to the handholds. I was daydreaming of a bench in the shade down by our Cornish stream and the murmur of the water; white wine in a tall misty glass and a plate of strawberries and cream. And I wondered whether I was wise to come to Mozambique in the wake of the disastrous Limpopo flood of 2001.

In Chokwe the floodwater has almost disappeared and it seems hardly possible that a bubbling brown flood could have surged so far over the land. We are 30 metres above sea level and the Indian Ocean is 150 kilometres away. The floodwater must drain gently into the Limpopo river then fall seawards by less than a hand's span every kilometre. The coastal lowland is still sheeted over with new lagoons.

Oxfam are clearing up the mess, giving roofing and plastic sheets and food for the present and hope for the future. We in a very small way are helping to restore water supplies.

Years ago every village had a borehole at least and several shallow dug wells. To grow more rice in the new utopia, Chinese experts were invited to extend a small existing irrigation network. Before the flood a barrage across the Limpopo river at Macarretane fed irrigation water to an area of about 400 square kilometres. The scheme was badly managed and over-irrigation caused saline water to accumulate in the aquifer so that the entire groundwater system was damaged. Shallow wells and boreholes were vitiated. As the distribution channels brought fresh water to the villages, wells and boreholes were no longer needed and fell into disrepair. This was not a serious problem so long as the villagers could draw their water from the channels.

But the flood surged along the channels, broke them down, then receded, leaving them blocked and dry. To compound the misery of losing livestock and homes, the returning villagers found they had lost their water supply. To drink brackish water is the lot of many people in arid parts of the world. In the central desert of Iran the people would find fresh water insipid and fall ill. In the Kalahari the accepted limit of potability is two per cent of salt; in Europe it is one quarter of that. In much of Africa, as in Europe, children are weaned on to fresh water and develop a body chemistry that makes it difficult to assimilate salt water.

So here we are, with our black boxes and our computer programs, trying to find fresh water. If there is none at shallow depth we must look deep. A borehole costing around US$12,000 and capable of supplying 5,000 people must be fitted with a hand pump to supply 500 people; crazy economics but there is no other practical solution.

At Macarretane the barrage survived the flood but the railway, the only link with Zimbabwe, was buckled and the bed torn from under it. The railway station was built on piles and survived: amid the wreckage of overturned ballast wagons it stands incongruous, proud and derelict, the walls ornately decorated with ceramic tiles from Lisbon and a big brass bell.

A tributary river can be crossed by walking on the railway sleepers and not looking down. There were two road bridges: the original blown up by the rebels in the civil war, the replacement Bailey bridge thrust downstream about 20 metres by the flood and tilted over. A high-powered expert from United Nations - a South African - accompanied by two Mozambican experts arrived one day to plan a new bridge. The South African sized up the damage and the necessary repairs remarkably quickly. The others were sceptical until he explained that during the war he had been flown in by helicopter to blow up the very bridge he now proposed to repair. A second helicopter had tried to land at the barrage a few hundred yards upstream but was shot down by a SAM missile. The wreckage is still there.

At Massevase village, a run-down relic of more prosperous times, the water tower, looms over two derelict boreholes. Water is trucked in by Oxfam in inflatable tanks and pumped up to the tower. The people wait patiently in line with empty plastic cans. An abandoned Russian tank stands guard over the school.

The British at the end of the 19th century displaced older African empires and hung on until around 1960. By contrast, Portugal colonised great coastal strips of Africa from the 15th century. They maintained an embassy to the court of the king of Benin in the 16th century and a Portuguese princess almost became one of the wives of the Oba of Benin. By the 20th century African territories were regarded as provinces of Portugal. To this day, published maps of Mozambique are titled 'Province of Mozambique, Portugal.' At the end of the Second World War Europe needed financial help to get going again. The US supplied it – at a price. As part of the price tag, Britain, France, Belgium and Portugal were to move out of Africa. Each retiring colonial power left behind its customs and by and large each emerging national government adopted them. One desirable part of the Portuguese legacy is seafood. Mozambican prawns are justly famous. Lorenzo Marques, the old name for the capital of Maputo, gave its name to the large local prawns and 'LM' prawns cooked Portuguese style are worth a pilgrimage. There is only one dessert in a Mozambican restaurant, an egg custard called 'pudding'.

When the time came to leave Mozambique and fly to Botswana, I left room in my suitcase for a few kilos of prawns but was sternly warned that an export licence was needed. So I filled the cavity with bananas. I arrived in Botswana but the suitcase – an old friend - did not. The report was that it was stranded in Johannesburg airport. It was hot and I was sustained for a week by ill-fitting borrowed raiment. On transiting back through Johannesburg I set about finding my case. Friendly concern was expressed but lips were pursed and the prognosis was thoroughly negative. Indeed, I was conducted to a huge store-room full of unidentifiable luggage. But with twitching nostrils I traced the scent of ageing bananas and (to the guide's bewilderment) rapidly and fruitfully identified the bag and bore it away to London.

Sierra Leone

There is a type of charity with the blanket title of Non-Government Organisation - NGO for short. In Britain the NGOs draw on consultants and volunteers to supplement their core staff. A pool of engineers is available from an international charity, Registered Engineers for Disaster Relief (RedR). Young professionals volunteer to spend time working for these charities, with generous leave of absence from their employers.

RedR is not my style. The training is too rigorous; lighting a fire with one match and digging latrine pits fail to attract. However I have been privileged to work with several of these NGOs in Africa and I have waxed on about them earlier in this narrative. The biggest has been Oxfam; the smallest must surely be our own little NGO, Afaka Initiative, working in northern Nigeria repairing hand-pumped boreholes. But the most exotic has been Peace Winds of Japan.

In 2000 and 2001 I had been involved with an operation near Bo, in the north east of Sierra Leone, at the request of Oxfam. The rogue Charles Taylor had wreaked enormous injury and damage in his deadly march from Liberia through the north east of Sierra Leone and down to the coast at Freetown. The little town of Bo was slowly recovering from the devastation brought about by the army of drug-crazed youths. Destitute, hungry families in and outside refugee camps were helped by Oxfam and later by Peace Winds to recreate the economy and keep folk from starving. No one asked whether they belonged to the oppressors or the oppressed; they all were in miserable straits.

One objective was to set up a local team with the capacity to site and drill successful water boreholes. My Nigerian colleague, Dotun, travelled to Freetown with a Nigerian driller to set it going. Oxfam had recruited 12 likely candidates; six were to learn enough geophysics to locate sites for boreholes, the others were to learn how to drill them.

The following year Peace Winds from Japan set up a parallel project. This time I was sufficiently intrigued to go myself. Travelling by a scruffy airline along the coast from Nigeria, I met in Freetown Peter Ball, an eminent drill systems engineer and an old friend. The flight to Bo in an open-sided juddering old aircraft flying low over the treetops was hair-raising and we were relieved to reach Bo and to be conducted to Madam Wokie's select hotel. This establishment, to be our home for some time, was good in parts. We were each awarded a penthouse suite and battled with armies of cockroaches, curious television sets and temperamental electricity powered by a stentorian generator four floors below. With the cockroaches we concluded an uneasy truce but did not care for the TV programmes of a very dubious nature relayed by the boyfriend of the resident hostess from a strange studio on the ground floor. Fortunately they were usually too scrambled to view.

The food was of a remarkably high standard considering that it was cooked on two small charcoal fires on the kitchen floor. As it was too dangerous to go outside after dark we spent long hours discoursing on everything under the sun and under the benign influence of the very good Star lager. At first there was the ritual disagreement with the waitress in the late evenings as to the number of bottles consumed. We solved this before going up to our rooms by lining up the bottle caps and conducting a serious count.

A big event in our social calendar was the arrival in a Land Rover of two enthusiasts from the British Council who were to retrain the local radio station staff. They were conducted to the last two penthouses. The redoubtable lady team leader uttered a refined scream and set forth to buy disinfectant, buckets and scrubbing brushes. We were soon assailed by a wave of aggrieved cockroaches looking for safe haven – in our rooms.

Our work concentrated on a refugee camp about 30 kilometres away in an abandoned school compound. First we had to decide who were to be trained geophysical technicians and who should become drillers. We introduced a simple arithmetic test with ten questions. The first question was: what should be added to two to make four. The average score was modest; the lower scoring half was to be taught drilling.

Twice a week the day started with the assembly below our windows of a UNHCR convoy that set off to Freetown for fresh fruit and vegetables. A huge armour-plated truck was sandwiched between two open Land Rovers crammed with helmeted guards, armed to the teeth and crouched dramatically behind mounted machine guns. They always brought back far more than could be consumed by the presiding geniuses and enterprising citizens hawked around the leftovers at agreeable prices.

Our more modest daily convoy left a bit later, carrying us to the nerve centre of our enterprise. Each Land Rover was equipped with a radio. As the driver passed listed landmarks he called up control along these lines: 'LR 333 passed checkpoint charlie, 0933 hours, two Europeans on board. Out.' Peter decided that we should be something more exciting than 'two Europeans' and dubbed us 'Mango 1' and 'Mango 2'. Ten years down the line this appellation appears in our email correspondence.

Our arrival on site was heralded by a surging mass of happy children who shouted what we thought were respectful greetings in their own language. It was some days before we learned that in reality they were shouting 'Give me money'.

Our outdoor training sessions were interspersed with breaks for reflection in our headquarters building, the school assembly hall. A sturdy warrior who had not quite passed the qualifying arithmetical test we appointed as tea maker. His product was a vigorous brew made from a little water, a large tin of condensed milk and a raft of teabags, all boiled up together.

In the villages bananas were cheap. The full realisation of just how poor the villagers were was brought home when I tendered paper money of low value and the vendors were reluctant to take it - as they had no money give us change. Though they owned nothing they were cheerful and optimistic - great qualities throughout black Africa and in shameful contrast to many of the grim-faced complaining folk in Britain.

At the end of our training course Peter concocted certificates for all the trainees complete with mug shots in glorious colour; and very impressive they were. The recipients became 'Geophysical Technicians' or 'Drilling Operatives'. The tea-maker demanded his own certificate and after some negotiation he settled for 'Chief Catering Supervisor'.

Our Japanese hosts were exquisitely charming. The head of mission, a California-trained lady, invited us to take tea and we felt it appropriate to treat the visit as a full-blown Japanese tea ceremony. We therefore tried to prepare a haiku (a three-line verse, supposedly impromptu, trotted out at high class tea ceremonies in the best Japanese circles) but inspiration would not come. When the time came, I explained that our tradition was for a simpler verse form, called a limerick. Challenged to produce a 'limerlik' I stumbled rather; the only presentable limerick that came to mind was:

> There was a young man of Japan
> Who wrote verses that never would scan
> When he was asked why
> He used to reply
> 'Well, you see, it's like this, I always like to try to get as many syllables into the last line as I possibly can.'

This simply would not do! In desperation, I fell back on a crusty old Edward Lear relic but it lacked conviction and oriental faces became inscrutable as our hosts sought inner meaning.

At the end of our mission we gave the Oxfam team, previously trained by Dotun and Sunday, a refresher course and were gratified at how well they functioned. Their driller subsequently attended at Cranfield University a seminar where he acquitted himself well.

When the time came for us to leave we were due to be picked up by a Russian helicopter; however, it had run out of fuel and crashed the day before (sadly for them but for us fortunate that we were one day late). So we endured the spine-jarring journey down a wet and potholed road in an Oxfam Land Rover.

Travel to the mysterious East

In 2006 I was introduced to an Islamic charity based in Birmingham and the experience was refreshing. Islamic Relief was a very young charity and wide awake. It has water-drilling rigs in several African countries and the latest was to move into northern Somalia in the Horn of Africa. This corner is called Puntland and covers much of the English speaking residue of Somaliland. It is semi-autonomous, relatively stable, though private enterprise involving hijacking of tankers has crept into local schedules. Puntland is very hot, with poor quality groundwater. My contribution was to steer them to where there was 'sweet' water at shallow depth.
The new rig was built in Thailand by Peter Ball, my pioneering colleague. The Islamic Relief team decided, reasonably, that it would be more agreeable to inspect the rig in Thailand than in Somalia, where there is no shortage of firearms and plenty of targets. At the beginning of November we all met in Bangkok. A delegation from Somalia included Ali, a venerable driller who had learned his art under the British and who claimed to be 91 years old.

For me Bangkok is memorable chiefly for the excellent quality of seafood served by the waterside in comfortable restaurants at low prices. However, it was good to get away from the smog northwards into the mountains at Khao Yai. Here we slept in a comfortable hotel and commuted to the location where we were to show the Somalis how to site a borehole using geophysics, then how to drill it. Commuting was simple; we walked a few hundred metres to a centre for appropriate technology, which is presided over by a distinguished academic. While the Somali delegation slept in the shade I demonstrated the geophysical techniques. Then Peter drilled a borehole while the Somali delegation slept even more deeply but woke to see it pumped and flowing copiously. Around us were birds - squacco herons and parrots – and in the background towering limestone cliffs. There had been talk of a packed lunch but when it arrived the lunch was more like a banquet. In an open-sided thatched building, a long table decked with flowers was crowded with about 30 different dishes. On one wing European style food; along the other wing hallal food for the Muslims; and in the centre Thai food. Surreptitiously shuffling between all three zones, I conducted extensive quality control.

The centre displayed a great variety of simple, energy-efficient gadgets and systems. For me the most impressive were the compact and simple devices for making charcoal and 'wood vinegar' (creosote).

The Afaka Initiative

Our Nigerian consultancy is run by Dotun Adekile (with bits of advice from me). In 2005, we registered as a Non-Government Organisation. The idea arose out of our discontent with the cut and thrust of competitive consultancy, preferring to choose and pursue worthwhile activities and carry them out our way. We would be free of political pressures and constraints imposed by clients. We would not be allowed to make a profit but we never made a profit in our consultancy work in any case. Fortuitously, my cousin William who administered a family trust fund was looking for a project connected with water and we put together a programme for renovating hand-pumped boreholes. In the Eighties and Nineties thousands of these boreholes for village water supplies had been drilled in the northern Nigerian states but no provision made for maintenance and repair.

With William's help we established a routine for bringing worn-out boreholes back to life and this ran well until the economic slump of 2008. Repairing each borehole cost £800, a small fraction of the £10,000 cost of drilling them. Moving on a bit, we noticed that clothes were being washed beside the borehole pump and dirty water left to lie and drain back into the ground, vitiating the groundwater, so we planned to build concrete wash pads a little distance from the borehole apron.

With little money for operating, in 2010 we encouraged students at Warwick University to visit Nigeria and work in two villages to popularise the use of simple water boilers that concentrated the sun's rays on a can of water.

Chapter 19. Domestic life at Little Margate

*Looking back, I marvel at surviving some spectacular life-threatening
scrapes and thank God that this soft machine is still alive,
with a lively though weather-beaten faith in that God.*

We jested that our decision to buy a country cottage buried deep in
Cornwall was influenced by a desire to make it difficult for relatives to
reach us. Indeed, comfortable journey time from the Home Counties
in those days involved an overnight stop half way. The fact was that it
seemed inevitable that, to make a living as a rock basher and water-finder,
I would be abroad frequently. There was little to be gained by living in
the smoke and having spent several holidays in Cornwall we had grown
to like it.

My cousin William had difficulty with the idea that anyone would wish
to live among rustic greenery when London with its incredible charm
was available for the taking. Dr. Johnson had two trenchant things to
say on the subject. 'A fellow who is tired of London is tired of life, Sir,
you may depend on it.' And 'A fellow who goes to bed before midnight
is a scoundrel, Sir, a scoundrel.' We disagreed and found Little Margate
Cottage, on the edge of a vast dark forest. Cecily at seven years old and
Jennie at five were less than enchanted. Every drop of water needed
pulling up from the well with a semi-rotary hand pump. Unsuspecting
visitors were sufficiently intrigued to try their hand; but after 10 minutes
they gave up with aching muscles. Bottled gas heated our food and
kerosene lamps lit our evenings. Septic tank drainage imposed a mild
constraint on loo flushing.

Kath only once complained of the isolation and loneliness when I was
overseas for weeks earning our crust. The school bus stop was nearly a
mile from home and in winter the trudge was tough going for two small
girls. After the first novelty wore off, the snow meant cold, wet feet.
Gradually we improved our utilities. We installed a diesel generator. This
was adequate for lighting but barely powerful enough for cooking so in
the early Sixties our community, with the help of our MP, secured for the
valley a line of electricity pylons and for the cottage a full-scale supply.

The cottage had an interesting history. In 1813 Napoleon's army began its retreat along the Spanish peninsula with the Duke of Wellington in hot pursuit. The Duke of Cornwall's Light Infantry overran and looted the baggage train of Marshall Jourdan. A big bag of sovereigns was shared out and in 1815 most private soldiers came home with gold coins sufficient to set them up in farming. Many two-up and two-down cottages were built having walls 18 inches thick of local stone with clay cores and Delabole slate roofs resting on mighty oak rafters. Around the middle of the 19th century ours was enlarged and, a hundred years later, a staircase installed in place of the traditional ladder. We had been puzzled by the streaks of red on the stone outer walls until we learned that left-over arsenical sheep dip was splashed around annually to kill bed bugs.

As the family grew so did the cottage. Seven rooms became 14, the stone cowshed became a chalet, the stone two metre-square pig house became the 'office complex', we built a well house, a conservatory, a greenhouse, a timber slate-roofed summerhouse and ultimately a giant woodshed with a roof garden. In the garden a swamp was dug out and became four spring-fed ponds and winter flooding from the stream was contained by making terraces and planting trees. Migrating sea trout and salmon were enjoyed, first as food during our early, hunter-gatherer phase and later, in our conservation-minded middle years, as a jealously preserved source of appreciation. An electric pump in the well carries water of such purity that in a perfect world it would carry the Chateau Margate label. The rich alluvial soil yields vegetables and fruit that in season threaten to engulf every work surface.

The years went by, with waves of sadness and happiness. Chateau Margate was by turns sad and empty, when the girls were away at Mayfield school, and happy in holiday times when the estate bulged with partying teenagers. There was inward sadness when we realised we could have no sons but much joy in having the girls.

Cecily became a lawyer and worked for large and prestigious London firms. Her mother once attended a court session concerning an insurance fraud. The complexity of the case intrigued her but her great memory was of her daughter's masterly presentation, which she recalled with pride for the rest of her life. Cecily rose as high as was practicable in a male dominated environment, then started a second career as a garden designer, becoming a medallist at Chelsea and Hampton Court. Her love of singing led to a Dublin wedding where she met Chris Larlham. So into the family came a first class lawyer, an ex-county cricketer, a bridge player of repute and a nose for good wines (as a cellar of 4,600 bottles of excellent vintage clarets testifies). Their son, Sam, has brought joy into all our lives.

Jennie, also known as Freckle (after the pop song concerning Jennifer Eccles) could have become a very competent actress. In the event, she chose to use her great talent for teaching languages and worked first in Italy (in Rome her local accent was uncannily accurate) then in Spain. Everywhere she lived life to the full. When very young she was abundantly considerate of others on the sports field. In the 100 metres sprint she would move aside to let the field thunder past. This great trust in the universal goodness of others, inherited from her grandfather, stayed with her and brought sadness when she was let down.

We were blessed that Cecily and Jennie came home often, when we all sang in the St. Endellion Festival choir. We were sad during inevitable domestic disappointments, joyous whenever our little inboard powered boat nervously put out to sea from Fowey, with a ham-handed captain and a pressed crew of landlubbers; and brief sadness when we caught no fish. There was hammer blow grief when Kath died suddenly and painfully but consolation that for a few years she had known a grandson. We were supported through the difficult times by good friends and gradually life returned to normal. There was great personal happiness when at last Ursula came into my life.

Now life flows by in a quiet and supremely contented existence, our only enemies being time, aches and pains and rapacious garden pests.

Looking back, I marvel at surviving some spectacular life-threatening scrapes and thank God that this soft machine is still alive, with a lively though weather-beaten faith in that God.

We still have little adventures. One fine Easter day when optimism triumphed over prudence, Ursula and I set out to cure a blockage in the loo cistern which even aspirin, that most ancient of medicines, had failed to shift. I described to Ursula how best to dismantle the inflow assembly. While I adopted my normal supervisory role she unscrewed the valve cover and battle commenced.

Being on a temporary biorhythmic low, I had forgotten to turn off the pump and drain down the delivery line. It is wonderful what a head of water can develop in a loo cistern; the refreshing spray was a bit like the Trevi fountain but colder. Ursula discovered that by holding the plastic screw cover hard against the inlet, we could keep pace with the flood.

My mind in an instant seized on the solution. Quick as a flash I realised that it would be good to switch off the pump and open up all the taps. I explained this at some length to Ursula and started to tell her the story that we all learned at elementary school about the little Dutch boy who kept his finger in a leaky dyke and saved the nation from catastrophic flood. In the legend, a neighbour gave the Dutch villagers a thumbs-up to mend the leak and the command rang out 'Pull your finger out boy!' Thus originating a catch phrase that has echoed down the ages.

Firmly launched into this narrative, I became aware of a certain tension; my dearly beloved was kneeling in a rather awkward position and her rejoinders were become a touch terse and tight-lipped. So without further ado I commenced the 10-minute process of simultaneously lowering the tension and the pressure, a paradoxical accomplishment indeed.

To her infinite credit Ursula's sunny nature broke through, she reassembled the apparatus and mopped the carpet. ....While I whimsically reflected on the enduring orderliness of life at Chateau Margate.

At a 'French evening' at the St. Austell Arts Club long ago the drama folk performed a sketch depicting a cabaret item in a louche Montmartre night club. A villainous looking type - garlic and disease ridden, on a crutch, a Gauloise glued to a supercilious sneer - flung his petit chou around in an apache dance with many a Gallic gesture. As a finale he hurled the lady into a chair. From the art group an artist immediately set up his easel, adjusted his beret and became furiously busy painting her. For this he was allowed 15 minutes while the poor girl recovered her breath and we all adjourned to the bar and topped up our glasses. I asked the artist what was the most difficult part of his job. "When to stop," he said. It was tempting, he added, to go on and on adding twiddly bits while not improving the outcome. Verbum sap – here I draw a line.

Acknowledgements.

The assistance of the following friends is gratefully acknowledged.

David Flynn, for sympathetic editing.
Peter Kwee for working magic on photographs.
Matt for creating cartoons.
Alan Gilliland for tidying up maps.
Roy Crocker for guidance through the minefield of printing.
My wife Ursula, for hours of proof reading.